TRACKS THAT SPEAK

The Legacy of
Native American Words
in North American Culture

Charles L. Cutler

HOUGHTON MIFFLIN COMPANY

BOSTON   NEW YORK

Visit our website: www.houghtonmifflinbooks.com

Library of Congress Cataloging-in-Publication data is available.
ISBN 0–618–06509–1
ISBN 0–618–06510–5 (pbk.)

Manufactured in the United States of America

MV 10 9 8 7 6 5 4 3 2 1

CONTENTS

PREFACE

Special thanks for inspiration go to Professor David P. McAllester and Professor William O. Bright. Professor Jack Weatherford provided valuable advice on various points throughout the manuscript. Edwin A. Hoey contributed incisive editorial counsel on a number of the essays. Elizabeth Frost Knappman made a crucial suggestion on the book's structure. Mark Noonan, editor in chief of *Columbia Journal of American Studies,* offered encouragement in the development of the book.

Thanks are also due to the following people, who helped in many ways: Thayne I. Andersen, James W. Baker, Peggy M. Baker, Robert Cumming, Ives Goddard, John Gray, Alfrieda Irwin, Susanne Javorski, Erhard Konerding, Kathy Lewis, Elizabeth Mainella, Frank Menchaca, Roger L. Payne, Diana Perron, Glenda Reed-Whitson, Lee Regan, Doris Sherrow, Kim Smith, Brian Southam, Elizabeth Swaim, Joan Tobin, Arthur Upgren, Pamela C. Wooding; the staff of Levi E. Coe Memorial Library in Middlefield, Connecticut, including Karen Smith, Lucia Ginter, Patricia White, Marilyn Sheehan, Laurel Carina, and Lynda Wlodarczyk; and the reference staff of Russell Library in Middletown, Connecticut, including Marcia Lewis, Gail Thompson-Allen, Catherine Ahern, Marcella Kenney, Martha Reid, Denise Macky-Russo, Deborah Rutter, and Phyllis Nathanson. Additional thanks and apologies go to any I may have omitted from this list.

CHARLES L. CUTLER
Rockfall, Connecticut

INTRODUCTION

The image of Native Americans has had many faces since Europeans first settled in North America, and these faces have appeared periodically in recent American culture. The Romantic notion of the noble savage gave way to the image of the fierce warrior and recalcitrant outsider who would not or could not negotiate the world of white people. Then came the caretaker of the forests and rivers and other natural resources, whose spirit was more deeply connected to the universe and whose religious impulses were worthy of imitation.

The persistence of these images vexes the subject of Native American influence on general American culture. If Indians are continually viewed as a series of stereotypes, it will always be difficult to determine authentic Native American contributions to American culture. But there are ways of identifying the abiding, if less readily apparent, cultural contributions of Native Americans, and perhaps the most important of these are their contributions to the English language.

You can hardly step outdoors without using words derived from Native American languages. So many of the plants and animals we refer to, across a variety of landscapes, have Native American names, from the *saguaro* cactus in the desert to the towering *sequoia* in the coastal rainforest. The *chipmunks* in the park, the *raccoons* rattling the trashcans, the shy *skunks* and *opossums* stealing about at night, all get their names from Indian languages, as do the massive *moose, caribou,* and *wapiti* that roam where humans are few.

The absorption of these words into English happened in the first instance out of necessity. English-speaking settlers in North

America were confronted with a new style of living when they encountered the continent's original inhabitants. Europeans had never before seen *wigwams, tomahawks,* or *wampum.* The early settlers and later arrivals learned to hunt the local animals. They ate native foods such as *hominy,* corn *pone, succotash, squash, pecans,* and *persimmons.* They also had to understand Indian society and social practices: they learned to call Indian leaders on the East Coast *sachem* or *sagamore,* and spoke of Indian women as *squaws* and Indian children as *papooses*—often using these terms loosely for non-Indians. Today, the use of many of these words, even in long-established placenames, can cause hard feelings and incite controversy.

As time went by, a rising fascination with native peoples led to the introduction into English of farflung words such as *potlatch, totem* pole, *kachina,* and *Shasta* daisy.

The settlers took up riding on *toboggans,* paddling *kayaks,* and wearing *moccasins.* They kept *Eskimo, husky,* and *malamute* dogs; and some rode *appaloosas.* They watched for the *Sasquatch*—and still do.

Meanwhile other terms were being derived from the myriad native-named places in North America—for example, *Canada* goose, *Catawba* grape, and *Chautauqua* program. In fact, the greatest number of borrowed North American native words are those that dot the U.S. map. Half the states bear native names, including *Alabama, Alaska, Arkansas, Connecticut, Idaho, Iowa,* and *Illinois* just from the first half of the alphabet. Many of the largest U.S. rivers carry Indian names, such as *Mississippi, Missouri, Ohio, Yukon,* and *Potomac.* The same is true of major lakes such as *Michigan, Erie, Tahoe,* and *Okeechobee.* Still others of the nation's scenic wonders relate to Native Americans—*Niagara* Falls, *Yosemite, Sequoia* National Park, and more. That is not to mention the thousands of Indian-named cities, towns, hills, and brooks. But examining these place names is beyond the scope of this book.

We also see and hear Native American loanwords in hundreds of commercial brand names, which further advertise the vitality of Native American words in modern American life. You can stay at a *Wigwam* motel, keep beer cold in an *Igloo* cooler, run *Sequoia* and *Appaloosa* software on your computer, and buy any of a dozen *Tomahawk* products from log homes to leather goods. And if you consider tribal names, your choice of products is breathtaking. You can buy *Apache* bicycles, boats, clocks, wet mops, or one of thirty other products. You can walk on a *Mohawk* carpet before paddling in a *Mohawk* canoe. You can ride around in a big Jeep *Cherokee* or a bigger *Winnebago* RV. Clearly, native loanwords not only enrich the English vocabulary, they also sell merchandise.

This bountiful harvest of words springs from the more than one thousand native languages currently and formerly spoken in the Western Hemisphere. The native languages of the Americas comprise dozens of separate families; many are as different from one another as English is from Japanese. At the dawn of European settlement, probably sixty separate families graced North America alone. Sadly, only about half of the continent's original stock of indigenous languages that existed at the dawn of European colonization are still alive today, many of them spoken by no more than a handful of elderly tribespeople.

Early explorers of North America's eastern coast palavered mostly with Indians who spoke one or another of the fifty or so languages in the Algonquian language family, a vast group of tongues that extended from the Northeast coast through the Great Plains to the Rockies and includes such languages as Abenaki, Cheyenne, and Shawnee. The explorers witnessed *powwows* and heard about *manitou*, borrowing these words along with those for other items already mentioned. The Algonquian languages contributed more words to English than any other Indian language family.

Then, as settlers spread in all directions and came into contact with other linguistic groups, the scope of borrowing expanded. The vast Athabaskan family, stretching from interior Alaska and western Canada on down into the American Southwest and Mexico, gave us the word *hogan,* a Navajo dwelling. The Muskogean languages of the Southeast, including Choctaw, Creek, and Seminole, gave us words such as *bayou, catalpa* and *tupelo.* From Iroquoian languages like Cherokee, Mohawk, and Cayuga, spoken across the northeastern and north-central U.S., we got the name of the *dowitcher* fish. The Siouan languages of the Great Plains, such as Dakota, Winnebago, and Crow, are the source of words like *tepee* and *yaupon.* The *coho* salmon and the clam called the *geoduck* are words borrowed from Salishan languages of northwest coastal areas. Uto-Aztecan, a language family stretching from the western U.S. down into Mexico and containing the Hopi, Paiute, and Comanche languages, gave us such words as *kiva, kachina,* and *sego.* We also got numerous words from Chinook Jargon, a lingua franca used in the Pacific Northwest that consisted of words from Salishan and Chinoookan languages. *Chum* salmon, *potlatch,* and *high muck-a-muck* are Chinook Jargon in origin.

Loanword borrowing from North American Native languages had its ups and downs, depending on the state of relations between settlers and native peoples. Indian uprisings in Virginia and King Philip's War of 1675–76 ended an early era of largely peaceful relations and halted the wholesale borrowing of native words into English. The westward movement of settlers in the nineteenth century increased contacts, both peaceful and hostile, with native peoples. Borrowing of native words reached a peak in the latter part of that century, diminishing after the last of the Indian wars. The acquisition of native loanwords declined during the twentieth century, but the full impact of the cultural revival of native peoples remains to be seen.

This book examines the most prominent of English words that were borrowed from North American Indian languages and explains their background and the significance of the things they refer to, both in Native American and in general American culture. For the words are signs, pointing to an elaborate web of cultural practices, each with its own unique tradition, extending into and influencing the present. When we follow their trail, we are re-minded of words a storyteller of the Slavey tribe in Canada once used to describe the wolverine: "His tracks go on and on." These are tracks that speak of an American past, present, and future, as American culture continues to find new meaning in the Indian legacy it has inherited.

ACKNOWLEDGMENT

On behalf of my late husband, I wish to thank Arthur Upgren, Middletown, Ct., for suggesting his agent, Sally Brady, at Brady Literary Management, and the following people at Houghton Mifflin: Joseph Pickett, Executive Editor; Ben Fortson, who edited the manuscript with the assistance of Uchenna Ikonné; Margaret Anne Miles, who oversaw the selection of art; Christopher Granniss, who oversaw the conversion of the manuscript to type; and freelancer Diane Fredrick, who copy-edited the manuscript.

KATHARINE CUTLER
November 2000

SHELTER

Native peoples of North America lived in shelters of many types. Varied designs reflected the various kinds of weather and terrain in which the peoples lived. The materials employed usually came from what lay at hand and included brush, bark, snow, timber, stone, animal skins, and earth.

Among the most impressive structures were those of the prehistoric Anasazi, who built stone towers and lofty cliff dwellings. The cedar-plank houses of peoples in the Pacific Northwest were as elegant in design as they were comfortable. The ancient, Hopi-named kiva — a chamber for religious ceremonies and social gatherings — remains in use among modern Pueblo of the Southwest.

This section focuses on three dwellings that retain their native names in English: the widespread and emblematic *tepee, igloo,* and *wigwam.* A concluding essay on the *Quonset hut* examines the World War II structure with an Indian name and a striking resemblance to the Iroquois longhouse.

TEPEE
Portable houses

At night, countless tepees once shone with a faintly reddish glow from the hearth fires within them. Sometimes one could see the shadowy shapes of people moving around inside. Smoke rose from the smoke holes. Under the starlit prairie sky, the tepees were at once home to their occupants and more than home — they were structures connecting them with the universe. Plains Indians still formed great circling encampments of the tents

tepee

*c. 1900 photograph by Frank B. Fiske of tepees at Standing Rock
Indian Reservation, Fort Yates, North Dakota*

during the nineteenth century. These encampments declined with
the Indian Wars as many Indians adopted white styles of housing,
through force or choice. But a sizable minority continued using tepees in good weather or for special events such as powwows.

The earliest European record of the tepee goes back to the
1540s when the Spanish explorer Francisco Vásquez de Coro-
nado encountered Southwestern Indian buffalo hunters. They
lived, he said, in beautiful skin tents. But the tepee goes back further in time, perhaps much further. People of the world's northern forests had been living in skin tents for many centuries. Not
enough is known about those early shelters to determine how
close in design they were to the historical tepee.

The Cree Indians are said to have introduced the tepee to
the northern Great Plains in about 1600. This movable home
was well suited to nomadic hunters who followed migratory
game such as buffalo. Its name originates with one of the

peoples who adopted the tent: The stem comes from Dakota *ti*, "to dwell." It is now often spelled *tipi* to reflect the term's origin more closely.

Plains Indians refined the tepee's basic design. Their tepee was not exactly cone-shaped but sloped to the rear to brace it against buffeting winds. Smoke flaps on top could be adjusted for wind and temperature. These features gave the tepee the versatility needed by people living on storm-swept terrain.

The tepee's assembly began with three or four long poles lashed together at the top, with additional poles added and secured to complete the frames. A three-pole starting framework was commonest in the northern Plains, a four-pole framework in the southern Plains. Next came the cover, consisting of about a dozen to twenty buffalo hides sewn tightly together with sinew. The assemblers raised the cover with a special pole so that it draped over the frame. Wooden pins held the cover together over the door, which was closed with a flap. Wooden stakes, or stones, anchored the tent firmly to the ground.

Some owners of tepees adorned them with symbols and pictures. In the 1830s, George Catlin described Crow tepees decorated with porcupine quills and colorful designs. One he obtained was, he said,

> highly ornamented, and fringed with scalp-locks, and sufficiently large for forty men to dine under. . . . This tent, when erected, is about twenty-five feet high, and has a very pleasing effect; with the Great or Good Spirit painted on one side, and the Evil Spirit on the other.[1]

Until the arrival of Europeans, the Indians used trained dogs to transport their tepees. These dogs, sometimes in the hundreds, carried packs or dragged lodge poles behind them. The introduction of horses revolutionized the tepee, leading to an increase in its size and the range of its use. The horse could drag a much heavier V-shaped travois — a device consisting of two trailing poles with a carrying frame slung between them.

Women made the tepees, packed them for moving, and set them up at the campsite. It took about an hour for a skilled group of women to assemble one. They then arranged the furnishings inside their movable homes. A lining around the bottom of the tepee kept it snug during cold weather. Buffalo hides, backrests, and cradleboards furnished the circular interior. Hung around the walls were bows and quivers, shields, and medicine bags. Among other objects compactly set in place were parfleches (hide bags) containing tools and other small items and sewing bags with a variety of awls and thread.

Apart from its practicality, the tepee held a deep religious significance for the Indians. Its rounded floor space repeated the giant disk of the Earth stretching all around. Its walls were like the sky. Its poles acted as trails for their prayers to the Spirit that over-arched them.

Paintings on the exterior of some tepees portrayed symbols that came to individuals in dreams or trances. The raising of a new tepee was a community event accompanied by a prayer and sometimes a feast.

Today the tepee has become more widespread than ever. Thousands are in use throughout the United States, not only among Plains Indians but among other Indians and non-Indians. The tepee has won greater recognition as a movable home that provides comfortable shelter under outdoor or wilderness conditions. People living in tepees say they can feel and enjoy the flow of nature around them. In *The Indian Tipi,* Reginald and Gladys Laubin suggest the peaceful atmosphere of the tepee:

> During the day it is cheerful and mellow. . . . Even on dark, gloomy days it is brighter than most houses. But especially are the nights wonderful. To lie there by the fire, listening to its merry crackling, watching the shadows flickering on the wall, the final dusky glow, with a few stars peeping down at you through the poles in the smoke hole, is beyond words to describe.[2]

Various companies have sprung up to help today's Americans share that experience. Nomadics Tipi Makers of Bend, Oregon, describes itself as the "world's largest maker of Native American tipis." It offers a complete array of materials for assembling and maintaining the tents — and it created those shown in the movie *Dances with Wolves*. Between 1970 and 1995, Nomadics sold more than ten thousand of its mail-order tepees.

IGLOO
Snowhouse

"Our astonishment was unbounded, when, after creeping through some long low passages of snow, to enter the different dwellings, we found ourselves in a cluster of dome-shaped edifices, entirely constructed of snow, which . . . admitted the light in most delicate hues of verdigris green and blue." So wrote George F. Lyon, the commander of a British ship, after visiting an igloo during an expedition to Hudson Bay in 1821.[1]

Lyon described only the most famous kind of igloo. Depending on location and season, Eskimo built their igloos from a variety of materials. Commonly they dug a pit about three feet into the ground. This they topped with a framework of wood (often driftwood), whalebone, or stone, covered with sod or whatever else was available in typically austere surroundings. A cold-trapping tunnel led to the house's living area, which contained platforms and alcoves for lounging and sleeping. A ventilator hole in the roof provided an outlet for smoke from seal-oil lamps, though many Eskimo suffered from respiratory problems caused by lingering soot. A pane of seal intestine admitted some light.

During the summer, many Eskimo moved into tents, or *tupiks*. These consisted of wood, whalebone, or narwhal-tusk frameworks covered by skins of animals such as caribou or seals. There the Eskimo remained until cold weather drove them back to their igloos.

One or two seal-oil lamps and the body heat of the occupants were sufficient to keep an igloo comfortable even during howling blizzards. "This type of sod *iglu* — which is simply the Eskimo word for 'house' — was a remarkable innovation, one that fostered a population explosion about a thousand years ago," says Arctic archaeologist John E. Lobdell.[2]

Despite its comparative rarity, the igloo built of snow blocks most vividly captured the popular imagination. The "snowhouse" was typical of Eskimo living in the northernmost regions of Canada. There a sheer lack of other natural resources forced them to build with the one material of which there was an inexhaustible supply. Furthermore, Arctic snow has qualities that make it uniquely suitable for such use — it is especially dense and hard.

Igloo builders used snow knives of ivory, bone, or (where available) native copper. Two men could work as a team. They would carve a supply of snow blocks, then together lay a foundation ring of blocks usually between six and fifteen feet across. Then, one in and one out, they would stack blocks upward in an inward-leaning spiral to form a dome. Next the builders constructed a passageway into the igloo. Meanwhile, women and children filled any chinks with loose snow.

Despite the artistry that had to be shown in the carving and fitting of blocks, experienced builders could complete an igloo in as little as an hour. Larger communal igloos might be built later for community gatherings; snow-block-covered tunnels could link igloos into clusters.

Many observers have praised the beauty of the snowhouse. Its symmetry and purity of color, its translucency within by day and without at night (from the lighted lamp inside), gave it the luster of "a hollow jewel" in one author's words. But the interior of the walls grew sooty with time. Its floor became foul from the butchering of seals. This soilure was not a serious problem, since the snowhouse was supposed to be only a temporary shelter, abandoned when its builders undertook one of their frequent moves.

Now igloos have largely been replaced by prefabricated housing. But Eskimo hunters and fishers still sometimes build snowhouses when on overnight trips. In 1998, author Stephen Harrigan traveled to Hudson Bay on behalf of *This Old House* magazine to see for himself how an igloo is constructed. He regarded the dwelling as "the most organic dome of all, a shape-shifting expression of snow, the quietest, purest building the human mind has ever conceived." His article "Igloo" tells of watching a 59-year-old Inuit elder — who learned his craft as a child — construct one of the snowhouses. The elder took a leisurely two and a half hours to complete the job. Harrigan spent the night inside on a snow sleeping platform covered with musk ox and caribou skins. "I wouldn't say it was the most comfortable night I have ever spent," he reported. But he did feel "reasonably safe and cozy."[3]

In the Valley of Alberta, Canada, people from many backgrounds still learn how to build their own snowhouses. Alf Skrastins, the University of Calgary's outdoor-programs manager, has taught the art to college students, winter campers, pilots, and even a stray Inuit. Some taking the course just want to know how to devise an emergency shelter; architects and engineers specifically want to study arch and dome construction. All find that managing snow blocks calls for practice.

WIGWAM
Lodges along the Atlantic

"We built us our *wigwam*, or house, in one houres space," wrote the explorer William Levett in a book published in 1628. "It had no frame, but was without forme or fashion, only a few poles set up together, and covered with our boates sailes which kept forth but a little winde, and less raigne and snow." Levett encountered wigwams in Maine, and he apparently was the first to write about them by name. But he and his companions got wet because they did not have the skill or time to construct one properly.[1]

Wigwam comes from the eastern Abenaki word for "house."

For Indians living throughout the eastern woodlands, it was a snug and practical shelter. One anthropologist calls it "the Algonquian lodge *par excellence*."[2]

Making a wigwam called for teamwork. In New England and elsewhere, men typically cut saplings for the frame. They set the ends at intervals in the ground and bent the tops to form arches over the wigwam's floor. The curved tops were lashed with material such as strips of basswood or walnut bark. Horizontal poles along the sides completed the frame. Women then covered the frame with overlapping mats made of reeds or grasses, slabs of bark, or hides. They left a smokehole in the roof with a flap that could be opened or closed by a string. A suspended mat or hide covered the low doorway. The finished structure was often domed, but it could be squarish, conelike, or shaped like a Quonset hut.

New England Indians sometimes pitched light wigwams while on hunting or fishing expeditions. But with the onset of cold weather, they and other northern peoples such as the Menominee would withdraw from the coast or lake shores to valleys and similar sheltered sites. There they would pitch substantial wigwams, often covering frames still standing from the previous season. An extra layer of mats around the inside of their shelter helped protect them as the weather grew more severe.

The occupants made the most of their often limited space, though the shelter could be expanded to twenty feet or more. They hung baskets and other light items from the rafters. Boxes made of bark (mococks) held tools, herbs, and other small articles. Depending on the dampness of the ground, hides or mats might be spread for sitting and sleeping. Sometimes low platforms were built upon which the occupants could rest. The fireplace consisted of a central pit or circle of stones.

How comfortable was the wigwam? Roger Williams called wigwams "smoaky holes." Other visitors complained about vermin and lack of privacy. But numerous observers, such as John Strachey while exploring Virginia in the sixteenth century, exclaimed at the shelter's snugness. Early settlers in New England often fashioned wigwams (apparently with more success than Levett) as temporary shelters until they could build houses.[3]

With time, the word *wigwam* came to be used more freely. Large buildings in the nineteenth century were sometimes so called, such as the huge two-story structure in Chicago where Abraham Lincoln was nominated for president in 1860. Members of the Tammany Society of New York and of the Kickapoo Indian Medicine Company of New Haven maintained the Indian theme of their organizations by referring to their headquarters as a "wigwam."

Not all Indian wigwams served as dwellings. The "shaking tent" is a telephone-booth-size wigwam used around the Great Lakes and elsewhere in the eastern woodlands. A medicine man, or shaman, inside the wigwam is believed to communicate with supernatural spirits that may cry out and shake the structure as they offer revelations. Another wigwam with a religious purpose is the widely used sweatlodge, in which water is poured over heated rocks to fill the interior with steam and spiritually cleanse the occupants.

The famed Kickapoo carried a kind of wigwam, the *wickiup,* from their northern homeland through the West and as far south as Mexico. A wickiup has a light framework covered with brush or the like, though the term may be applied to any roughly assembled shelter. (*Wickiup* comes from the Algonquian language of the Fox, Sauk, and Kickapoo. It is cognate with *wigwam* and, like it, means "house.")

Indian tribes sometimes used the wigwam while also adopting white styles of housing. Archaeologists have discovered that on Connecticut's Mashantucket Pequot reservation, three-fourths of the dwellings were wigwams up to the middle or late eighteenth century. Subsequent houses may have been intermediate between wigwams and frame houses, with earthen floors and smokeholes. By the mid-nineteenth century, all or almost all the Mashantucket Pequot dwellings were frame houses.

But wigwams continue in use in North America, though mainly among Indians. Besides the wickiups of the Kickapoo, the sweatlodge and shaking tent play a deeply significant role in the lives of Indians today who may live in frame houses or apartments. In the 1990s, the Aquinnah Wampanoag of Martha's Vineyard, Massachusetts, incorporated wigwam themes in their tribal housing. Architects planned a development for them that echoes the kind of dwelling that their ancestors had lived in. Houses in this development have a curved roof and vaulted interior, with a central living room-dining room, like the traditional wigwam.

QUONSET HUT
Reversion to type

The Quonset Surplus Store, located off a four-lane highway in Portland, Connecticut, offers a hoard of outdoor-living supplies. Heaped on its shelves and counters are pac boots from Canada, military overcoats from Europe, and old U.S. Army gear. Actually two Quonset huts twinned, the store is one of many such survivors from World War II. The Quonset's designers intended the corrugated steel hut with semicircular cross section to be primarily a shelter. But even during the war it found other uses, such as machine shop and church. And after the war, mustered-out Quonsets showed even more versatility as they became student apartments, bowling alleys, barns, and banks.

If the surviving huts make some people think of the last big war, they remind others of the famed Iroquois longhouse that reached up to one hundred feet long or more, with curved sapling poles supporting a barrel-shaped, bark-covered roof. (In the nineteenth century, a gable roof replaced the traditional rounded shape.) Families of the same clan lived on either side of a central aisle. Each had a sleeping platform covered with furs or the like, storage shelves, and access to a fire with a smoke hole in the roof above. "Today," says an authority, "the longhouse remains a symbol of the persistence of Iroquois culture."[1]

Quonset hut
c. 1946 photograph of a residential Quonset hut in Mansfield, Ohio

At first blush, there seems to be no link between longhouse and Quonset. The U.S. Navy developed the latter at Quonset Point, Rhode Island, in 1941. Coincidentally, the name of the site comes from the Narragansett word said to mean "long place." The navy's requisites were for a shelter "that could be mass-produced, that could be used in tropical and arctic climates and the climates in between, that would require a minimum of shipping space, that could be set up and taken down by the men who lived in it, and that would be rotproof, verminproof, waterproof, and any other proof that circumstances called for."[2]

The building that came closest to those specifications was the British Nissen hut, devised and widely deployed in World War I. Navy engineers kept the overall shape of the Nissen but added many improvements, such as a plywood floor and an inside wall of Masonite finishing board with wood-fiber insulation separating it from the outer steel wall. Within the year, Quonsets were being shipped as part of lend-lease aid the United States contributed to a Great Britain struggling to resist Nazi Germany. When the United States joined the war, more Quonsets followed the nation's armed forces abroad.

United States factories produced about 170,000 Quonset huts during the war. The services adapted the huts to circumstances. In northern climates, snug end walls featured two windows and a door. In the tropics, screening covered open end walls while extra openings along the sides aided ventilation. Seabees linked Quonset huts into vast assemblages, as longhouses once were connected. The most spectacular was a 54,000-square-foot warehouse on Guam known as the Multiple Mae West.

At the war's end, thousands of Quonsets returned to the United States to join others as yet unshipped. A building-hungry public welcomed the economical, durable, practical structures. New York City announced plans to erect at least two thousand Quonsets at a cost one-third of that for conventional buildings.

But what of the hut's resemblance to the longhouse — can that be just a case of cultural coincidence? The designer of the Nissen hut was Lt. Col. Peter N. Nissen, a Canadian engineer officer who had studied at Queen's University in Kingston, Ontario. He must have been familiar with the Iroquois longhouse; it is hard to believe he was not influenced by it, consciously or unconsciously. In 1917, the *Architects' and Builders' Journal* called Nissen's creation a "reversion to type, to the type of the beaver's hut or the Esquimo's." Or, the journal might have added, to the longhouse.[3]

CLOTHING

Native American clothing varied from one people to another. The continent's range of climate and abundance of raw materials made many styles possible. Local customs further diversified ways of dressing.

In *Indians of North America,* the anthropologist Harold E. Driver offers a survey of this subject, the highlights of which are:

- Inhabitants of the most northern regions favored caribou-hide hooded coats (parkas or anoraks) and fur trousers. Boots, or mukluks, of sealskin or other material provided snug footwear. Along the relatively mild and moist Northwest coast, Indians often wore coats of woven plant fiber in the summer and robes of fur in the winter.
- Plains Indian men frequently wore simply a breechcloth and moccasins in the summer. Leggings and a buckskin shirt might be added for travel wear, with a buffalo robe available for added warmth. Women wore moccasins and a dress made of buckskin or elkhide. Early Southwestern Indians wore sandals of woven yucca and had blankets of feather cloth.
- Pueblo Indians wore cotton clothing and leather moccasins as well as sandals.
- Southeastern Indian men favored a buckskin breechcloth and moccasins, with a robe added during winter and on special occasions. They often donned leggings when traveling. Women wore a knee-length skirt made of buckskin, woven bark, or other materials, and leggings that reached to the knee. Indians

of the northeastern woodlands often fashioned buckskin into shirts, skirts, breechcloths, leggings, and moccasins. Sometimes they made lightweight robes of feathers sewed onto netting.

This section examines types of Native American clothing so artfully designed that they have won international recognition. The *moccasin, mukluk,* and *shoepac* or *pac boot* are rugged kinds of footwear well suited to modern leisure and outdoor uses. The closely related *parka* and *anorak,* with refinements, offer unparalleled comfort and warmth in the winter. The *mackinaw coat* apparently grew out of the blankets Indians in northern Michigan wore during harsh winter weather.

MOCCASIN
In the footsteps of the Indian

"Don't judge a man until you have walked a mile (or two moons) in his moccasins," goes an old saying. These slipperlike shoes epitomize the American Indian way of life. For thousands of years, moccasin-clad feet have threaded the trails of North America.

With a breechcloth, moccasins were the minimum wardrobe of the male American Plains Indian. They protected feet during hunting trips and on migratory journeys. Supple leather enabled wearers to feel their way silently through wilderness while stalking game or even following the warpath at night. Silence was vital: In some tribes, a warrior who was so careless as to snap a fallen branch underfoot had to carry the pieces in his hand for the rest of the expedition.

The first appearance of the word in English occurs in a 1609 translation of the Frenchman Marc Lescarbot's *Nova Francia, a description of Acadia:* "Besides these long stockings, our savages do use shoes, which they call *mekezin,* which they fashion very properly, but they cannot dure long, specially when they go into watery places, because they be not curried nor hardened, but only made after the manner of buff, which is the hide of an elan [moose]."[1] Women made moccasins, but the men carried extras or an awl and leather thongs for repairs on the trail.

Variations of the word *moccasin* occur in a number of languages in the Algonquian family. Some examples are *mockasin* in Virginia Algonquian, *mocussin* in Narragansett, and *makisin* in Ojibwa. But speakers of other languages applied their own names. Each tribe displayed its individuality in the design of the shoe. A soft, or continuous, sole prevailed in the east and most of the north. A hard, or separate, leather sole found greatest favor in the west and the extreme north. Height ranged from below the ankle to above the knee. The cut of the leather varied as well, often showing considerable elegance. Nez Perce Indians fashioned a seam running along one side of the shoe from big toe to heel. The northern Athabaskans employed a T-seam at toe and heel. The distinctive shape of many moccasins often allowed Indians to tell by an imprint the tribe of the person who had made it.

Identifying tribal moccasins indicated to members that they were on the right path or that another was one of them. After the Deerfield massacre of 1704, Indian raiders gave their captives "Indian shoes" for their long journey to Canada. Native footwear enabled the whites to travel more swiftly through the wilderness than did stiffer European-style shoes. But the gift also asserted ownership of the captives until they were ransomed or possibly adopted. During the Iroquois and Omaha ceremonies of adopting an outsider, the person received a pair of tribal moccasins specifically to signify membership in the tribe.

Intricate decorations turned dress moccasins into works of art. The makers used moose hair, porcupine quills, or beads to embellish their footwear with designs that were ornamental and sometimes symbolic. Instead of being left a natural brown or tan, the moccasins might be stained — those of the Hopi traditionally a red brown. A young Pawnee was entitled to wear black moccasins after he killed a buffalo and consecrated it to the holy Tirawahat. A Crow warrior flaunted wolf tails at the heels of his moccasins after he accomplished that most daring of Plains Indians feats — scoring a *coup,* or touching an enemy's body without injuring him.

And moccasin customs could be poignant. Right after a baby was born, Menominee parents placed moccasins with holes cut in them on its feet. The holes were protection against wandering spirits who might try to lure it to the Otherworld: The baby could plausibly refuse because its moccasins were inadequate for such a long journey. In the 1970s, Mexican Kickapoo were still protecting their infants in this way.

Meanwhile, moccasins gained popularity with the American public in general. "Moccasins appeared during the nineteenth century as an all-American fashion item for men, women, and children," notes the book *Dress in American Culture* (1993). The woodland Indians remaining in New England, the book adds, sold non-Indians "decorative moccasins with beadwork, quillwork, or silk embroidery."[2]

The nearly worldwide influence of the moccasin's construction can be seen in the Loafer, or "moc front slip-on," of the twentieth century. This is a comfortable step-in shoe with a moccasin upper or even a full moccasin construction. "Like the shoes of an era in which craftsmanship thrived, the Polo Loafer is hand-sewn in Maine using generations-old shoemaking techniques," goes a 1995 Ralph Lauren ad. "The full moccasin construction, for example, wraps the foot in a single sheet of leather, yielding a personalized, custom fit that only becomes more comfortable with age."[3]

Moccasins and their offshoots now appear not only on trails but also in city streets and offices. The continuing influence of the American Indian is reflected in the way more people than ever before walk in the Indian's moccasins.

MUKLUK

'Most comfortable things'

Along with the parka and anorak come Eskimo boots — primarily mukluks — built to withstand the world's coldest temperatures. A century ago, the *Medicine Hat News* of Medicine Hat, Alberta, Canada, celebrated one who wore them:

> *Her parkee, made of Caribou, it is a lovely fit.*
> *And she's all right from muck-a-luck unto her dainty mit.*[1]

Mukluks are still common in Arctic and subarctic regions. And during the winter, Park Avenue matrons today wear snow boots directly descended from those of the Eskimo.

With differences, of course. The word *mukluk* comes from the Yupik Eskimo name *maklak* for the bearded seal. Though styles of mukluk varied, the boot typically had a sealskin sole.

Some surprising materials went into mukluks or other snow boots. Yukon Eskimo made soles and uppers of chinook salmon skin. These were lightweight and warm over grass liners, but they tore easily and deteriorated when exposed to a fire's warmth. In 1854, the explorer Elisha Kane encountered a polar Eskimo wearing boots made of a bear's lower legs — with soles and claws still attached!

Eskimo women more commonly made true mukluks with sealskin or caribou skin uppers.

The style of boots varied, often within the same region. An anthropologist has noted fifteen different styles in one society of Kotzebue Sound, each with a different name. Yet all were made of seal and caribou materials only.

Mukluk tops were often sewn directly onto oil-tanned

mukluk

sealskin soles crimped upward around the edges with a special ivory tool. But additional sealskin or other material might be used to join the sole to the rest of the boot. On the western coast of Alaska, tops consisted of white deerskin shaved to a velvety texture. The skins of beaver or wolverine might be added for decoration or to strengthen the boots. In the northern part of Hudson Bay, women's mukluks had a wide top where an infant might be carried, facing the mother and leaning back. Inside mukluks, ankle-length socks of deerskin or sealskin with hair still attached, or sometimes socks of woven grass, supplied insulation.

Eskimo have tended to retain their handmade mukluks longer than other traditional clothing because commercial boots cannot match the mukluk's warmth and lightness. Some modern Eskimo don skin mukluks for ordinary wear but use a rubber-soled kind when hunting or trapping in wet snow.

Among the non-Eskimo people who have adopted mukluklike boots are the Athabaskan Kutchin of northern Alaska. They wear a boot like the mukluk, but with a tanned moosehide sole and canvas top. This is tied around the ankle and opening. Heavy lining and several pairs of wool socks provide the warmth that canvas lacks. Richard K. Nelson, an anthropologist who lived with the people, says under wet conditions many wear commercial cloth boots with rubber soles but regard them as too clumsy for ordinary use.[2]

John McPhee writes in *Coming Into the Country* of trying on traditional mukluks during his excursion into Alaska:

> Mukluks, with their soft moosehide bottoms, thin leggings, and layered contents of felt, are the lightest, driest, warmest, most comfortable things I have ever had on my feet.[3]

He met one trapper who combined native mukluks with L.L.Bean felt insoles and wool socks.

L.L.Bean has offered a modified women's Bean Mukluk to the general public. It has a thick rubber bottom, full-grain leather top, and shearling (sheepskin or lambskin with wool left on) lining and cuff. These snow boots and other modern adaptations follow a design perfected over centuries of struggle against bone-chilling cold.

SHOEPAC, PAC BOOT
Hunting shoes

"Outside of your gun," said L. L. Bean, "nothing is so important to your outfit as your footwear. You cannot expect success hunting deer or moose if your feet are not properly dressed."[1]

The founder of the L.L.Bean sporting-goods enterprise knew what he was talking about. He had hunted and trapped in the Maine woods as a young orphan to provide himself with food and clothing. Often suffering from cold feet on his expeditions, he began experimenting with rubber shoe bottoms stitched onto lightweight leather tops that would shed water from around the foot while allowing "breathing" higher up on the leg. In 1912, he had one hundred pairs of his Maine Hunting Shoes made up. He marketed these through the mail from Freeport, Maine, with a money-back guarantee. Ninety came back after the bottoms pulled away from the tops.

Lesser men would have given up, but Bean developed a better boot. He kept improving it, ultimately adding a split backstay to eliminate chafing, a chain-tread sole, insulation, and other refinements. Other Bean boots followed for various specific purposes such as hiking, fishing, summer outings, and extreme-cold-weather activities.

The Bean Boot, as the company's premier product came to be known, did not directly imitate hunting boots that Indians had fashioned for themselves. Rather, it arose from a parallel need — one some Indians chose to ignore. Many had simply endured the icy water that drenched their feet while hunting. The Kutchin, for example, wore moosehide moccasins lined with rabbit skins.

Ice water soaked right through the moccasins, but the hunters kept moving and warmed up when they could. (Today the Kutchin wear warmer boots patterned on those of the Eskimo.)

Other Indians fashioned more-or-less waterproof boots and stuffed them with the skins of animals or dried grass or moss. Often such boots were hard to distinguish from moccasins that could sometimes rise high on the leg (as with the Apache), even up to the knee. The Iroquois version consisted of a moccasin with a sole turned up and sewn to an upper; its leather was boiled in tallow and wax.

The Lenni Lenape (Delaware) developed one of the most successful boots. They called it *seppock,* meaning "shoe," from the Delaware jargon. This became in English *shoepac(k)* or *pac(k)* boot, the first form undoubtedly influenced by *shoe.* A fellow officer used the word in a 1755 letter to young George Washington, who was leading the colonial militia defending Virginia's western frontier against Indian raiders. The two forces were playing a deadly game of hide-and-seek through mountainous terrain in which surprise could be crucial. "The Indians discover our Parties by the Track of their Shoes," the officer warned. "It would be a good thing to have Shoepacks or Moccosons for the Scouts."[2]

Shoepac and *pac boot* are now somewhat loosely applied. They commonly mean a waterproof, laced boot for cold-weather wear. The L.L.Bean catalog does not commonly use the terms, though in World War II, Bean himself developed a "Shoe Pac," based on his Maine Hunting Shoe, for the U.S. Armed Forces. In 1996, the Bean catalog limited use of the loanword to its all-rubber "Sub-Zero Pac Boots."

Several hundred other companies have produced their own pac boots. Some of the best-known brands carry names reflecting rugged and cold-resisting qualities — such as Kodiak, Point Barrow, Alaskan, Yukon, Rocky, and Chinook. Sorel boots from Canada are famed for their warmth in severe cold, including one model guaranteed to provide comfort at minus eighty-five degrees Fahrenheit.

Bean Boots, of course, are by far the most widely known — among outdoors people and perhaps even more among fashionable suburbanites.The early Indians who gave the shoepac/pac boot its name might find these modern versions somewhat strange, but they'd almost certainly welcome them.

PARKA, ANORAK
Arctic jackets

A sled-dog driver approached the Anchorage clothing designer Deborah Ives in 1988 with an urgent request. He was going to enter the Iditarod, the annual race in Alaska, and wanted her to replace his old Eskimo-style pullover with one in a similar style. Ives went into a "creative frenzy," she recalled. She made an outer shell, then tested various removable liners to meet the trail's harsh and changeable conditions. The driver showed his finished coat to friends, who admired the garment's comfort and warmth. Word spread. Ives's fur-trimmed nylon or natural-cloth coat has since been worn not only by Iditarod drivers, but by a wildlife biologist, a leading mountain climber, a paraglider, and numerous other sportspeople.[1]

The coats are a modern adaptation of ones used in the Arctic for centuries or millennia. They had to be warm enough to withstand blizzard winds and minus-seventy-degree Fahrenheit temperatures, yet ventilated enough to minimize sweat inside the coat. The two main styles of Eskimo-Aleut coats are the parka and the anorak. A *parka* is a hooded coat with an opening that reaches down the front. The name comes from the Aleut language but ultimately, through Russian, from a native language of northern Russia. An *anorak* strictly means a hooded pullover with an opening that reaches only partway down the front. Its name comes from Greenland Eskimo *annoraq*.

Women produced these sturdy coats. "A man is the hunter his wife makes him," went a Polar Eskimo saying. Only a hunter wearing weatherproof clothing could endure Arctic cold for the long hours needed to bring back food for his family. The coats, typically worn over baggy trousers, often displayed matched furs with elegant fringes.

Some Aleut and western Eskimo fashioned coats out of seabird and marmot (a small rodent) materials. Poor Eskimo even resorted to salmon skin. Around the Bering Strait and elsewhere, Eskimo often favored caribou fur — one of the warmest in the world because of its hollow hairs. (See **Caribou**.) But they also used muskrat, white and blue fox, mink, and other furs. Wolf or wolverine fur made a trim for sleeves and coat bottoms, with a fringe encircling the face like a halo.

The pairing of parkas, or a parka with a jacket, kept the wearer warm partly because of air trapped between the layers. The inner parka would be worn with the hairs pointing inward. The hairs of the outer parka would point outward. During summer, a person typically wore just one parka.

Clothing had to be waterproof in wet weather and during excursions out to sea. Some of the best parkas for such purposes were made of seal intestine, with a skirt that could be tied around the manhole of a kayak (which see) and thus render a kayaker impervious to waves washing over his craft. A whale's bladder or a great whale's tongue also made effective rainwear, though the latter was heavy and tore easily. So concerned were Eskimo about wet garments that some beat parkas with a special stick before entering an igloo to remove the least snowflake that would melt.

The cut of parkas and anoraks varied from region to region, and it is often hard to tell from descriptions which coat type is being referred to. Around Hudson Bay, a parka reached almost to the knees. Copper Eskimo wore coats short at the wrists and the bottom. Eskimo around the Bering Strait and in west Greenland wore coats reaching to or below the knees. Some Canadian Eskimo wore parkas waistlength in front and curving down in back to the ankles. The coats of Eskimo women resembled those of men.

With the movement to towns and availability of machine-made goods, Eskimo and Aleut now typically wear cloth coats. It is mainly hunters and those in remote villages who still don traditional skins and furs. But the *design* of the Arctic coats has spread throughout the world. The L.L.Bean company sells both parkas and anoraks on a large scale. Its 1996 spring catalog advertised an Alpine and Mountain Classic Anorak for hiking, biking, camping, or fly fishing.

Modern mountain parkas may face even more rugged tests than their anorak relative. The L.L.Bean All-Conditions Parka, with its Primaloft lining, has warmed members of expeditions to Everest and Cho Oyu in the Himalayas, and climbers in the Pacific Northwest. It boasts special features such as an interior zipper for the full length of the coat's front and durable stretch cuffs.

Despite the careful distinction made by L.L.Bean and some others between *parka* and *anorak,* the two words now often appear interchangeably. In his *New York Times Magazine* column "On Language," William Safire has observed the difficulty of keeping the two separate and notes, "Dictionaries don't make these fine distinctions about outerwear."[2] Both words, however, serve as reminders of one of several notable contributions that Eskimo and Aleut have made to our culture — the finest coats ever devised for cold-weather wear.

MACKINAW
Almost impervious to rain

Summer guests rocking on the vast porch of the Grand Hotel on Michigan's Mackinac Island may be pardoned if they are too engrossed in the tranquil view before them to reflect on the

mackinaw

bloody, hand-to-hand fighting that took place when the island was a frontier trading post. The hotel boasted the world's largest hotel porch (627 feet) when it was built in 1887. Today it is the world's largest summer hotel, offering guests antique-furnished rooms, a superb cuisine, and ballroom dancing in the evening — plus grounds that include two nine-hole golf courses.

But the island's name hints at quite a different past. The Ojibwa called it *michilmakinac,* "island of the great turtle," from its humped, turtlelike appearance. Indians regarded the island as sacred and made an offering of tobacco as they passed it in their canoes. The French and English shortened the name. Now the atlas lists Mackinac (pronounced *MAK-in-aw*) Island but Mackinaw City across the straits from it.

The strategic location of Michilmackinac made it a target for the European countries seeking a vantage point for their trappers and traders. The island lay in the straits between Lake Michigan and Lake Huron. It provided access to the busy trade route through Niagara and served as a gateway to the Pacific Northwest.

Father Jacques Marquette established a mission near Michilmackinac in 1671, and the area developed into an emporium for the fur trade. The British took control in the following century. But in 1763, Indians entered the British fort under the pretext of retrieving the ball in a game of lacrosse. They then proceeded to massacre the garrison but spared French inhabitants of the fort. The British resumed control a year later until the United States won the island after the American Revolution. After losing the island in the War of 1812, the United States finally gained permanent possession in 1815.

Blankets developed into the premium trade item at Mackinac,

as the island came to be known. These were draped over winter clothing for added warmth in the bitter northern weather. Pieces of blanket were fashioned into socks and mitten liners. When hunting thinned out the best furbearing animals, Indians substituted blankets for their animal-skin clothing.

By the early nineteenth century, blankets had become the leading article of exchange in much of the Northwest as well. These were graded for quality by "points," marks on a blanket's edge indicating its value in beaver skins. Thus a three-point blanket equaled the skins of three beavers. Major traders such as the Hudson's Bay Company maintained a high standard in the blankets, marking them fairly. Indians knew they could count on their quality and traded widely for and with them. In the early nineteenth century, for example, Chinook sold a male slave for the price of four or five blankets; a female slave fetched somewhat more.

Heavily felted blankets from Mackinac came to be a preferred kind. In 1822, a visitor to Michigan wrote:

> The heavy Mackinac blankets are almost impervious to the rain, and are universally worn by the Indians in this quarter. They are large enough to cover an Indian completely.[1]

And a coat made from the blanket came in for its share of fame. That type of coat dates back more than two centuries. When the British trader Alexander Henry neared Michilmackinac Island in the 1760s, he disguised himself in Canadian French clothes because the Indians hated Englishmen. His new outfit included a loose shirt, a red worsted cap, and a "blanket coat."[2]

But a British officer in the War of 1812 is sometimes given credit for developing what came to be called the mackinaw coat. Captain Charles Roberts, who commanded troops on St. Joseph's Island, couldn't obtain greatcoats for his shivering men. So he had a coat designed that used a blanket from nearby Mackinac.

The coat, often in red-and-black plaid, became standard winter wear for lumberjacks and outdoorsmen. In its most basic form, it was a short coat of heavy fabric. A rhyme celebrated the coat's popularity:

When can its glory fade?
Stout little coat of plaid,
All the North wondered.
Honor the coat they made
Down at the old stockade,
Still made by the hundred.[3]

The character Nick Adams in Ernest Hemingway's "The Last Good Country," set in northern Michigan, wears one. Having covered his sister with his coat while they were camping, he watches her sleeping "with the collar of the warm Mackinaw coat under her chin."[4] But the mackinaw also became standard for men working in factories. Archie Bunker of TV's *All in the Family* goes out on winter days wearing a plaid mackinaw.

At the end of the twentieth century, the mackinaw may be fading in popularity — at least in name. Yet the C.C. Filson Company of Seattle, Washington, founded in 1897, was still offering a line of deluxe Mackinaw Coats a century later. It also carried a Mackinaw Wool Vest and a Mackinaw Cap.

Related words include those for the flat-bottomed *mackinaw boat* used on the Great Lakes, the plaid woolen *mackinaw shirt,* and the *Mackinaw* (or Lake) *trout.* "By the holy mackinaw" has long been an oath in some northern regions.

FOOD FROM PLANTS

"North American Indians had at least 1112 food plant species," says ethnobotanist James A. Duke. Another ethnobotanist, Daniel E. Moerman, places the number higher — at 1886 Native American food plants. Many of the plants would now be regarded as weeds, but the Indians, eminently skilled at living off the land, found nourishment in them.[1]

Food plants varied from one part of the continent to another. Camas bulbs and wapatoo tubers were eaten mainly in the Northwest, tuckahoe in the Southeast, and saguaro cactus in the Southwest. Other plants, such as corn, beans, and squashes — the famed "three sisters" — eventually sustained people across much of North America.

Bruce D. Smith, an archaeologist at the Smithsonian's National Museum of Natural History, says that eastern North American Indians were growing plants for food as long ago as four thousand years. Among those plants were sunflower, lamb's quarters, and at least one kind of squash. Corn, from Mesoamerica, did not arrive in the region until around A.D. 200, and became a staple there only centuries later.

Hominy and *corn pone,* among the five key foods or food sources examined in this section, were both sophisticated products of corn. The widely eaten *succotash* consisted of corn with other ingredients. *Squash* in many varieties enjoyed widespread popularity among Native Americans. Because of its regional occurrence, however, the *saguaro cactus* appears in the diet mainly of Southwestern peoples such as the Tohono O'odham.

HOMINY
True grits

In 1993, more than fifty thousand people gathered in St. George, South Carolina, for the ninth annual World Grits Festival. This celebration of hulled corn, known also as *hominy*, harked back to a colonial and Indian past thousands of years old — and looked forward to a continuing lively interest in the grain.

The festival started in the 1980s after a Quaker Oats salesman showed Bill Hunter, manager of the local Piggly Wiggly grocery store, a map of the Southern grits belt curving from lower Texas to Washington, D.C. "It just hit me," said Hunter. "We looked like we are right in the middle of the grits belt." His enthusiasm led to the establishment of the festival in the town of two thousand people. Participants sing and dance on Main Street, watch a Miss Grits beauty pageant, and join in such activities as shelling corn and (of course) eating grits. Money raised by the events goes toward projects helping youngsters.[1]

The festival recalls some of the Western Hemisphere's most ancient rites involving corn, native to the Americas and a sustainer of the peoples there. Maize gods of Central and South America presided over civilization after civilization. The Maya maize god still receives offerings in the more remote parts of Central America. A Mother Corn ceremony linked the Arikara of South Dakota to the universe. Sometimes sacrificing a maiden at planting time, the Pawnee continued honoring Mother Corn at each stage of the plant's growth.

Corn reached eastern North America about two thousand years ago, becoming a major crop of the Indians there. It saved the Jamestown settlers and the Pilgrims from starving, and they soon learned from Indian purveyors how to raise the grain that became their staple.

Settlers followed the Indians in roasting fresh corn (still wrapped in its inner husk) in the ashes of a fire or under a layer of earth covered with hot coals. Stripped, ears of corn were propped in front of a fire and baked. The settlers boiled corn, though in metal rather than clay pots. And they learned from Indians how to preserve corn by parching it — partly cooking and then drying the kernels.

Readying corn for cooking could be an art in itself. Indians showed settlers two techniques for divesting corn kernels of their tough jackets to obtain the nutritious inner part called *hominy*. This word comes from Virginia Algonquian *uskatahomen,* probably meaning "that which is ground."

The most direct way to make hominy is to crack the corn and winnow away its husks, a procedure referred to in the Southern folk song:

> Ginny cracked corn and I don't care
> Ginny cracked corn and I don't care
> Ginny cracked corn and I don't care
> My master's gone away.

This process may have given rise to *cracker* as a disparaging term for poor Southern whites.

The more nutritious way to make hominy called for wood ash. This was added to water and boiled to produce the alkaline liquor called lye. The preparer soaked corn in the lye for hours, which loosened the hulls. Repeated rinsings enabled the hulls to be rubbed off by hand while washing away the lye. The process was well worth extra trouble because it causes a chemical change that boosts the protein value of corn, which added to its importance as a staple throughout the ancient Americas. (The people of Central America and Mexico use lime for the same purpose.)

New Englanders called their coarsely ground hominy — or a mush made from it — *samp* (from Narragansett *nasàump,* corn mush). In 1643, Roger Williams praised the settler version of this dish:

> *Samp,* which is the *Indian* corne, beaten and boild, and eaten
> hot or cold with milke or butter, which are mercies beyond the
> *Natives* plaine water, and which is a dish exceeding wholesome
> for the *English* bodies.[2]

Southerners showed much ingenuity in preparing hominy dishes. In *Shucks, Shocks, and Hominy Blocks,* Nicholas P. Hardeman describes some of them:

> Rural chefs simmered hot hominy over slow heat for many
> hours, enriching it with butter and perhaps cream, and salting
> and sugaring it to suit the taste before serving. Southerners
> were notoriously fond of hominy and meat gravy. Other popular
> dishes were hominy fritters — grits mixed with milk, flour, and
> a beaten egg, and fried-hominy muffins, and hominy mush.
> Grits were eaten as a main part of the meal or sweetened and
> served as dessert.[3]

Pork with hominy was so cheap and tasty that "hog and hominy" became a Southern term for poor fare. "Hominy men" plied the streets in East Coast cities and elsewhere in the nation until early in the twentieth century. Grits are still standard food in the grits belt, commonly served steaming at breakfast with dollops of butter. But in *The Story of Corn,* Betty Fussell calls hominy today "a minor branch of corn cooking."[4]

Nielsen Marketing Research nevertheless found that Americans ate nineteen million pounds of grits in 1993, a three percent increase over the preceding year. "In the past five to ten years, the grits business has picked up substantially," confirmed Mason Adams of Adams Milling Company in Midland City, Alabama, which sells grits to grocers and mail-order customers.[5] The Quaker Oats Company reported in the mid-1990s that its 800-number for queries about grits cooking was receiving calls daily from all over the country. Hominy, a staple for millennia, endures as one of the most cherished traditional foods of the Americas.

CORN PONE
America's original bread

"You tell me whar a man gits his corn pone, en I'll tell you what his 'pinions is," said Mark Twain, indicating the bread's importance. Yet he also suggested corn pone's sometimes low repute. Huckleberry Finn refers to "baker's bread," or wheat bread, as "what the quality eat — none of your low-down corn-pone."[1]

Valued or despised, bread made with corn has been a basic American food for millennia. It was often the only thing that stood between Indian or settler and starvation — a staple that was nourishing and easy to prepare. Forms of corn bread still appear on dinner tables across the United States, in sticks, cakes, or slabs.

The term *corn pone* is redundant since pone was always made with cornmeal. But Virginia Algonquian *poan* or *appoans* originally meant "thing roasted or baked." In 1612, the explorer William Strachey described how Indians made this basic pone:

> [They] receave the flower [flour] in a platter of wood, which, blending with water, they make into flatt, broad cakes . . . [called] apones, which Covering with Ashes till they be baked . . . and then washing them in faire water, lett dry with their own heate.[2]

This simple recipe has given rise to an array of refinements and variations. *The American Heritage Dictionary* (Fourth Edition) defines basic pone or johnnycake as "Cornmeal bread usually shaped into a flat cake and baked or fried on a griddle." It lists some of the names of pone and its near relatives: *johnnycake* (also known as *journey cake* and *Shawnee cake*) in New England; and *ashcake, battercake, corn cake, cornpone, hoecake,* or *mush bread* in the Southern states. The dictionary goes on to point out that ingredients, batter consistency, and cooking methods differ from region to region.

From the first, settlers felt the same ambivalence toward pone

as Twain. "The want of English graine ... proved a sore affliction
to some stomacks, who could not live upon Indian bread," complained Edward Johnson in *Wonder-Working Providence* in 1654.
Some cooks lightened corn pone by mixing cornmeal with wheat
or rye flour. Such was the recommendation of Amelia Simmons
in the nation's first cookbook a century and a half later.[3]

In *Walden* (1854), Henry David Thoreau described how he
reached the same conclusion:

> Bread I at first made of pure Indian meal and salt, genuine hoe-
> cakes, which I baked before my fire out of doors on a shingle or
> the end of a stick of timber sawed off in building my house; but
> it was wont to get smoked and to have a piny flavor. I tried flour
> also; but have at last found a mixture of rye and Indian meal
> most convenient and agreeable.[4]

Hoecake, incidentally, was at first literally baked on the blade of a
hoe.

Modern corn bread recipes commonly include eggs and short-
ening, and they rarely recommend covering the batter with ashes.
Yet some purists still turn out a johnnycake that is pretty close to
the original pone. Nowhere is the early version defended so vigor-
ously as in Rhode Island. There the Society for the Propagation of
Jonnycake Tradition meets twice a year to bake and eat the bread.
(In the 1890s, the Rhode Island legislature prescribed the *h*-less
spelling of the name.) But even within this society, factions heat-
edly debate the true version. One of their simplest recipes calls for
just four ingredients: Rhode Island stone-ground flint corn,
sugar, salt, and water — cooked on a hot griddle as the earliest settlers probably did.

Today corn pone may be as common in figurative speech as it
is on the table. The term can mean "folksy and homespun."
William Safire in his *New Language of Politics* (1972) sees the noun
as meaning, especially in the South, "'sweet talk' and gentle persua-
sion." He observes that in 1960, vice-presidential candidate Lyndon Johnson named his campaign train "the Corn Pone Special."[5]

Though often taken for granted or demeaned, this ancient bread continues to be firmly rooted in American life.

SUCCOTASH
Forefathers' meal

Early on the morning of December 23, 1996, a cannon boomed from a hill in Plymouth, Massachusetts. Thirty-five men doffed their top hats and cried, "Hip, hip, Hooray!" three times. Then they paraded back to their clubhouse.[1]

Participants were members of the Old Colony Club — New England's oldest social club — gathered for their annual Forefathers' Day celebration of the Pilgrims' landing in 1620. (December 21 is the precise date according to today's calendar.) Members came together again in the evening for a dinner that included succotash — perhaps New England's most tradition-laden dish. Indeed, the club's first such dinner in 1769 offered as its second course "A dish of Souquetash." And two days before the modern Old Colony Club celebration, the Pilgrim Society — keeper of the relics from the first settlers — had presented its 177th Annual Forefathers' Day Dinner for more than a hundred people. The meal featured Plymouth's unique version of succotash.

The Plimoth Colony Cook Book of 1957 affirms that succotash is as "sacred to Forefathers' Day as turkey is to Thanksgiving."[2] But just what goes into this classic dish? In 1643, Roger Williams narrowly defined *msíckquatash* — the Narragansett form of the name — as "boild corne whole."[3] The evidence is that Indians in New England and across North America introduced settlers to corn and beans boiled together. To this basic succotash the Indians and settlers added other vegetables and meat as available.

Combining the two main vegetables was natural, since they were grown together (often with squash). According to the Iroquois, the spirits of the two "sisters" wanted to remain together even when being cooked and served. And nutritionally, corn with beans provides "all the protein requirements of working males," according to an authority on ancient American cuisine.[4]

Travelers in many parts of colonial America reported succotash as an important part of the Indian diet, with many regional touches that gave the dish a distinctive flavor and appearance. Writing in 1767, Jonathan Carver described a version made by Indians in Wisconsin:

> One dish which answers nearly the same purpose as bread, is in use among the Outagamies, the Saukies, and other eastern nations, where corn grows . . . is reckoned extremely palatable by all Europeans who enter their domains. This is composed of their unripe corn, . . . and beans in the same state, boiled together with bear's flesh — which renders it beyond comparison delicious. They call this food succotash.[5]

Another traveler reported in the early nineteenth century that the Mandan kept a large pot of corn-and-beans succotash bubbling in their dwellings for visitors to dip into. To the south, the late-nineteenth-century anthropologist Frank H. Cushing described Zuni succotash as "the delicacy of the year" — a soup or stew of corn, beans, and pieces of meat thickened with sunflower seeds or ground piñon nuts.[6]

Modern Americans typically eat succotash in its basic form of corn and beans — a dish that early North American Indians would recognize. That is, except for lima beans, which originated in ancient Peru (whose modern capital gave them their name) and Mexico. The Pilgrims almost certainly used native kidney beans and flint corn.

But many people of Plymouth today scorn a succotash composed merely of two vegetables. James W. Baker, head of Plimoth Plantation, that fascinating reconstruction of the original town, writes:

> Plymouth may be unusual in that the town has its own unique dish (one in which most of the rest of the country seems unac-

countably uninterested) which it defends against pallid pre-
tenders to the name elsewhere. I am of course speaking of Plymouth Succotash — that sacrament of the true Plymouthean
and triumph of the traditional Forefathers' Day table![7]

The Plymouth Succotash that Baker extols is a hearty stew
with corned beef, fowl, salt pork — preserving the Indian custom
of often including meat — and several vegetables besides the
original two. "Plymoutheans" once served the meats separately,
but now all the ingredients are usually mixed together. This is a
meal well suited to a wintry day on the Massachusetts coast.

SQUASH
Halloween and all that

One of the vegetables that intrigued and bewildered early
American colonists was squash. Indians widely cultivated this native American plant, which now includes varieties such as acorn,
butternut, summer, crookneck, and more than a dozen others.
These come in white, yellow, green, blue, and orange hues; and in
shapes like globes, clubs, tubes, turbans, acorns, bowling pins,
and some too grotesque for comparison.

At first skeptical, settlers learned from the Indians to eat
squashes baked or stewed. One of the most popular was the
pumpkin. New Englanders made a primitive pumpkin pie by
filling a pumpkin shell with apples, sugar, spices, and milk
before baking it. The vegetable's importance to settlers during a famine can be judged from a seventeenth-century
rhyme:

> *Instead of pottage and puddings and custards and pies,*
> *Our pumpkins and parsnips are common supplies;*
> *When have pumpkin at morning and pumpkin at noon;*
> *If it was not for pumpkin we should be undoon.*[1]

American Indians had been growing squash for thousands of years before Europeans arrived in the New World. Remains of the pumpkin family of squash (species *Cucurbita pepo*) found in Oaxaca, Mexico, date back to about 8000 B.C. Rind fragments and seeds apparently of the same kind of squash from Missouri date to about 2000 B.C.; and other evidence suggests a still earlier date for North America, making squash possibly the first plant cultivated on the continent.

Squash was one of the "three sisters" of Indian agriculture, along with corn and beans. Northeast Indians planted corn in little mounds. Then they added bean seeds, which put out runners that clung to the cornstalks. Squash seeds planted close by developed into vines that protected the roots of the corn and kept weeds out. The three sisters not only grew harmoniously with each other but together provided a nutritious diet, with squash adding vitamins A and C to the protein and other nutrients of the other two.

Indians in widespread parts of America, besides those noted above, grew squash. George Catlin observed in the 1830s that the Mandan of the northern Great Plains cultivated pumpkins and other squashes.[2] Peoples of the Southwest showed an especially keen appreciation of the vegetable. They ate the seeds and blossoms as well as the flesh. Hopi painters used chewed squash seeds in mixing their colors. Squash-blossom effigies adorned the headdresses worn by dancers at Hopi sacred ceremonies. Girls of that people wore their hair in loops, called squash blossoms, over their ears. The Navajo fashioned necklaces and other jewelry in classic squash-blossom designs.

The first English comments on squash, however, come from the East Coast. John Smith wrote in 1612 that Virginia Indians planted "pumpeons" [pumpkins].[3] In 1643, Roger Williams praised squash in a comment that recorded the modern form of the Narragansett name:

> *Asqutasquash*, their Vine aples, which the *English* from them call
> *Squashes* about the bigness of Apples of severall colours, a
> sweet, light wholesome refreshing.[4]

Today squash plays a cherished role in two American holidays. Squash and pumpkin pie have been traditional Thanksgiving desserts since colonial times. The jack-o'-lantern made its grinning appearance early in the nineteenth century. In Ireland on Halloween, people had placed a candle inside a hollowed turnip with a carved face. They carried this skull-like lantern from house to house while celebrating the holiday. Irish immigrants introduced the custom to America, with the larger and more gaudy pumpkin as a New World twist to the ancient Celtic custom.

And pumpkins are the center of some later autumn celebrations. Circleville, Ohio, sponsors a Pumpkin Show annually that is Ohio's oldest (since 1903) and largest festival. It takes place on the third Wednesday in October through the following Saturday and draws crowds of up to half a million. Among the treats offered are pumpkin cookies, pies, bread, pancakes, waffles, burgers, chili, doughnuts, pizza, taffy, fudge, and brittle. Each year, a local baker produces the world's largest pumpkin pie — five feet across and weighing 350 pounds. Public activities include a pumpkin-pie-eating contest and a competition for the largest pumpkin grown (sometimes close to 600 pounds). Farmers from around Circleville sell tons of whole pumpkins during the festival.

American supermarkets carry a half dozen or so of the most popular other squashes for everday use — often the butternut, buttercup, turban, spaghetti, Hubbard, or zucchini. Specialty seed companies, like Native Seeds/Search of Tucson, Arizona, list up to about thirty squash varieties. Many of these unusual squashes carry names indicating an Indian background, such as Pima bajo and Hopi pumpkin.

Squash, one of the most ancient cultivated foods of the Americas, still offers new possibilities to gardener and cook.

SAGUARO
Symbol of the Southwest

The boy was going to throw a stone to knock down fruit growing atop the towering saguaro (pronounced *sa-HWAH-ro*). "No!" cried the old woman with him. "The saguaros — they are Indians too. You don't ever throw anything at them. If you hit them in the head with rocks you could kill them. You don't do anything to hurt them. They are Indians."[1]

Nor are Indians alone in regarding saguaros as more than mere cacti. So human can they seem in desert expanses that non-Indians sometimes find themselves talking to them.

Saguaros are unique to the Sonoran Desert stretching from central Arizona to northern Mexico and the tip of southeastern California. They rise majestically to about fifty feet when fully mature and can weigh several tons. At the age of a half-century or so, they start sprouting upward-curving branches. Some many-branched saguaros live to be three hundred years old.

The Pima and Tohono O'odham (formerly Papago) Indians found a use for almost every part of the saguaro. The word *saguaro* itself is probably of Piman origin.[2] A saguaro's heated flesh has relieved the pains of rheumatism. Vinegar made of its juice can etch seashells. The tough ribs of the saguaro have served as a framework for mud-plastered thatch houses. Calluses, formed where the Gila woodpecker drills its holes in the cactus, have been crafted into boxes.

Most of all, Indians prized and still prize the saguaro's fruit. The cactus starts blooming at sunset late in April, putting forth white blossoms (Arizona's state flower) that stay open through the night and into the following afternoon. The red, two- or three-inch fruit typically follows late in June. So crucial has this fruit been to the Tohono O'odham that their New Year begins with its appearance. Using a pole (often saguaro ribs tied together), some gatherers knock the fruit off while others catch it in a basket. The

Indians eat the sweet fruit fresh. They turn it into syrup and jam, and they use the seeds to make porridge or candy.

When fermented, the saguaro fruit becomes a key element in the Tohono O'odham rainmaking ceremony. (Specific ceremonies vary from community to community.) An elder traditionally mixes saguaro syrup and water in large jars inside a council house. As he does, he addresses the brew:

> Be strong!
> Let us get well drunk!
> Hither bring the wind and its cloudiness.[3]

Fermentation takes about two days. An official taster assures the proper degree of potency.

Meanwhile the people come together. Elders begin the first nightlong round of singing and dancing to assure the start of the rainy season and the planting of crops. A stanza from one of their songs welcomes the dawn:

> At the edge of the world,
> It is growing light.
> Up rears the light.
> Just yonder, the day dawns,
> Spreading over the night.[4]

The opening ceremonies end at daybreak.

During the second night, celebrants resume their singing. Toward dawn, they begin drinking the mild wine in great quantities. Their object is to cause vomiting, which mimics rain clouds and stimulates rain. Cupbearers pass along brimming cups, saying:

> Drink, friend! Get beautifully drunk!
> Hither bring the wind and clouds.[5]

The saguaro is closely linked not only with the lives of Indians but with a wide range of desert animals and plants. Woodpeckers and other birds drill holes in it, and some such as the elf owl nest in the cavities. The long-nosed bat flies from Mexico to sip nectar from the saguaro and incidentally pollinate its flowers. Ground animals such as coyotes and foxes feed on the fallen fruit while ants and other insects eat the seeds.

The saguaro's priceless value to Indian folkways and desert ecology has led to concern about its future. Vandals hack, shoot, and steal the cactus. Urban sprawl is an ever-present threat to its habitat. But botanists say the durable saguaro is not about to disappear.

Congress established the Saguaro National Monument in 1933 to shelter the cactus in Arizona. In 1994, President Bill Clinton signed a bill upgrading the monument's status to Saguaro National Park. The bill also provided for the addition of more than three thousand acres to protect saguaros against spreading suburbs. More than two million people a year were then hiking, biking, and driving through the park. At the same time, the Tohono O'odham continued to follow their hallowed tradition of setting up a camp there each July and August to harvest the saguaro fruit.

/\

ADDITIONAL
PLANTS

\/

An early settler of America who was sick or injured often lacked even the rudimentary medical care available in Europe. So it is hardly surprising that Euroamericans tried and often adopted remedies using native plants. These were plentiful and varied, for the original inhabitants of the continent had developed an intimate knowledge of their surrounding plants.

Virgil Vogel, in his *American Indian Medicine* lists a "minimum" of 161 species of North American plants that have been or are drugs approved by the U.S. Food and Drug Administration. The ethnobotanist Daniel E. Moerman places the number of plants Native Americans used for medicines at 2874, with thousands more put to other practical uses.[1]

This section deals with three key plants that provided Indians and then settlers with medicines — *pokeweed, puccoon,* and *pipsissewa.* (Other medicinal plants that retain Indian names include *cohosh* in several varieties; *senega,* or *seneca root;* and *wahoo,* or burning bush.) An additional plant examined here is *tuckahoe,* which Indians and some settlers used to make a kind of bread.

POKEWEED, PUCCOON
Vagabond weed

It grows abundantly throughout the East — at the back of yards, along meadows, beside highways. One herbalist calls *pokeweed* (or simply *poke*) a "vagabond among weeds." The four- to ten-foot stalks of the far-flung plant turn purplish red in autumn.

Around fifty different kinds of birds, including doves and cedar waxwings, gorge themselves on the deep-purple berries it then displays. The birds excrete and thus disperse the seeds in their travels, sometimes leaving purple splashes on cars.[1] In "Vacant Lot with Pokeweed," Amy Clampitt notes one of the plant's random appearances:

> *raw-buttoned, garnet-rodded*
> *fruit one more wayfarer*
> *perhaps may salvage from*
> *the season's frittering. . . .*[2]

Indians prized this native American plant, and its name may be related to Virginia Algonquian *poughkone,* or puccoon. But a host of other names testifies to its widespread popularity among settlers as well:

pokeberry	puccoon (see below)
Virginia poke	pigeonberry
poke salad (or sallet) —	inkberry
the cooked shoots	scoke

Pokeweed eaten carelessly is highly poisonous: it can cause nausea, convulsions, and sometimes death. But the Virginia Pamunkey and the Iroquois drank a potion of the berries to cure rheumatism. Other tribes are said to have taken tonics including pokeberry as blood purifiers or emetics.

Indians also made a dye with the plant's berries. Connecticut Valley natives stained baskets with it. Other Indians used pokeweed to color clothing, wooden ornaments, and sometimes their own skin.

Settlers learned from the Indians to eat pokeweed. Especially in the South, they made "poke salad" — young shoots boiled in several changes of water to eliminate toxins. An eighteenth-century traveler in the United States, noting the lack of vegetables in one locality, commented, "We adopt the custom of the inhabitants who gather the leaves of the poke-plant, just as they shoot above the ground and are tender and soft."[3]

A curious use for pokeweed emerged during James K. Polk's campaign for the presidency in 1844. Supporters, making a pun on the name, marched through city streets flourishing pokeweed stalks. Tennessee ox drivers stained the horns of their oxen with pokeweed juice to advertise their loyalty to the Democratic candidate; drivers favoring his Whig rival, Henry Clay, plastered clay on the horns of their oxen.

As a medicine, the plant greatly impressed settlers. Early on, and into the twentieth century, older Americans drank a tea made from pokeweed berries to treat rheumatism. From 1820 to 1916, the *United States Pharmacopoeia* — the national official list of drugs — designated pokeweed root as a treatment for pain and inflammation; sometimes a preparation for this purpose came in the form of a wine. Extracts of the plant allegedly relieved cancer, respiratory diseases, and laryngitis.

Settlers learned that pokeweed berries yielded still another bonus — a long-lasting red or purple ink, causing the plant to be nicknamed *inkweed*. (The great Sequoya would use pokeberry juice and a quill pen to transcribe the Cherokee language for the first time.) One eighteenth-century recipe for pokeberry ink called for boiling together pokeberries, vinegar, and sugar. In the twentieth century, country people still sometimes used the concoction for special writing purposes.

The person most responsible for piquing interest in pokeweed during the late twentieth century is the naturalist and best-selling author Euell Gibbons. In *Stalking the Wild Asparagus,* he describes how to cook the young shoots and serve them with butter, margarine, or bacon. The dish "so closely resembles asparagus that some may be fooled," he says. Gibbons also offers tips on frying and pickling the shoots.[4]

True to its vagabond reputation, pokeweed was carried to Europe two centuries ago. There it is not scorned as a weed, but honored as a cultivated plant.

Puccoon requires separate mention. The word comes from Virginia Algonquian *poughkone* and is akin to *pokeweed*, both perhaps ultimately from an Algonquian root *pak*, "blood." The word may refer to any of several plants yielding a red dye. One is pokeweed. Another, more common one is bloodroot — a delicate white-blossomed plant whose roots contain bright red sap. Indians applied the sap as a dye and a paint for skin. "*Pocones*," John Smith wrote in 1612, "is a small roote that groweth in the mountaines, which being dryed and beate in powder turneth red: and this they use for swellings, aches, annointing their joints, painting their heads and garments." He added: "At night where his lodging is appointed, they set a woman fresh painted red with Pocones and oile, to be his bedfellow."[5]

Although the unmixed sap is poisonous, Indians treated a number of internal diseases with medicines made of it. In the twentieth century, other Americans also took bloodroot potions as expectorants, emetics, and tonics.

Warning: Pokeweed and puccoon may be highly toxic if consumed. Beware of careless use.

PIPSISSEWA
Flower of the woods

Inspired partly by learning that Indians and then Euroamericans used the trippingly named pipsissewa as a remedy, Virgil Vogel wrote his monumental *American Indian Medicine*. Vogel observes that the plant remained in officially sanctioned medical use well into the twentieth century. It continues to be gathered in regions with a living tradition of folk medicine.

Henry David Thoreau admires pipsissewa in his journal:

> The back side of its petals, "cream colored tinged with purple," which is turned toward the beholder, while the face is toward the earth, is the handsomest. It is a very pretty little chandelier of a flower, fit to adorn the forest floor.[1]

Pipsissewa belongs to the wintergreen family and sometimes even goes by that herbal name. There are two kinds of pipsissewa. The medicinal kind, *Chimaphila umbellata*, reaches a height of about four inches in deep dry woods throughout much of North America and also grows in Europe and Asia. It has evergreen leaves and white-to-pink five-petaled flowers.

pipsissewa

Dictionaries once translated *pipsissewa* as "it breaks it [a gallstone]," from the plant's medical use. Now the word's origin is conjectured to be "flower of the woods," from Eastern Abenaki *kpi-pskwáhsawe*. Nicknames include *prince's pine, king's cure, love-in-winter*, and *dragon's tongue*.

Indians sought out the medicinal pipsissewa for a variety of external and internal purposes. A few of the tribes that used it were: the Ojibwa (as a stomachic); the Menominee (for female complaints); the Catawba (for backache); the Montagnais (to promote perspiration); the Penobscot (to draw out blisters); and the Shawnee (for consumption). The list of Indian applications for pipsissewa could easily be expanded.

Settlers took up the versatile plant. Doctors in the early nineteenth century reported that it worked as a diuretic and relieved intermittent fever. In the Civil War, the eminent Dr. Francis P. Porcher of Charleston recommended that the Confederacy use pipsissewa as an emergency substitute for mercury and as a tonic and diuretic. The dried leaf of pipsissewa was officially listed in the authoritative *United States Pharmacopoeia* until 1916 and in the *National Formulary* (issued by the American Pharmaceutical Association) from 1916 to 1947 as an astringent, tonic, and diuretic. Into the twentieth century, pipsissewa beer was made by adding sugar for sweetening, ginger for flavor, and yeast for fermentation. It was taken as a beverage and as a treatment for what were called "scrofulous affections."

Today inorganic medicines have replaced pipsissewa in common medical practice. Yet Nelson Coon, in *Using Plants for Healing*, reports that herb gatherers in North Carolina and other mountain regions were preparing and selling it in the 1960s. One can still obtain it at health food stores. People who maintain terrariums keep pipsissewa and other woodland herbs to enjoy flowers that are as charming as their names.

TUCKAHOE
Wild potato

Many a far-flung town, river, or street in the United States bears the name of an Indian staple that the explorer John Smith noted among Virginia Indians in the early 1600s. *Tockawhoughe* Smith rendered the name, but it is better known now as *tuckahoe*, or sometimes familiarly as *wild potato*. The plant is the arrow arum (it has arrow-shaped leaves), found in freshwater marshes on the East Coast.

Smith reported that an Indian could gather enough of the tuckahoe's starchy, potatolike roots in a day to last a week. These were sun-dried in slices or baked for twenty-four hours under a layer of leaves covered with earth to rid them of their irritating acid. The dried roots would at last be pounded into a meal used to make what one historian calls "a passable bread." Virginia Indians depended on this food in the months before corn ripened.

Settlers tried eating tuckahoe but apparently didn't acquire a fondness for it. The word became a nickname for people living east of Virginia's Blue Ridge Mountains, especially on the poor land there. By extension, poor whites in some parts of the South were called "tuckahoes." Somewhat like "Podunk," the name also came to be applied to backwoods places, although the names-

authority George R. Stewart considers this usage to be more humorous than derogatory.

Today thirteen U.S. communities, at least twenty-six streets,
and scores of other sites bear the name *Tuckahoe.* Most lie in the
South, especially in Virginia and North Carolina; others are as far
away as California. When connected with a watery location, the
name is likely to refer to the plant. In other cases, it may well have
been adopted because of its humorous associations or catchy
sound.

A few edible plants other than arrow arum, especially at least one
other arum, are also sometimes called *tuckahoe.* So is the edible
part of certain fungi. *Tucket,* meaning a green ear of corn, is related to the word *tuckahoe.*

FOOD FROM TREES

Nothing expressed the fruitfulness of North American forests more than the nuts that annually rained down in a variety of shapes, sizes, and flavors. Among those that Indians prized were acorns, black walnuts, butternuts, chestnuts, chinquapins, hazelnuts, and piñon nuts (pine nuts).

Acorns appear to have been the most widely eaten nut, with fifty-nine native species of oak growing to tree size. The kernels of sweet acorns were enjoyed fresh or pounded into a flourlike substance used to make porridge or a kind of bread. Indians processed the bitter acorns by crushing the kernels and filtering water through them to remove the offending tannic acid.

Especially in the eastern half of the United States, Indians ate *hickory* nuts, which retain a native name. They mixed a "hickory milk" into stews and breads, greatly enhancing food value. Curiously, settlers did not seem to take to this nourishing ingredient. But the related *pecan,* which also retains a native name, has become a major U.S. commercial crop. Indians in the Southwest gathered piñon nuts as a major part of their diet, and these nuts are still relished.

A blight has killed off most chestnut trees in modern times, but hazelnuts and black walnuts, as well as piñon nuts, are popular today as they have been for millennia. *Chinquapin* nuts, on the other hand, once commonly eaten by Eastern Indians and then settlers, have more recently lost popularity. Among tree-borne fruits, the Indian-favored *persimmon* remains a largely regional delicacy, although it is sold in national supermarkets. An essay on each appears in this section.

HICKORY
Forest abundance

> The shagbark [hickory] seems like a symbol of the pioneer age, with its hard sinewy limbs and rude, shaggy coat, like the pioneer himself in fringed deerskin hunting shirt. And the roaring heat of its fires, the tang of its nuts . . . stand for the days of forest abundance.[1]

So writes that connoisseur of trees, Donald Culross Peattie. But he also points out that Indians appreciated and used the hickory in resourceful ways long before the arrival of Europeans.

The approximately seventeen species of hickory are nearly all native to North America, growing mostly in the central and eastern parts of the United States. Hard of wood and plentiful of nuts, they are related to the walnut, and sometimes so called by early settlers. The pecan, which ranks first among the hickories in economic importance, is discussed separately in this book.

The hickory's name reflects the tree's most important Indian use. It comes from Virginia Algonquian *pawcohiccora,* which means food prepared from pounded nuts, with the basic idea being "pounded" or "beaten." The naturalist William Bartram, traveling in Georgia in 1773, saw one Indian family storing more than a hundred bushels of hickory nuts. He said that Indians would pound the kernels to pieces and throw them into boiling water. They strained out the rich, oily part of the liquid. This hickory milk would be blended into the ingredients of stews and breads, enhancing their nutritiousness and flavor.

Earlier in the century, Elizabeth Hanson witnessed the nutritive value of hickory milk while a captive of Indians (unspecified) in Canada. When her own milk, on which her nursing baby depended, dried up, an Indian woman had her beat up some hickory kernels (called by Hanson "walnuts") with water. She was told to add some fine Indian cornmeal and boil the mixture. Upon sipping the gruel, the infant "quickly began to thrive and look well."[2]

Settlers followed the Indians in eating the nuts of the shagbark and other hickories producing sweet kernels. Youngsters joined in shelling bees, where joking and pranks lightened the tedious chore of extracting kernels from thick shells. Hickory nuts lent a uniquely American tang to breads, cakes, and puddings. Pignut hickory nuts, too bitter to eat, yielded an oil believed to be good for rheumatism.

Indians valued the resilient hickory wood as well. Like the Pawnee and other tribes, the Menominee employed it to make bows. A craftsman blocked a length of wood from a tree, preferably the shagbark hickory. He carved the wood to its final shape, rubbed it with bear grease, and put it away to season. Once the bow was in use, applications of deer brains kept it from cracking.

Hickory wood, dense and tough, found many uses in the growing country. Americans fashioned it into the hubs and other heavily stressed parts of covered wagons. They used it to make unsurpassed handles for axes and other tools. They turned it into rail fences and barrel hoops. The broom hickory furnished them strips for brooms. Not least, cords of hotly burning hickory logs heated drafty colonial houses.

Hickory's toughness was proverbial. During the War of 1812, General Andrew Jackson ignored orders to demobilize his troops in Mississippi, far from their homes. He marched them 500 miles to a more convenient location, and they admiringly called him "Old Hickory" because of his toughness. This nickname helped create his political identity. During the election of 1828, local committees supporting him, called "Hickory Clubs," developed the theme with a thoroughness worthy of a Madison Avenue advertising agency. They passed out hickory brooms, canes, and sticks; many of these emblems went up on steeples and signposts. Jackson won a sweeping victory.

And *hickory* remained conspicuous in other ways. A hickory referred to a switch of that or other wood used to strike an errant child. The noun could also mean a walking stick. A *hickory shirt* was one made of strong twilled cotton fabric with vertical stripes, so named because of its strength and its pattern — as vertical as the tree.

Today hickory still occupies a significant place in American life. Its wood continues to be valued for its exceptional hardness and density. The best tool handles come from the hickory tree. As firewood, hickory is unequaled. Hickory-flavored ham — smoked in hickory fires for ten days or more at a temperature of more than ninety degrees — is considered among the tastiest of meats. The sweet-kerneled hickory nuts are still gathered in rural areas by people with the patience to crack them, and one can sometimes buy cakes or other desserts with a haunting shagbark flavor at country fairs.

Current names for species of the tree include *sand hickory, shagbark hickory, big shellbark hickory, red hickory, white hickory* (mockernut), *black hickory,* and *pignut* (or *bitternut*) *hickory.* Many people enjoy the hickories simply for their shade and beauty. The shagbark and pignut soar almost as gracefully as an elm, and their autumn leaves turn a soft golden color that lingers after maple leaves have fallen.

PECAN
Vanilla, chocolate, and . . .

The people of San Saba in central Texas are connoisseurs of the nation's most popular native nut — the pecan. They call their small town, with a population of less than three thousand, "The Pecan Capital of the World." Apart from the ample commercial orchards that give the town its distinctive character and flavor, evidence of the pecan can be seen at every turn. Pecan trees shade the two main streets and many neighborhood yards. Stores feature a number of the several hundred varieties of pecan. And, as Regina Schrambling reported in the *New York Times* after a visit, the town's specialty appears in the fudge, pralines, coffee, breads, waffles, and pies available in local shops.[1]

Pecan pie, of course, is a national favorite. Crunchy butter pecan ice cream ranks third in popularity among Americans after vanilla and chocolate. Pecan pralines and caramel "turtles" nestle on thousands of the nation's candy counters. But many Americans enjoy whole kernels right out of the shell, especially at Thanksgiving or Christmas.

After being shipwrecked on the Texas coast in 1528, the Spanish explorer Núñez Cabeza de Vaca came upon Indians eating pecans. He called the unfamiliar nuts walnuts, to which they are related. Seeds and leaves of the pecan have been found together with human artifacts in Texas locations dating back at least five thousand years. From ancient times, tribes combed the bottomlands of what are now Texas and the lower Mississippi Valley each fall for the nuts. They ate them whole and extracted oil and pulp from them to enrich stews and bread. (See **Hickory** for similar use.) In historical times, the Choctaw were one of the tribes noted for cultivating the nut.

The early English name for pecans was *Illinois nuts,* but the French adopted what would become the current name for the Illinois Indian *pakani,* changing it to *pakane.* The word is akin to Ojibwa *paka·n* meaning a hard-shelled nut. *Pecan* would later become a popular place-name, with more than seventy brooks and rivers of the name flowing in Texas alone.

Colonists quickly took to the nourishing, delicately flavored nuts. They gathered them by the bushel, storing sacks for trade and later use. Sometimes (the forests seemed endless) they chopped down great pecan trees to harvest the nuts more easily. George Washington raised pecan trees at Mount Vernon. In 1790, Thomas Jefferson asked a friend "to procure me two or three hundred Paccan nuts from the Western country." The third president planted pecans at Monticello and distributed them in Virginia, creating a legacy still to be seen on the grounds of many homes there.[2]

The nuts of earlier trees had harder shells and smaller kernels compared to those of today's cultivated trees. Around the middle of the nineteenth century, a Louisiana slave named Antoine improved the pecan by developing trunk-grafted trees. His work became the foundation for the development of the meaty, "papershell" nut we enjoy today. Thanks to improved methods of cultivation as well, pecan orchards have spread over much of the southeastern United States and reached the West Coast and some northern states. Georgia (outside the original range) ranks first among states for pecan growing. The pecan is the state tree of Texas, and most of that state's counties boast commercial pecan orchards.

The Brownwood (Texas) station of the U.S. Agriculture Department has painstakingly produced at least twenty varieties of pecan, with Indian names paying tribute to the nut's original gatherers. Some of these, with the number of years required for their development, are: Choctaw (13 years); Mohawk, Sioux, and Wichita (19 years each); Pawnee (21 years); Kiowa (23 years); Cheyenne (28 years); Houma (31 years); Oconee (33 years); Osage (41 years); and Caddo (46 years) (*Houston Chronicle,* 4 April 1994).

Today the processing of pecans is no less sophisticated than their cultivation. They may be blown through a specialized air system and sorted electronically. The automatically shelled nuts are sterilized in water and refrigerated or frozen. The process ensures a long-lasting, flavorful nut.

Of less importance, though significant, are other uses of the pecan tree. It is prized as a lofty shade tree; and its hard wood goes into furniture, flooring, and tool handles. Even pecan shells, pulverized, find uses as mulch and poultry litter.

Curiously, the pecan nut has never found the same popularity abroad that it has enjoyed at home. It is grown mainly in the United States and northern Mexico, and its leading importer is Canada. In Europe, the nut has long been regarded as a "luxury or treat" and an "exotic, premium ingredient," according to a dairy industries report in 1995. One of the most delicious contributions Indians have made to cuisine has still not, centuries after its

discovery by Europeans, won the international recognition admirers say it merits.[3]

CHINQUAPIN
A great daintie

In the early 1600s, the explorer John Smith wrote that Virginia Indians considered certain small acornlike nuts, which they
called *chechinquamins*, "a great daintie."[1] They ate the nuts fresh,
or boiled them with chestnuts for soups and breads served at their
feasts. Settlers too enjoyed nuts of the *chinquapin* (or *chinkapin*),
as the name was Anglicized, and markets in some Southern
towns carried them at least into the second half of the twentieth
century.

Smith's chinquapin is the shrub or small tree now often called
the *Allegheny chinquapin*. This tree resembles the chestnut and
can be found from New Jersey south to Florida and Texas, and
west to Indiana and Missouri. Indians gathered its nuts for more
than food. The Iroquois made a kind of coffee out of roasted chinquapin nuts. The Cherokee brewed a tea out of the leaves and
treated feverish people with it; the Mohegan drank such tea for
colds and rheumatism.

Settlers found the Allegheny chinquapin almost as useful.
They, too, patiently gathered and cracked the little nuts. Southerners thought chinquapin
helpful in treating ailments
such as ague. Sometimes they
made fence posts and the like
out of the larger trees. Yet the
nut's popularity faded over
time.

An article in the journal
HortScience (1994) suggests
that the chinquapin merits renewed consideration. It states

chinquapin

that the chinquapin "may well be our most mistreated and mis-
represented native North American nut tree." The authors say
that it:

➤ yields a sweet and edible nut;
➤ is a "wood source for fuel, charcoal, fence posts, and railroad
  ties";
➤ produces nuts that can be used as a coffee or chocolate substitute;
➤ provides food for wildlife;
➤ can be used for hybridizing with other chestnut species to
  heighten their resistance to blight;
➤ grows a root sometimes used "as an astringent, a tonic, and to
  treat fevers."[2]

Modern Americans seem largely to have forgotten the "daintie" that Virginia Indians introduced to the settlers. The time
may have come for a new look at the underrated Allegheny
chinquapin.

The *evergreen chinquapin* is found along the West Coast from
Oregon to California. It grows to be much larger than its distant
Allegheny relative, ninety feet or so, and sports a mass of evergreen foliage. Nuts from this tree are edible but tough to extract.
"A well-plumped-out edible nut is hard to come by, and though
the kernels are sweet to the palate, what a task to extract them
from their spiny prisons!" comments Donald Culross Peattie.[3]

The Omaha and other Indians regarded the unrelated *water
chinquapin,* or American lotus, as sacred — much as the peoples
of Egypt, India, and China revered their lotuses. The yellow-
blossomed plant grows in ponds or sluggish streams. Its flowers
rise above the water's surface along with seed-bearing cones. The
Omaha, Iroquois, and other Indians ate almost every part of the
plant, including the seeds. Some modern writers on edible plants
recommend the water chinquapin to people interested in sampling foods from the wild; others warn that it is nearly extinct in
some regions.

PERSIMMON
'Misunderstood and neglected'

President Thomas Jefferson served continental cuisine and fine French wines at the White House, but also the best fare his country produced, such as his *persimmon* beer. This became so famous that Jefferson's recipe for it appeared in the magazine *American Farmer* (15 April 1819). Commonly called "simmon beer" by Southerners, the beverage represented only one of many delightful ways the orange-colored, date-flavored fruit was being served. Americans, especially Southerners, turned persimmons into pudding, biscuits, cookies, bread, and fudge; and they ate them fresh or dried.

Early colonists had found Virginia Indians eating the North American variety of the fruit (*Diospyros virginiana*) like figs and baking it into breads and puddings. The newcomers painfully learned that a persimmon could not be eaten prematurely. "If it be not ripe, it will drawe a mans mouth awrie, with much torment, but when it is ripe, it is as delicious as an Apricock," cautioned John Smith in 1612.[1]

The Indians customarily dried persimmons on mats spread over frames. This led to the Algonquian term *pasemenan*, meaning "fruit dried artificially." Smith transcribed the name as *putchamin*, and his contemporary William Strachey wrote *pessemin*. By the end of the seventeenth century, *persimmon* became the standard, more pronounceable form in English.

The North American persimmon tree grows from Texas and Florida to Connecticut. It is a member of the ebony family, with exceptionally hard wood that was useful to the Indians. In modern times, this wood has been made into shoe lasts, furniture veneer, and golf-club heads. Indians used the fruit's flat, hard seeds in playing a dice game.

The persimmon tree was known in the South as *possum-wood* because of the fondness that animal has for the fruit. The fruit's lusciousness earned it a prominent place in the region's lore and language. "The longest pole knocks down the most simmons" was a way of acknowledging that the stronger party tends to win. "To rake up the persimmons" was an expression for success in gambling. "That's persimmons" meant "Great!"

But attempts in the early twentieth century to widen the popularity of persimmons met with limited success. Perhaps because of unhappy experiences with unripe persimmons, the public tended to regard them as a novelty or a specialty fruit. When the culinary writer Raymond Sokolov traveled to Gnaw Bone, Indiana, for some of its much-praised persimmon treats, he happily discovered a source of superb persimmon fudge. But he learned that nobody around there cultivated the tree, and it was with difficulty that he located a tree and gathered up some neglected fruit.[2]

Nevertheless, a persimmon festival held in Mitchell, Indiana, for more than twenty years has helped win the fruit some badly needed recognition. Toward the end of September, the festival occupies two blocks of the small town. Contestants vie for prizes in best-persimmon-pudding and persimmon-novelty-dessert competitions. Local groups serve persimmon cakes, fudge, ice cream, pies, and puddings — along with more standard fare such as chicken and dumplings. Thousands of spectators look on as judges select a Persimmon Festival Queen and three Miss Persimmons, who take part in a large parade on the last day of the event.

A disappointment to some, the two persimmon varieties most commonly sold in the United States are of Japanese origin — the Fuyu and the Hachiya. Persimmons enjoy so much popularity in Japan that they have been called the country's national fruit. One of Japan's greatest poets, Masaoka Shiki (1867–1902), wrote:

> *Remember me*
> *as a persimmon eater*
> *who loved haiku.*

Fuyu is nonastringent. "When really well-ripened on the tree, it's sweet; you can eat it like an apple, but it's smoother than that, it's almost buttery," says Kay Ryugu, professor of pomology retired from the University of California, Davis. Still, he feels that the astringent Hachiya has more persimmon flavor if allowed to ripen.[3] In fact, Hachiya persimmons are the most common in American supermarkets.

Sokolov passionately argues that the North American persimmon of the Indians is "clearly superior" to those of Japanese origin. The native persimmon "remains misundertood and neglected," he laments.[4]

OTHER TREES

We found shole water, wher we smelt so sweet, and so strong a smel, as if we had bene in the midst of some delicate garden abounding with all kinde of odoriferous flowers, by which we were assured, that the land could not be farre distant.

So Arthur Barlowe reported after reaching the North Carolina coast in 1584. As Richard Ketchum observes in *The Secret Life of the Forest,* the fragrance of a wilderness informed Barlowe and other European voyagers that they had neared the North American coast. Those who ventured inland discovered vast forests as far as they could travel — all the way to the Mississippi River.[1]

Native Americans made the most of the more than 680 species of trees on the continent. The main limit on their use of wood was the amount of effort that cutting with stone tools entailed. Wood was their typical fuel. They hollowed out logs into dugout canoes, bent saplings into frameworks for dwellings such as wigwams and longhouses, raised plank houses in the Pacific Northwest, and fashioned handles of wood for tomahawks and other tools or weapons. Native carvers made wooden bowls, paddles, masks, religious images, and totem poles.

Nor did bark go to waste. Wigwams were often covered with slabs of bark, such as that of elm. Indians of the Northeast made canoes out of paper-bark birch. Those of the Yukon subarctic region and elsewhere shaped boxes from bark (called *mococks* by Algonquian speakers) to hold food or small items. Those of the Northwest coast, the Southeast, and elsewhere wove bast (inner bark) into material they then used to make clothing.

The trees examined in this section illustrate a variety of uses Native Americans and settlers found for this abundant resource.

Tamarack-root thread held birch-bark canoes together, while the tree's wood went into native and Euroamerican dwellings. The *giant sequoia, catalpa,* and *tupelo* also all find a valued place in modern American society as they have in its native past.

SEQUOIA
God's first temples

What Niagara Falls is to flowing waters, the giant sequoia is to the world's forests. The *big tree,* as it is commonly called, has produced the largest tree anywhere in volume of wood, with an age of about 3500 years. Christopher Isherwood described the impact of a sequoia on one of the twentieth century's great composers:

> We drove up once to the sequoia forest, and I remember Stravinsky, so tiny, looking up at this enormous giant sequoia and standing there for a long time in meditation and then turning to me and saying: "That's serious."[1]

The giant sequoias had been known and venerated by Indians in the Sierra Nevada mountains countless centuries before a hunter named A. T. Dowd followed a wounded grizzly into the wilderness in 1852. At last he came up short before the largest tree he had ever seen. He tricked his incredulous companions back at camp into viewing the tree themselves and sharing his wonder.

Before long, loggers were felling trees so huge that it took five men working twenty-two days to bore through one. Sometimes a severed tree would refuse to fall for several days, poised as if contemplating its fate until a mighty gust finally toppled it. Loggers sometimes just dynamited a tree, splintering much of its wood in the process. Thirty-two people danced a cotillion on the stump of one harvested tree. The bark was shaved off a tree and reassembled as a gargantuan curiosity in New York and London. A road was tunneled through one standing giant, and a home carved out of another that had fallen.

Local Indians — the Mono, a Paiute people — stood aghast at the devastation. They knew the sequoia as *woh-woh´-nau,* a name imitating the hooting of the owl held to be the guardian spirit and deity of the tree. Indians believed it was bad luck to cut down a sequoia, to mock or kill a tutelary owl, or even to shoot a weapon in such an owl's presence. Whenever the Mono saw a teamster hauling a wagonload of sequoia lumber away, they called out a warning that the owl would bring him bad luck.

It is curious that the big tree now bears the name of an Indian from the East who never saw one. The decision came from Europe. Stephan L. Endlicher (1804–49) was one of the nineteenth century's leading botanists and a curator of the Vienna Museum of Natural History. A man of wide-ranging interests, he named the coast redwood in honor of the Cherokee leader and language pioneer Sequoya. (Endlicher would come to a tragic end after spending all his money on his museum and the scientific publications of himself and his friends: facing starvation, he committed suicide.)

Discovery of the big tree in the Sierra Nevada complicated matters. A leading English botanist proposed that the new find be called *Wellingtonia gigantea* after the Duke of Wellington, who defeated Napoleon at Waterloo. American botanists patriotically countered with *Washingtonia gigantea.* The French botanist Joseph Decaisne broke the deadlock with *Sequoia gigantea* (modified by modern botanists to *Sequoiadendron giganteum*). Yet the coast redwood and the giant sequoia have often been confused, as will be discussed. Frequently both are called "sequoia."

Despite the controversy, Sequoya's name seemed especially fitting. Sequoya (1760–1843) was the son of Nathaniel Gist, a Revolutionary War veteran, and Wurteh, a sister of the head chief of the Cherokee Nation. He was brought up by his mother as a Cherokee and, together with her, fled from American militia attacks during the turmoil following the Revolution. Sequoya distrusted whites but admired aspects of Euroamerican culture, including one the Indians called "talking leaves" — written and printed materials. For twelve years, he labored to create a written language for the Cherokee. He at last formulated a syllabary, or set of eighty-six characters standing for syllables, that enabled the Cherokee language to be transcribed. It was an extraordinary feat.

Within months, the Cherokee had become literate in their own language, producing a newspaper, a constitution, and subsequently books. But the persecution of the Cherokee forced many of them to move westward from the southern Appalachian Mountains, and Sequoya lived as a tribal leader in Arkansas and then Oklahoma. He disappeared into Mexico in 1843 while searching for a Cherokee band living there. Sequoya's achievement placed him among the cultural giants not only of the United States, but of the world — surely the reason Endlicher chose his name for a monumental tree.

Yet botanists long debated the exact designation of California's giant trees and a Chinese relative. These trees today are held to fall into three classifications:

➤ Giant sequoia, or big tree — *Sequoiadendron giganteum*. Growing only on the western slopes of the Sierra Nevada when discovered, it flourished millions of years ago throughout the earth's northern hemisphere. Today it is confined to about seventy groves, nearly all on state or federal land. It belongs to the pine family and has narrow pointed leaves. Though not the tallest, it is the biggest tree: The General Sherman giant sequoia could furnish enough wood for 40 five-room houses. But the tree's wood is so brittle that it has little commercial use.

➤ Redwood, or coast redwood — *Sequoia sempervirens*. This is now native only to the Pacific coast of northern California and Oregon. Like the giant sequoia, it grew far more widely in ancient times. Also a member of the pine family, it displays leaves like the hemlock's. The redwood is the world's tallest tree, growing to twice the height of the Statue of Liberty. The Yurok and other Indians near the coast made finely crafted seagoing dugouts forty-two feet or more in length from redwoods that had fallen naturally and floated down on rivers. Loggers have cut down ninety-seven percent of the ancient coast redwood forest. National parks preserve many of the remaining ancient redwoods, and conservationists are working to save others from being used in construction or for furniture, shingles, or fence posts.

➤ Dawn redwood — *Metasequoia glyptostroboides*. Once thought to have been extinct for 20 million years, the dawn redwood was discovered alive in China during the 1940s. It resembles the coast redwood but sheds its leaves.

Statistics on the giant sequoia and coast redwood can be stupefying, and the trees' greatness has inspired the people associated with them. None was closer to the trees than John Muir (1838–1914). A native of Scotland, he grew up mostly in Wisconsin and attended the University of Wisconsin. He devoted himself wholeheartedly to nature and eventually hiked thousands of miles on five continents, experiencing many extremes of weather and terrain. He deliberately strode through gale-ravaged woods, beard streaming, as branches flew past his head; he survived a nighttime blizzard on a mountaintop; he risked his life on trackless glaciers and sheer cliff sides.

At the insistence of friends, the thirtyish Muir began writing about his adventures and observations. His rhapsodic essays struck a chord among Americans beginning to recognize the priceless value of their natural environment. The giant sequoias were a favorite of Muir's, and he called their groves "God's First Temples." In an influential essay, he described the tree:

> The immensely strong, stately shafts, with rich purplish-brown bark, are free of limbs for a hundred fifty feet or so, though dense tufts of sprays occur here and there, producing an

ornamental effect, while long parallel furrows give a fluted, columnar appearance. The limbs shoot forth with equal boldness in every direction, showing no weather side.[2]

Ralph Waldo Emerson met Muir at Yosemite in 1871. "You are yourself a sequoia," Muir assured him in Mariposa Grove. "Stop and get acquainted with your big brethren." Asked to name a giant sequoia, Emerson recommended "Samoset," in memory of the Indian who first greeted the Pilgrims. Later, other dignitaries, including President Theodore Roosevelt, visited Muir to see for themselves the wonders he celebrated. Through his writings and personal advocacy, Muir played a major role in the defense of the giant sequoias and in the establishment of national parks such as Yosemite, Rainier, Grand Canyon, and Petrified Forest. In 1892, he helped found the Sierra Club, and he served as its president until his death. More places in California carry his name than that of any other person.[3]

Today the giant sequoia has spread as an ornamental tree far from its home. Found throughout Europe and as far away as New Zealand, it embodies a U.S. national treasure and commemorates the Indian genius who gave his language a written form.

CATALPA
Indian bean tree

Scraggly and messy according to some but beautiful to others, the catalpa thrives in diverse environments from grimy cities to royal estates. Its snowy white flowers tinged with yellow and purple markings in late spring "rival the finest orchid," says a naturalist. But slender, foot-long seed capsules hanging down afterward lend the tree a weirdness that turns many people off. Its resulting odd appearance has helped win it nicknames such as "Indian bean tree" and "Indian cigar tree."[1]

The catalpa is an American native with a northern (or hardy) species originating in the central Mississippi valley and a southern species from the Southeast. It displays a rounded crown, spreading branches, and large, heart-shaped leaves. For nearly three centuries, it has been planted across the United States as a fast-growing shade tree that offers protection from both sun and wind.

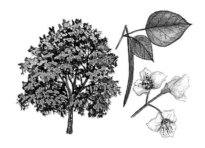

catalpa
a Southern catalpa with details of its leaves, a fruit pod, and flowers

In the 1720s, the English naturalist and traveler Mark Catesby discovered the catalpa among the Creek Indians (Muskogee) inhabiting prosperous villages deep in Georgia and Alabama. Catesby came upon the tree while on an expedition to study the plants and wildlife of southern America. He appears to have been a largely self-taught naturalist who became eminent in his field through hard work and doggedness. A friend called him "tall, meagre, hard favoured, and [with] a sullen look," and "extremely grave or sedate, and of a silent disposition." Yet "when he contracted a friendship [he] was communicative and affable" — evidently enough at least to receive backing for his second visit to America in 1722 to 1726, during which he collected the catalpa, among other specimens, and painted illustrations for his classic *The Natural History of Carolina, Florida, and the Bahama Islands.*[2]

Catesby took special pride in the catalpa. "The Catalpa Tree . . . was unknown to the inhabited parts of Carolina, till I brought the seeds from the remoter parts of the country . . . ," he wrote. "It is become an ornament to many . . . gardens."[3] He also borrowed its Creek name *katalpa* meaning "head with wings," from the shape of its flowers.

The catalpa rapidly became widespread in America and popular in Europe. George Washington wrote in his diary for 1785 that he had planted two large catalpas "West of the Garden House." Frederick the Great planted hundreds on his Potsdam estate, and more than two centuries later, they or their descendants still adorned the grounds with showy flowers and pendulous pods.[4]

The toughness and low cost of the catalpa led to its establishment in countless American neighborhoods of all kinds. "The first tree that many an inner-city child climbed was a catalpa," observes a naturalist. Its usefulness as a shade tree and windbreak made it popular on the prairie, where large stands defy both blizzards and harsh summer weather. The catalpa's wood also makes long-lasting fence posts and can be used to build a crackling fire. Carvers prize the wood for its grain pattern and sheen.[5]

Many Americans admire the catalpa, yet there seems to be little recognition that the tree's name and its curious presence are a heritage from the Creek.

TUPELO

Tree of the swamps

Cupola Pond in Missouri's Mark Twain National Forest features a remarkable stand of water tupelos. The pond is a five-acre limestone sinkhole 23,000 years old lying in the uplands of the state. The nearly five hundred tupelos crowding the ancient pond with their leaves are believed to be descended from ancestors that have grown there for a good part of the sinkhole's existence, probably well before the arrival of Indians. The stand is prized not only for its great age and its associated mosses and flowering plants, but also for its unusual occurrence at a high elevation. One typically finds the trees in low-lying swampland.

The English naturalist and traveler Mark Catesby reported the tupelo family of trees in the 1730s. (See **Catalpa**.) "The Tupelo Tree . . . the Grain of the Wood is curled and very tough, and therefore very proper for Naves of Cart-Wheels, and other Country-

Uses," he wrote. Catesby borrowed the name from the Creek Indian *'topilwa*, literally "swamp tree."[1]

It is hardly surprising that Catesby observed the tupelo among
the Creek. This people established villages along tupelo-haunted
rivers and streams. Settlers nicknamed them Creek probably because of their association with flowing water.

One can find tupelos across most of the eastern half of the
United States. They come in three main varieties:

➤ The *water tupelo* follows wetlands along the Atlantic coast from
  northern Florida to Virginia and along the Gulf coast; and it
  extends up the lower Mississippi Valley.

➤ The *black tupelo* is the commonest — a medium-size tree with
  a rounded crown, dense branches, and glossy, pointed leaves.
  It comes into its glory each fall when its leaves turn scarlet over
  the moist or swampy sites it loves. Many people know it by
  names such as "sour gum," "black gum," or "pepperidge."
  The latter name was borrowed for the Pepperidge Farm bread
  company from a stand of trees on a Connecticut farm the
  founders owned.

➤ The *Ogeechee tupelo*, named after Georgia's Ogeechee River, is
  the least common of the three, growing in extreme southern
  South Carolina and Georgia and in northern Florida. "There is
  no tree that exhibits a more desirable appearance than this, in
  the autumn, when the fruit is ripe, and the tree is divested of
  its leaves; for then they look as red as scarlet, with their fruit,
  which is of that colour also," wrote the eighteenth-century naturalist William Bartram.[2]

➤ This fruit yields a limelike juice used to make Ogeechee-lime
  preserves.

Tupelo timber has found widespread use for flooring, gun-
stocks, scaffolding, and chopping bowls. The hollow trunks of tupelos make excellent beehives. Bearing a Creek name, tupelos are

enjoyed as a shade tree and an ornamental far beyond the homeland of those Indians.

TAMARACK, HACKMATACK
Golden tree of the north

Northernmost of North American trees, the tamarack is
among the loveliest and the most desolate, depending on the season. Its light blue-green needles turn gold in October before they
fall off. Leaf watchers drive hundreds of miles to view what one
writer calls its "golden spires" at this magic time of year. But during winter, a stand of the swamp-haunting trees can shock a hiker
with its stark, leafless appearance.[1]

The tamarack is also known as the American larch. Its range
runs from the Midwest and Mid-Atlantic states up to the northern
limit of trees in Canada, where it grows in muskeg (which see)
and on storm-blasted slopes. It has a cone-shaped crown sometimes reaching eighty feet in height, though with a scraggly look
compared with trees such as maples. The shedding of needles in
the fall and their renewal in the spring is a peculiarity the tamarack shares with only one other cone-bearing tree, the bald
cypress.

The ruggedness of the tamarack and its preferred habitat are
described in a note by William Clark of the Lewis and Clark Expedition (1804–06):

> The Mountains which we passed to day much worst than yes-
> terday the last excessively bad & thickly Strowed with falling tim-
> ber & Pine Spruce fur Hackmatak & Tamerack.[2]

Indians found the tamarack valuable, and its name probably
comes from an Algonquian language. An alternative name, ap-
pearing in the quote above, is *hackmatack,* perhaps from Western
Abenaki. Indians, and colonists after them, applied the sticky
tamarack sap to cuts and bruises. Both used the tree's crooked
roots in constructing the frames of canoes and boats. But Indians

found tamarack roots especially helpful in sewing together birch-bark canoes, with a seam that held tight even after constant soaking in water. Longfellow's Hiawatha addresses the tree:

> *Give me of your roots, O Tamarack!*
> *Of your fibrous roots, O Larch-Tree!*
> *My canoe to bind together,*
> *So to bind the ends together*
> *That the water may not enter,*
> *That the river may not wet me!*[3]

Tamarack lumber today finds use in home construction, railroad ties, telephone poles, and pulpwood. But the tamarack's staunchest admirers laud its beauty, and many — willing to overlook its winter bleakness — cultivate the tree. They celebrate the tamarack's green needles in spring and summer and its "glorious golden splash of color" in the fall.

FISH AND SEAFOOD

Lobsters five or six feet long, foot-long crabs, and oysters of over a foot reportedly amazed the first colonists on the Atlantic coast. Gigantic shell heaps along the continent's two main coasts — one covering twenty-four acres on the Connecticut shore — testify to the abundance of shellfish that Indians enjoyed. Seafood including great shoals of fish, notably cod, supplied a major European industry and afforded colonists a food so common they often despised it. Pilgrims ate lobster only as a last resort.

Indian familiarity with marine fish can be seen from the Narragansett-named *menhaden, mummichog, scup,* and *tautog.* The *quahog,* with a name of the same origin, provided both tasty food and shells, used to make wampum and hoe blades.

In the Pacific Northwest, vast salmon runs provided Indians and then Europeans with not only a food staple but also an article of trade that brought wealth to the region. Major salmon species — *chinook, chum, coho,* and *sockeye* — keep Indian names while retaining their significance in native diet and culture. The Indian-named *abalone* has been harvested as a delicacy for millennia, with the also Indian-named giant *geoduck* and *Yaquina* shellfish providing additional food sources.

Fish played a smaller role in the diet of most inland native peoples. But the *muskellunge,* so named by the Ojibwa and discussed here, remains a food-and-game fish still eagerly sought by fishers of all backgrounds. Among other freshwater fish with native names are the *chivey, cisco, cui-ui, kokanee, namaycush, oquassa, sacalait, siscowet,* and *tullibee.* The Algonquian-named *terrapin* and other turtles further supplemented the food supplies of many Indian peoples.

Significantly, most of the fish and shellfish examined in this section have been threatened with depletion. In 1999, the federal government announced the listing of nine types of salmon under the Endangered Species Act. Vice President Al Gore pledged $100 million in government aid to carry out this most sweeping application of the law in area and in economic impact. An agreement the same year between Canada and the United States committed the two countries to regulate salmon catches each year by the abundance of runs. These steps offered new hope for a fish that the *New York Times* has called "virtually a cultural icon" for the Pacific Northwest.[1]

ABALONE

The 'magic, romantic animal'

For ten thousand years, divers have plunged into California coastal waters for the *abalone*. Ancient and modern gourmets have esteemed it as a food. Craftsmen continue the Indian tradition of fashioning its iridescent shell into jewelry and other decorative objects. "Abalone is one of the few animals out here with a significant place in California culture," says Armand Kuris, a zoology professor at the University of California at Santa Barbara. "It's one of those magic, romantic animals in California history."[1]

The abalone is a large sea snail that feeds on kelp and other seaweeds. Zoologists call it *Haliotis* ("sea ear"), but its more popular name, *abalone,* comes from Rumsen, an Indian language of Monterey Bay, California. The abalone's foot, growing up to twelve inches long, clings so tenaciously to rocks that crowbars are sometimes required to pry it loose. Tenderized, this foot provides the gourmet's delight. Abalone shell shimmers with every color of the rainbow — an effect produced by light reflected through many layers of lime and horny material.

Great shell heaps along the Channel Islands off the coast of southern California prove that early Indians relished the abalone. On San Clemente Island, these heaps date back as far as ten thousand years. Abalone shells outnumber shells of the next most common shellfish four to one in the lower layers of ancient heaps on Catalina Island. Upper layers reveal that Indians ate a progressively higher percentage of other shellfish as they thinned out the abalone population. At last, Indian fanciers of abalone would move to unspoiled parts of the coast.

The Indians used abalone shell to make or decorate "ear plugs, bracelets, rings, lip ornaments, necklaces, belts, and other articles of personal adornment."[2] An exquisite necklace acquired by a Russian traveler in the early 1800s features abalone pendants gleaming from a band of clamshell beads. A portrait of the explorer Meriwether Lewis shows him wearing a cape of otter skin embellished with ermine fur and abalone shell, "the most elegant piece of Indian dress I ever saw," he commented.[3]

Indians put abalone shell to practical uses as well. They made bowls, fishhooks, knives, and scrapers out of it. Abalone provided material for the more valuable kind of shell money circulated in California and Oregon before 1850. Abalone shell was traded as far away as Colorado and Arizona. The Tewa of northern New Mexico initiate children into a tribal division by holding an abalone shell filled with sacred water to their lips and having them drink while they are given new names.

Despite the popularity of abalone among Indians, their consumption of the shellfish did not threaten its survival. Newcomers moving into California in the 1850s, however, took a heavier toll on the abalone. Abalone-loving Chinese laborers opened new markets for the shellfish. Within a few years of their arrival, they were harvesting quantities of abalone — most of it for export to China. Japanese immigrants joined the industry subsequently, bringing with them skills they had developed diving for abalone in the waters of their homeland.

Other California settlers also found abalone cheap and tasty.

Its inexpensiveness in the early twentieth century can be gauged by these lines from the "Abalone Song" by George Sterling, friend of Jack London and other California writers of the period:

> Oh! some folks boast of quail on toast,
> Because they think it's tony;
> But I'm content to owe my rent,
> And live on abalone.[4]

Meanwhile, the popularity — and cost — of abalone was starting to grow worldwide.

The career of master chef Yeung Koon Yat illustrates the lofty position of abalone in world cuisine now. Yeung enjoys international fame as the "Abalone King of Hong Kong" and belongs to the elite Le Club des Chefs des Chefs. He spends more than a day and a half soaking, boiling, and braising whole dried abalone to prepare it for the table. Connoisseurs of his abalone have included former French president Jacques Chirac and the Chinese leader Deng Xiaoping (the latter is reported to have deemed abalone to be "a precious item"). Unfortunately, the increasing cost of abalone tends to restrict the enjoyment of Yeung's cooking to the rich and the famous. At a 1995 banquet that he prepared for Harbor Village Restaurant of Monterey Park, California, the cost of the abalone in his superb meal ran to about $140 per person, and higher grades of the shellfish would have cost more.

For various reasons, abalone numbers have been declining. Sea otters crack abalone shells to get at the meat; oil spills and other forms of pollution have harmed abalone stocks; a disease has devastated the black abalone. But overfishing is largely responsible for the decline, which has driven up prices sharply. In 1994, commercial fishers in California harvested only about 750,000 pounds of abalone, less than fifteen percent of the yearly amount taken in the 1950s and 1960s.

Seekers of abalone can no longer move from a depleted area to another part of the coast. So Californians are witnessing steps to bring the shellfish back. In 1995, about fifteen commercial fisheries in California were engaged in abalone farming. This is a demanding occupation in which abalone must be constantly swirled in seawater and fed fresh giant kelp. The government and private diving clubs have also worked at restocking abalone beds to restore the population. Abalone lovers have applauded these efforts, hoping for a larger supply of the delicacy enjoyed by countless generations of Californians.

QUAHOG
The clam with its own festival

"Little has changed in the [clamming] industry since the Narragansett Indians scratched the fertile bottom of Narragansett Bay for the clams . . . that lie in its rich silt," wrote a United Press International reporter in 1983. "The name the Indians gave their succulent catch, *quahog,* is still preferred in Rhode Island over *littlenecks* and *cherrystones.*" *Quahog,* the general name for the clam, comes from Narragansett *poquaûhock.* It is pronounced *KOH-hog* (especially if you are a Rhode Islander) or *KWOH-hog* or *KWAH-hog. Littleneck* (from Littleneck Bay, Long Island) and *cherrystone* refer to tender young quahogs, considered the best eating. Large quahogs, which can grow to six inches long, may be called *hens* and are chopped or ground for chowder and the like.[1]

In 1983, about three thousand people were licensed to harvest quahogs from Rhode Island waters. Shell heaps along the Atlantic coast from Florida to Maine testify that Indians had been doing the same thing for thousands of years. Roger Williams, first recorder of the name *quahog,* identified the clam in 1643 as "a little thick shel fish which the Indians wade deepe and dive for."[2] After eating the meat of the clams, the Indians used the small purple part of the shells to make *wampum* (which see). They turned large shells into blades for their hoes.

Curiously, the Pilgrims did not esteem quahogs. They ate the clams reluctantly and regarded them as "poverty fare." Possibly the commonness of quahogs caused them to be taken for granted, as with the lobsters fed to hogs. The lack of condiments among the Pilgrims, further, may have made quahogs a monotonous food.

Times have changed. So popular is the quahog in modern Rhode Island that the town of Wickford declared the First International Quahog Festival in 1983. The rollicking success of this celebration led to more such festivals. Thousands of visitors have flocked to the town for events that grew to include boat tours of clam beds, demonstrations of clam digging, shucking contests, quahog cook-offs, and a competition for the "most useless quahog object." By the time of the twelfth annual festival in 1995 (one year was skipped), sponsors expected an attendance of up to thirty thousand people.

Most often, small quahogs (littlenecks and cherrystones) are eaten raw. But the quahog lends itself to a variety of tasty dishes. A favorite at the quahog festivals is the "stuffie" — a concoction of quahogs, bread crumbs, and onions, with Tabasco sauce and a wedge of lemon. The quahog often appears in New England clam chowder and, with tomato, in Manhattan clam chowder. Quahog pie, consisting of chopped and seasoned clams between pastry crusts, has long been a New England favorite. The American public more commonly enjoys quahogs as fried clams. Beyond their distinctive sea-scented flavor, quahogs provide diners with generous amounts of low-fat protein and dietary iron.

In recent years, pollution and overfishing have threatened the quahog harvest. The clams used to be so plentiful along Florida shores that clammers harvested tons a day. Finally, though, the number of quahogs dwindled, leading some seafood companies to go into aquaculture, raising quahogs in carefully controlled hatcheries. "The clam boom led to the aquaculture market because we overfished the water at the same time we built up a demand," said a partner in one such enterprise. By 1990, about sixty aquaculture quahog businesses were operating in Florida alone. These farms, though modern and scientific in their methods, were continuing one of the most ancient occupations on the nation's Atlantic coast — harvesting the versatile quahog.[3]

GEODUCK, YAQUINA, UMPQUA
Stalking the giant clam

Toward the end of the twentieth century, one of the world's strangest black markets challenged police in the Pacific Northwest. Planes were illicitly flying thousands of pounds of clams a night to Japan and other far-flung parts of the world. But the planes carried no ordinary clams. Their cargo was the *geoduck* (pronounced *GOO-ee-duck*), the largest burrowing clam in the United States and perhaps in the world. A geoduck commonly weighs two and a half to three pounds but can grow to sixteen pounds. Although it is tasty cooked or as sushi, Asian men prize it chiefly as an alleged aphrodisiac — a notion based on its long, phallic-shaped siphon.

The geoduck lives only on the upper West Coast, from California to Alaska. There is no mistaking the bizarre-looking clam once it has been harvested. Its siphon is attached to a plump body bulging between shells the size of soup bowls. The name comes

from the Puget Salish word meaning "dig deep." Indians of the Northwest ate it fresh, or they smoke-dried it for winter eating or as a trade item. So important was the clam to the Indians that they called the lowest tides of the year — the best for harvesting the clams — "geoduck tides."

Euroamericans took up geoduck hunting for food and for sport. In *Stalking the Blue-Eyed Scallop*, Euell Gibbons de-

geoduck

scribes the strategy for gathering geoducks. The clams lie two and a half to three feet below the surface of sand flats exposed by low tides, but they display a siphon that reaches to the surface. Two people working together watch for water squirting out of the siphon's end. One person grabs the siphon and slides his hand downward so as not to snap it off. The other digs away the sand to expose the clam, sometimes surrounding it with a bottomless barrel to keep sand from crumbling back.[1]

Companies have mechanized the process. They send divers with vacuumlike machines to suck the clams right out of their beds. In 1997, black marketers defying state restrictions were harvesting more than 2000 pounds of geoducks daily just from southern Puget Sound.

"It's close to being out of control," said Ed Volz, a detective with the Washington State Department of Fish and Wildlife. "They take the clams at night, put them on a plane, and the next day they appear in a fresh fish market someplace from New York to Singapore." In Asia, the geoducks fetch more than $10 per pound wholesale. Rivalry among the "clam runners" has led to death threats, violence, and convictions for such crimes as extortion and conspiracy.[2]

To those who legitimately dig the clams or buy them at the market, Gibbons offers recipes for geoduck cutlets and chowder. Restaurant goers, especially in the Pacific Northwest, find that the giant clam seems to inspire chefs. Diners enjoy it as sushi or sashimi (raw, served with a sauce for dipping), poached or grilled. At a Japanese restaurant in Seattle, the food writer Melissa A. Trainer called geoduck sautéed with quartered mushrooms "tender, buttery, and sweet." It was a sentiment that could be echoed in many parts of the world. The clam that was once mainly an Indian staple has become an international delicacy.[3]

Nevertheless, a 1994 court ruling reserved half of Washington's shellfish, including geoducks, to local Indians. Toward the end of the century, they were harvesting more than two million pounds of the giant clams each year.

Still another prized shellfish of the West Coast is the *Yaquina oyster* (*Ostrea lurida*), which carries the same name as Yaquina Bay on Oregon's coast and the Indian people who lived around it. The small, tasty oysters were a principal food of the Indians, who harvested them at low tide as they did the geoducks. Overharvesting by Euroamericans (200,000 pounds in 1895) and pollution had nearly wiped them out by 1900. Recently biologists discovered that Yaquina oysters prefer to anchor themselves on the shelves of their ancestors; but commercial harvesters and their customers had been discarding the shells elsewhere. So the biologists have bred millions of the oysters and deposited them on shell heaps in local bays, a move they hope will lead to a population spurt among the mollusks.

Oyster farms in the region cultivate the *Umpqua oyster,* which has the same name as a local river and the Indian tribe. "The younger Umpqua oysters have a nutty richness and a dash of salt, while the two-year-olds seem more intense, sweeter," says a writer in a travel magazine.[4]

CHINOOK SALMON
The king

"I have lived!" Rudyard Kipling exulted after a day spent catching chinook salmon in the Columbia River. "The American Continent may now sink under the sea, for I have taken the best that it yields, and the best was neither dollars, love, nor real estate."[1] The *chinook* (or *king* or *quinnat* or *tyee*) *salmon* has been called the soul of the Pacific Northwest. Its silvery grace makes it one of the most beautiful creatures in a region still filled with wild beauty.

The chinook is the largest of the salmon — about three feet long and weighing an average of twenty-two pounds in the Columbia River. (For the Indian background of the name, see **Chinook**.) It has shimmering silver sides and belly, with a dusky back. The rich red flesh of the chinook makes it one of the most delectable salmon, whether fresh, smoked, pickled, or canned. It is a traditional staple of Indians in the Northwest. Few people of any background can resist a baked chinook or one poached and served with egg sauce.

Over thousands of years, the chinook arrived in seemingly inexhaustible numbers. As members of the Lewis and Clark Expedition canoed down the Columbia in October 1805, they were amazed at the multitude of salmon in the water. "The number of dead Salmon on the Shores & floating in the river is incredible to say," wrote William Clark.[2] Most of the fish (which had died after spawning) were chinook salmon, one of the most abundant fish in the Northwest.

During a six-month period, the chinook makes two major spawning runs up rivers along the Pacific coast. It heads for countless familiar streams and nooks, sometimes far inland. The female lays eggs that the male fertilizes before both parents die, leaving the young to travel a cycle that swings far out into the Pacific and ultimately back.

In the mid-1800s, up to 16 million salmon and other food fish were swimming up the Columbia each year. These enormous runs had begun declining seriously during the 1920s. Gone were the old Indian customs of releasing the trapped salmon a village did not need and, at least in some cases, sparing salmon that had not spawned. Heavy fishing to supply canneries along the coast took a toll. Logging operations fouled some of the key spawning rivers and admitted glaring sunlight into shadowy spawning grounds.

The most devastating blows, however, began to fall in the 1930s with the building of huge hydroelectric dams across rivers that the salmon had been climbing for so long. Grand Coulee Dam, on the Columbia River northwest of Spokane, was begun in 1933. It has a crest almost twice as high as Niagara Falls and a width equal to fourteen city blocks. Along with thirteen other large dams on the Columbia, it supplies electricity to much of the Northwest, as well as irrigation for millions of acres of land. Its price has been the loss of countless salmon spawning grounds. Fish ladders at several of the dams only partially help, by enabling some salmon to return to the places of their birth.

By the mid-1990s, wild chinook (as opposed to hatchery fish) that run in the spring and summer had become extinct in almost two-thirds of their range and were threatened in much of the rest. Fall-run chinook were a little better off, extinct in almost a fifth of their range and threatened in most of the rest.

The attempt to offset the decline of Northwest chinook salmon by breeding them in hatcheries has enjoyed only qualified success. Hatchery chinook lack the smarts of their wild kin when it comes to navigating river currents and evading predators. Biologists say that the hatchery fish are unlikely to make up for the massive loss of chinook born and bred in the wild.

The Canadian and U.S. governments have established restrictions on the taking of chinook and other salmon in areas where the fish are most seriously endangered. Canada fisheries minister Brian Tobin cut his country's 1995 chinook harvest quota in half and invited Alaska (where the chinook is still plentiful) to take a similar step. At the same time, the Columbia River Intertribal Fish Commission proposed that the U.S. federal government turn over control of the salmon and their habitat to the Indians, who regard the fish as a spiritual resource — a suggestion not likely to be followed. Yet the Indian practice of restrained harvesting, enforced by the government in recent years, is helping to preserve what is left of one of the Northwest's greatest treasures.

SOCKEYE
'Lonesome Larry'

In 1994, Idaho governor Cecil Andrus displayed in his office a mounted sockeye salmon nicknamed Lonesome Larry. It was the last sockeye to have returned to the Snake River, two years before, to spawn. The forlorn fish was both a sign of despair and an emblem of hope. Sockeye salmon, along with the four other salmon species of the Pacific Northwest, have declined in numbers alarmingly during the twentieth century. But area Indians, whose culture is traditionally based on salmon fishing, and white neighbors, who derive much of their prosperity from the fish, have joined in an effort to restore and preserve the historically enormous salmon runs.

The *sockeye* (also known as the *blueback* or the *red salmon*) gets its name from the Salish (dialectal) *suk-kegh*. As with so many other Indian names, English speakers adapted it to fit their tongues. The kokanee is a small landlocked version of the sockeye, also with an originally Salishan (Shuswap) name.

The sockeye is one of the smallest salmons at an average of about six pounds in weight and two feet in length. It has a slender body, blue along the top and glittering silver on the sides, but it turns red at spawning. Born in freshwater, the sockeye migrates to the far North Pacific before returning to its birthplaces to spawn and die.

Gourmets prize the sockeye. Even after canning, it retains a fine flavor and oily richness. About half of canned Alaska salmon belongs to this species.

No people have been closer to the sockeye than the Lummi Indians of northwestern Washington. For uncounted centuries, they have greeted the sockeye's first spawning run of the season with an elaborate ceremony. When the men bring in the fish, each child carries one to a bed of winter fern. The women place spice plant, duck down, and red paint in front of the fish to welcome them. Meanwhile an elderly member of the tribe sings a spirit song. The fish are baked, and each person partakes of them. After this feast, the bones are returned to the river so that the sockeye, having been honored, will return another season.

Millions of salmon did arrive year after year. With European settlement of the region in the nineteenth century, whites started to join in harvesting the teeming runs. The first commercial salmon cannery in Washington began operation in 1866, and others soon followed. Sockeye was a favorite with the entrepreneurs. Improved nets and traps boosted the efficiency of catching salmon. Factories processed vast amounts of the fish. In 1901 alone, more than 25 million sockeye were caught in and around Puget Sound.

But in 1913, the sockeye migrating through Puget Sound to nearby British Columbia received a devastating blow. A rockslide triggered by blasting for the Canadian Pacific Railway blocked salmon trying to swim up the Fraser River to major spawning grounds. The river was cleared in about a year, but the damage had been done. Far fewer sockeye returned in the following years. Government-built dams near the Pacific coast, as well as logging operations, would spoil numerous other spawning sites.

Meanwhile, many Indians who had depended on the sockeye and other salmon found themselves crowded out of their traditional occupation of fishing. A 1913 government report on one of the tribes in the Puget Sound area explained:

> They have not in the past been accustomed to depending upon Mother Earth for subsistence, for in primitive days the adjacent waters rendered them self-supporting. That condition, however, does not exist to such an extent today having been diminished by the commercial exploitation by the white man's fish traps.[1]

A court ruling in 1974, however, assured Indians of western Washington the right to take half of harvestable salmon and forbade the state to impose regulations on the fishing except to protect fish runs. "The fish resource is on the rebound throughout the Pacific Northwest because the state and tribes have learned to work together and leave behind the confrontation of the past," said Billy Frank, the Nisqually head of the Northwest Indian Fisheries Commission, in an optimistic observation in the late 1980s.[2]

But a century of massive abuse could not all be undone in a few decades. In 1995, the sockeye was still extinct over more than half its historic range in the Pacific Northwest. Then the

Canada–United States fishing agreement of 1999 brightened the prospects for the future of the sockeye and other salmon throughout the region.

MUSKELLUNGE, MUSKIE, MASKINONGE
Great fish

"Muskies don't give a rip for you or your boat," says a Michigan muskellunge guide. "They don't know fear." Muskellunge are, in fact, one of the fiercest freshwater fishes in North America. That's why seasoned anglers spend hours and days of monotonous waiting to tangle with one of them.[1]

The muskellunge is a giant, broad-headed member of the pike family reaching up to about seventy pounds and more than five feet. Its name comes from Ojibwa *maashkinoozhe,* said to mean "large fish." It lurks in the weeds of lakes and slow-moving rivers of the Northeast, feeding on other fish as well as frogs and animals such as small ducks.

Anglers call the muskellunge "the fish of 10,000 casts." It will calmly ignore sometimes garish lures or, allegedly, flick them back at fly-fishers. Once hooked, the muskellunge may fight for three hours or more before succumbing. Many anglers throw them back to ensure the future of the fish's population.

At least some Indian peoples liked sturgeon, walleyed pike, whitefish, or trout better. Longfellow's Hiawatha showed an apparently widespread preference when a muskellunge interfered with his quest for the sturgeon, "King of Fishes":

> Full of scorn was Hiawatha
> When he saw the fish rise upward,
> Saw the pike, the Maskenozha,
> Coming nearer, nearer to him,
> And he shouted through the water,
> "Esa! esa! shame upon you!

You are but the pike Kenozha,
You are not the fish I wanted,
You are not the King of Fishes!"
  Reeling downward to the bottom,
  Sank the pike in great confusion . . .[2]

Yet other Indians actively sought the muskellunge. In 1794, Elizabeth Simcoe, wife of the first governor of Upper Canada, described Indians (perhaps Iroquois) fishing for muskellunge, which she called "a superior kind of pike," in a lake during winter. For shelter, the Indians draped a blanket on posts above holes chopped through ice. Then they dangled wooden fish in the water. When muskellunge and pickerel swam up to investigate, the Indians speared them.[3]

Modern anglers probably work as hard to catch muskellunge, but call their activity sport. One favored kind of muskellunge is the tasty, white-fleshed Chautauqua muskellunge, found in New York State and adjacent areas; the northern pike is a closely related sport and food fish.

The muskellunge's nicknames, besides those given above, include *musky, lunge, longe,* and *great pike.* Canadians call the fish *maskinonge*; and Maskinongé is the name of a town and county in Quebec.

TERRAPIN
Earth upholder

The preparation of terrapin in an exclusive Chesapeake Bay restaurant can require three days' notice to permit its securing, washing, boiling, deboning, chopping, stewing, and seasoning. Eating such a delicacy is typically surrounded by customs that go back to plantation days. At one Baltimore home, the savory stew with hints of cayenne pepper and salt marsh arrives at the table in a silver tureen. Diners munch beaten biscuits (dough lightened by beating and folding) and sip dry sherry with the meal as their ancestors did.

terrapin

The ceremonial eating of terrapin goes back to early colonial and ancient Indian days. *Terrapin* comes from the Algonquian language family. "I have caught with mine angle [fishhook] ... the Torope or little Turtle," an Englishman reported from Virginia in 1613, using the Virginia Algonquian term. *Terrapin* and *turtle* are used interchangeably today, with the first commonly applied to hard-shelled, edible turtles from fresh or brackish waters.[1]

Indians respected the turtle as deliberate, calm, steadfast, and long-lived. Many revered it. A widespread belief among Indians in the Northeast and others as far away as California was that Earth is Turtle Island — an island resting on the back of a giant turtle. Cheyenne legend relates that Earth's creator piled mud on the back of Grandmother Turtle until she was hidden from view. Trees and grass sprang up as her hair, flowers as her ornaments, seeds and fruits as offerings to the creator, and so on. Today Grandmother Turtle and her descendants must move slowly because they carry the weight of Earth and its inhabitants on their backs.

American Indian attitudes toward the turtle bear an extraordinary resemblance to those of the Asian world. The Chinese traditionally honored the turtle on much the same basis as the American Indians, for its perceived steady character and longevity. According to one Chinese legend, a giant turtle's four feet stand as pillars between heaven and earth. Another legend holds that a turtle supported each of the five islands where Immortals lived. The second incarnation of the Hindu god Vishnu is a turtle that bore the earth up out of a great flood. Stone and bronze turtle statues throughout Korea, Mongolia, and other parts of Asia reflect the theme of the animal as sacred or divine. It seems possible that the American Indian regard for turtles arises from a heritage shared with Asian peoples.

But American Indians also sought turtles, with due respect, as relief from a sometimes monotonous diet. The ferocious, though tasty, snapping turtle was a favorite, especially for sacred feasts in the case of the Menominee. Indians ate a number of different kinds of turtles, among them the painted and map turtles, and the esteemed diamondback terrapin. The Huron cooked turtles in apparently typical Indian fashion by burying them in hot ashes or boiling them with legs sticking up.

Aside from food, Indians found other parts of the turtle useful. The Menominee fashioned turtle claws into arrowheads, which were considered especially deadly in battle because of the turtle's magic power. They and other Indians scraped out the inner ribs and sometimes trimmed the edge of the shell to make a handsome bowl. Turtle shells also became rattles when pebbles were sealed inside and handles attached to them. Huron chiefs would shake such rattles and sing all night to heal a sick person. During ceremonial dances among various tribes, turtle-shell rattles were used to accompany the participants.

Because of the turtle's character and sacred associations, Indians portrayed it often. They carved counters for games and maple-sugar molds in turtle shapes. Similar designs appeared on totem emblems among groups such as the Iroquois. One stunning portrayal of the sacred animal is the modern Turtle Museum near Niagara Falls, a building shaped like the animal that houses exhibits of the Iroquois League's history and culture.

Colonists followed the Indians in dining on certain turtles. Snapping turtles, some weighing up to sixty pounds, were a favorite served as steaks or in turtle soup. The diamondback terrapin, however, seems to have been a special treat. It is named for the sharply etched plates of its shell. Found along much of the

East and Gulf coasts, its seven subspecies became a common part of local settlers' diets.

So familiar was the animal in the early Republic that the War of 1812 became known as the "Terrapin War" because opponents claimed that hostilities cut off trade the way a terrapin defensively withdraws into its shell. Plantation slaves sometimes had to eat so much terrapin that they grew sick of it — one of the grievances that led to revolts. Ward McAllister, the nineteenth-century New York society leader, reminisced, on the other hand, that terrapin stew was "a dish for the gods, and a standard party dish when a Charleston and Savannah party was an event to live for."[2]

Terrapin became a national symbol of sumptuous eating. It was an item on the menu of the Silver Palace Hotel cars of the Central Pacific Railroad in 1869, along with antelope and pheasant en casserole. Mark Twain mentioned terrapin as one of the American foods he yearned for while in Europe (he also listed chitterlings). Gourmands such as Diamond Jim Brady included terrapin among the numerous delicacies they gorged themselves on at vast, multicourse meals.

At last the diamondback terrapin started becoming scarce — and expensive. A terrapin sold for as little as twenty-five cents in 1880; the price had gone up to seventy dollars a dozen by 1900, and only the well-to-do could afford terrapin à la Maryland or terrapin Newburg at the four-dollar-a-plate price that fine restaurants were charging.

In 1902, the U.S. Bureau of Fisheries started looking for ways to replenish the disappearing diamondback. Biologists learned that it could be artificially propagated, and "diamondback farms" began producing hundreds of thousands of the animals. Several states further passed laws protecting them, and that protection has been extended. New York, for example, established a code in 1983 that regulated the catching and sale of diamondbacks. In 1998, New Jersey installed 600 feet of snow fencing near the

Meadowlands in its northeast to prevent diamondbacks from wandering onto a highway and getting killed. The diamondback population has rebounded. By 1990, a biologist estimated that at least 10,000 diamondbacks per year were being sold in New York City – mostly to Asian-Americans, whose cuisine features turtle meat. In other places, such as Louisiana, local fishers still catch small numbers of the turtles for family and friends, as Indians have done for millennia.

GAME ANIMALS

When Europeans began arriving, according to the anthropologist Harold E. Driver, native peoples in over half of North America "lived exclusively by hunting, fishing, or gathering wild plants."[1] Meat was basic to the diet of many, and they also found practical uses for animal hide, sinew, brain, bone, antlers, teeth, and other parts.

Native hunting techniques may look cruel to a compassionate modern observer. Eskimos left as bait pieces of meat with bone splinters coiled within them that would spring open in an animal's stomach and puncture it. Elsewhere, deer wounded by arrows sometimes had to be tracked until loss of blood finally slowed them down so a coup de grâce might be administered. Animals trapped, snared, or bashed by a deadfall might linger at length bef re a trapper found and killed them.

Yet paradoxically (at least in the perception of many non-Indians), the hunters regarded their prey as not necessarily inferior to themselves, but, in many respects, as equal. An animal embodied a manitou (which see) or the equivalent and could influence the success or failure of one who slew it. Hunted animals even willingly yielded themselves to hunters who approached them respectfully — and jinxed those who failed to do so. The Cherokee, for example, believed that maltreatment of deer could cause disease among human beings. The Koyukon held that failure to honor a wolverine (carcajou) carcass would lead to other wolverines' avoiding hunters in the future.

This respect for animals helped conserve the animal population. Killing was commonly kept to a minimum and slain animals utilized fully, as among the caribou hunters of northern Alaska.

The coming of settlers sometimes upset a long-standing ecological balance, as when the European demand for beaver skins led to a depletion of that animal's numbers in the Northeast during the eighteenth century. On the other hand, some Plains Indians stampeded buffalo herds off cliffs, killing far more of the animals than they could fully use.

This section offers a sampling of key game animals still hunted — the *moose, caribou,* and *wapiti* (elk) — plus a discussion of *pemmican,* a way of preserving surplus meat that came to be widely used by Euroamerican hunters and trappers. Deer, buffalo, and bear are among the numerous other animals crucially important to the economy of Indians and then settlers. The next section, on furbearers, includes some additional game animals such as the *muskrat, raccoon,* and *opossum.*

MOOSE
North American behemoth

The insult to the nation was too much for Thomas Jefferson. Comte de Buffon, the great French naturalist, had sneered that a "degenerative" tendency in North American people and animals made them smaller and less vigorous than those of Europe. In 1787, Jefferson asked Governor John Sullivan of New Hampshire to obtain the largest moose he could find. Sullivan spared no expense (Jefferson's) to fulfill the request. His troops bagged the moose and then cut a road through twenty miles of forest to convey the animal to the nearest house. Jefferson triumphantly had the moose's antlers, hide, and skeleton shipped to Buffon in Paris.[1]

The moose, largest member of the deer family, is closely related to the European elk. But English explorers borrowed the Eastern Abenaki name *mos* in 1603 perhaps because the animal was central to the existence of many northern Indian peoples. The name apparently refers to the way moose strip bark off trees for food: compare Narragansett *moos,* "he strips off." Despite its huge proportions, the moose lives on a vegetarian diet — up to sixty pounds a day of bark and twigs.

A moose may stand nearly eight feet high at the withers and weigh more than half a ton. Indians hunted it using a birchbark horn to imitate its mating call, but they approached it cautiously. Hunters paddling canoes often killed the water-loving animal in a lake or river, where it was relatively defenseless. Killing the moose during winter, when deep snow slowed its movements, was perhaps easiest — stalkers wearing snowshoes could then run it down. Even then, though, it was dangerous. The antlers of a bull moose may spread six feet, and it can be so aggressive as to attack a locomotive.

Yet Indians found the rewards of a kill well worth the risk. The moose was, and sometimes is today, a massive source of meat, leather, and bone. The Koyukon still hunt the animal and eat it from nose to tail. They use its hide with fur as a mattress, and without fur for clothing and sled lashings. They fashion its antlers into articles such as awls, spoons, platters, and knife handles.

The moose occupies a special niche in American lore. Moose names abound in the United States, including those for the towns of Moose (Wyoming) and Mooseheart (Illinois, founded by the fraternal Loyal Order of Moose), as well as Moosehead Lake in Maine. According to the names-authority George Stewart, Minnesota has about ten Moose Lakes. The moose was a favorite animal of Henry David Thoreau, and he uttered its name in 1862 during his deathbed delirium. Theodore Roosevelt once told a reporter that he felt "strong as a bull moose." This comment led to the animal's becoming the emblem of his third-party movement in 1912 that threw the presidential election to the Democrats and Woodrow Wilson.

Canada, with four-fifths of North America's moose, enjoys an even closer relationship with the animal. Numerous items including a premium Canadian beer and the country's coinage have borne the moose's name or image. No fewer than 662 official moose names dot Canada's atlas. Among them are Moose Island,

Moose Creek, Moose River, and, of course, Moose Lake. Then there are villages and cities such as Moose Factory and Moosonee, as well as Moose Jaw. An authority on Canadian names, Alan Rayburn, calls the latter "the most extraordinarily crazy name for a town in the world."[2] Indeed, Moose Jaw may be on its way to becoming the Podunk of Canada.

One problem with moose is that they can be a nuisance in some places and a sought-after rarity in others. Moose commonly roam the streets of Anchorage, Alaska, during heavy snows, foraging on ornamental shrubs and peering in windows. Such behavior turned out to be no laughing matter in 1995 when a female moose, accompanied by a calf and fleeing from a snowball barrage thrown by students, stomped a professor to death on the University of Alaska's Anchorage campus. Still, the moose were clearly losers in their encounters with people that year, with more than 700 killed on Alaska's roads and another 175 killed in train collisions.

Almost coincidental with these happenings, though, Michigan had initiated a program to restore moose to its forests, where they had been hunted to extermination a century ago. A wave of moose mania swept over Michiganders. Highway signs announced "Moose Country." A dairy offered Moosetracks Ice Cream. People wore "Moose Booster" caps. Bumper stickers boasted, "Michigan, Where the Moose Run Loose."

Elsewhere, too, more moose have been making themselves at home. Today, despite threats such as the brain-worm parasite and the automobile, the million-strong moose population seems to be gaining in numbers and spreading in territory. Second-growth forest (filling in the logged-over areas that had once sheltered earlier generations of moose) provides the animal with the young leaves and twigs it loves to browse upon. Moose are multiplying not only in Alaska, but also in northern New England, especially in Maine.

Yet Canada continues to spend more than a million dollars a year studying moose, and U.S. biologists also continuously monitor the moose in Alaska and south of Canada's border. Both governments are determined to protect an animal that is vital to northern Indian peoples and an enduring presence in North American culture.

CARIBOU
Last frontier

Caribou, with their great arching antlers and big hooves, have been fondly described as "goofy" by one nature writer. The gangly animals, typically weighing three to four hundred pounds, are given to wandering and browsing harmlessly. A further endearing trait is that they are American cousins and look-alikes of Eurasia's reindeer.[1] For thousands of years, caribou roamed the North American wilderness all the way from what is now the northern United States to the Arctic. Their practice of pawing through deep snow to feed on the grass underneath gave rise to their name — from the Micmac *ĝalipu,* scraper or pawer (of snow).

caribou

Native peoples and then sportsmen regarded caribou as among the most desirable big game. In fact, overhunting, together with logging and other adversities, has caused the caribou to become one of the most endangered mammals in the lower forty-eight states. In the late twentieth century, the U.S. Fish and Wildife Service was struggling to maintain a herd of fifty woodland caribou in northern Idaho. Attempts to restore the animal to Maine, where it vanished in 1908, failed because of brain-worm infestation and bear attacks. But a vast herd of the closely related Porcupine caribou still migrates near the northernmost areas of North America, sustaining about seven thousand Gwich'in Indians in seventeen villages there.

Each spring, approximately 180,000 Porcupine caribou start their migration northward from wintering grounds in Canada and Alaska. Their specific name comes from the Porcupine River many swim in this journey. Their destination is the Arctic coastal plain, where the pregnant females give birth just as the nourishing new grass is sprouting. The caribou feed on the lush vegetation in June and July, then they stream back to their wintering grounds.

During this migration, wolves, grizzly bears, and Gwich'in harvest the herd. The animals take mainly the old and weak. The Gwich'in kill (now with rifles rather than spears) only as many caribou as they need, up to about ten thousand a year. With each kill, they perform ceremonies to honor the animal's spirit. They keep their harvest at a minimum by using as much of each caribou as possible.

Sarah James, a Gwich'in, calls those northernmost caribou "the lifeline of our people in the same way the buffalo, before they were wiped out, were the life of the Plains Indians. The Gwich'in are caribou people. For thousands of years we have lived with caribou right where we are today. They don't just determine what we eat; they determine who we are. They're in our stories, dances, songs, and the way we see the world."[2]

The methods of preparing caribou for most of the Gwich'in's

food and clothing have been passed down from generation to generation. Seventy-five percent of their protein comes from caribou: heads — roasted, baked, or boiled — are a special treat. "Some of our Northern Indians eat raw the marrow of the Arctic reindeer, as well as various other parts, including the summits of the antlers, as long as they are soft," wrote Henry David Thoreau. "And herein, perchance, they have stolen a march on the cooks of Paris . . . . This is probably better than stall-fed beef and slaughterhouse pork to make a man of."[3]

Caribou fur, with hollow hairs, is among the warmest in the world and ideal for cold-weather clothing. Gwich'in fashion caribou skins into coats, pants, shirts, boots, and mittens. Sinews in the caribou's back become threadlike babiche (from a Micmac word meaning "thread"). Bones become awls and tool handles.

These traditional ways still suit the Gwich'in. "I'm still a hunter, so I know where my food comes from," says Kias Peter, the chief of Arctic Village in northern Alaska. "I know who is living next door. I like to play the fiddle and dance the jig, and I can do that when it suits me. We have something to teach the world about simpler living."[4]

But the Gwich'in worry about their independence. Arctic Village lies next to Alaska's Arctic National Wildlife Refuge. This 19-million-acre reserve in the northeast corner of the state harbors an immense variety of wildife. Geologists say it is also rich in oil. Throughout the 1980s and into the 1990s, the Gwich'in fought oil exploration on the refuge's coastal plain, where the caribou calve. They fear pollution from oil spills and argue that elsewhere migratory caribou have shown a reluctance to cross pipelines and roads that lie across their routes.

In 1997, Secretary of the Interior Bruce Babbitt visited the north Alaska coast and called it "the last frontier where we see a genuine subsistence form of life." But whether the United States government will continue to recognize their concerns in the face of pressure from the oil industry remains to be seen.[5]

Other native peoples in northern Canada, some dependent on their own huge caribou migrations, share Gwich'in concerns for the animal. In 1998, the Eighth North American Caribou Workshop held its meeting in Whitehorse, capital of Canada's Yukon Territory. Its motto was "A future for an ancient deer." Native participants planned to link their traditions to high-tech mapping techniques that closely track caribou migrations and life cycles. Wildlife scientists at the meeting felt that such cooperation could serve as a model for the protection of other natural resources vital to native peoples.

WAPITI
Lordliest of the deer

With the coming of fall, valleys across North America used to resound with the bugling of the *wapiti,* or American elk. This call can still be heard in parts of the West. It rises up the musical scale to a clarion tone, then falls to a series of grunts. "The pealing notes echo through the dark valleys as if from silver bugles," wrote wapiti-hunter Theodore Roosevelt, "and the air is filled with the wild music."[1] To rutting bulls, it is a challenge to battle for harems of wapiti cows. Soon forest glades fill with the clatter of antlers as the bulls fight, occasionally to the death, for dominance.

Roosevelt called the wapiti "the lordliest of the deer kind in the entire world."[2] A bull may stand five feet high at the withers and weigh a thousand pounds. The smaller cow lacks antlers, which in the bull start growing in the spring until they spread up to five feet or so in the fall.

Victorious bulls and their harems migrate from mountain valleys to lower wooded slopes and valleys in the winter. In the spring, bulls shed their antlers and get ready to migrate back to the mountains. Cows give birth to usually one calf in May or June.

Early English settlers confusingly called the animals "elk" because of their general resemblance to the European moose known by that name. The scientist B. S. Barton corrected this mis-nomer in the *Scientific Monthly* in 1806. He proposed *wapiti* in-stead, from Shawnee *wa·piti,* meaning "white rump," because of the distinctive rear-end patches on the mostly reddish brown ani-mal. "As the elk has not to my knowledge been described by any systematic writer on Zoology, I have assumed the liberty of giving it a specific name," he explained. "I have called it Wapiti, which is the name by which it is known among the Shawnees."[3] *Elk* still prevails, but careful writers often use *wapiti.* (The red deer of Asia and other parts of the world is sometimes also called *wapiti.*)

Large herds of wapiti once roamed much of the United States and southern Canada. When Prince Maximilian of Wied was touring North Dakota in the early 1830s, he saw wapiti antlers scattered "in all the forests and prairies." Subsequently he came across a pile of antlers that Blackfoot Indians had heaped up measuring sixteen or eighteen feet high and twelve or fifteen feet in diameter.[4]

Despite their apparent carelessness with the antlers, Indians found many uses for them. Maximilian reported wapiti-antler war clubs (an antler weighs up to sixty pounds) and had heard tell of whip handles of the same material among more Western tribes. He noticed wapiti canine teeth ornamenting the leather blouses of Blackfoot women. Other observers reported that Crow women wore dresses trimmed with up to eleven hundred of the teeth.

Mandan and other Indian groups prized tough wapiti hide as material for the soles of their moccasins. According to Maximil-ian, only the skin of wapiti cows was typically used for clothing be-cause the thick skins of bulls could not be easily worked. The mas-sive animals also served as an important source of meat for the Indians.

But bagging wapiti was no easy task. Indians employed several techniques to kill them without having to pursue the swift ani-mals or risk injury from the antlers of a bull. The Cheyenne and various tribes of California snared wapiti by hanging nooses in their path: when an animal's neck was caught, the victim instinctively jumped with fright and strangled itself. The Arapaho would drive wapiti over a cliff into a pit below, where they slaughtered and butchered the animals.

With the arrival of whites, the wapiti population began declining. Settlements cut into the ranges of wapiti, which need about 128,000 acres for each herd. Professional hunters took large numbers of the animals for their meat, hides, antlers, and the upper canine teeth men sported as a fob ornament in the nineteenth century. The estimated ten million wapiti in North America at the time of the white man's coming have dwindled to about five hundred thousand today.

Warnings from conservationists (sometimes also hunters) such as Theodore Roosevelt helped save the wapiti from extinction. Olympic National Park of Washington was founded mainly to protect the Roosevelt elk, the subspecies that was named after the former president and is the largest of the wapiti. In the 1990s about five thousand lived in the park. Most U.S. wapiti today inhabit zones extending from British Columbia to New Mexico and Arizona, and along the Pacific coast from northern California through the Pacific Northwest. Attempts are being made to restore them to other states, including Arkansas, Michigan, Pennsylvania, and Wisconsin.

The valley of Jackson Hole, Wyoming, however, is regarded as the country's center for wapiti. Each year, up to eighteen thousand of the animals descend from the mountains and forests of Grand Teton National Park to the valley's National Elk Refuge. The town of Jackson revels in its wapiti associations. "The town square is decorated with four large arches made entirely from thousands of bleached white [wapiti] antlers," wrote *New York Times* reporter Jim Robbins. He noted that some of the town's restaurants served wapiti meat. (Although the animals are protected in their refuge, hunters still cull herds in the region.)

In the spring, Boy Scouts gather thousands of antlers shed in Jackson Hole. These are fashioned into chandeliers, chairs, tables, knife handles, belt buckles, and the like. Still more go to dealers who buy them for export to Asia, where they are ground up for medicinal purposes. The sale of antlers in 1995 produced nearly $100,000, says Robbins, a fifth of which went to the Boy Scouts and the rest to the refuge.[5]

But for many tourists, the unforgettable experience at Jackson Hole is the age-old bugling of bull wapiti. "The sound echoes from the Tetons for miles across the valley of the Snake," says Charles Kuralt. "It sends chills down the spine."[6]

PEMMICAN
Bread of the wilderness

Inland Indians and the trappers who followed them into the northern wilderness often shouldered heavy packs of pemmican. On journeys during harsh winter months, they dined and thrived on this concoction of dried meat pounded fine and mixed with melted fat. Berries might be added but were not needed to make the food palatable, according to many who subsisted on it.

Pemmican comes from Cree *pimihka·n,* "he makes grease." The Cree people ranged from Quebec to the Rocky Mountain foothills. They sometimes faced a feast-or-famine problem when they killed large numbers of animals, as by stampeding a herd of buffalo over a cliff. One solution was to process surplus meat into pemmican that could keep for years.

The Arctic explorer and author Vilhjalmur Stefansson believes that drying strips of meat to make jerky was a first step toward the invention of pemmican. Natural jerky is so tough that native peoples pounded it to make it chewable. They ate this dry food with liberal amounts of fat for palatability. Combining the two ingredients as pemmican was a logical second step.[1]

How, specifically, did Indians prepare pemmican? The Englishman Charles Alston Messiter, who toured the Far West in the 1860s and 1870s, gives a vivid account of pemmican manufacture:

> The buffalo-meat is first cut up into thin slices and dried in the sun or over smoke until it is as hard as leather; then the skin is taken raw, cut square, and sewn into a bag about three feet long by eighteen inches wide, with the hair outside. The meat is then taken and beaten with a flail until it is all fibres, and the fat is melted in large kettles and about three inches of the bag is filled with boiling fat; an equal quantity of fibre is then put into it and is beaten down with a heavy stick used as a rammer, then more fat is poured in and more fibre; and so on until the bag is full. It is then sewn up with raw hide or sinew and beaten flat, and is ready for use.[2]

Pemmican came in four sometimes overlapping kinds, according to Stefansson: summer, winter, plain, and berry. Summer pemmican was preferred because meat dried more efficiently in hot weather. The meat of "winter pemmican" (actually made in autumn) did not dry out so thoroughly and thus did not keep as long. Plain pemmican, the basic kind, consisted of lean meat with added fat usually from the same kind of animal. Various meats such as venison, caribou, beef, or even fish might be used besides buffalo. Choke cherries, saskatoon berries, or other berries could be added. These were possibly first introduced to please European appetites.

The pemmican-filled leather sack, called a "piece," weighed around ninety pounds. A trapper or wilderness laborer had to carry at least one piece on the trail along with his other gear. Heavy though a piece was, it offered more food energy for its weight than any alternative: a pound and a half of pemmican a day could easily sustain a laborer, and (Stefansson asserts) it did not become monotonous. Further advantages of the packed food were its resistance to soaking when a canoe overturned and a freshness that lasted throughout a long trip.

When potatoes were available, however, trappers sometimes

found variety in a dish they called "rubbiboo." This was made by putting pemmican in a frying pan with some fat. Then they mixed in mashed boiled potatoes and salt and pepper, frying the mixture. "Eaten hot, and taking care to be very hungry, it is not bad," said Messiter, perhaps not fully attuned to wilderness living. "And the hungrier you are, the better it will be."[3]

The records of fur traders and travelers refer to pemmican as "the bread of the wilderness." Priests in early North Dakota actually used pemmican as the host in communion when bread was lacking. It was a staple so critical to the fur trade that shootouts occurred in the early nineteenth century between the Hudson's Bay Company and the rival North West Company over control of the pemmican supply.

In 1849, Gail Borden started to manufacture a version of pemmican he called a "meat biscuit" for those seeking gold in California. He sold six hundred pounds of his food product to forty-niners and some to the Arctic explorer Dr. Elisha Kent Kane. His meat biscuit won a medal in 1851 at the International Exhibition in London, and he established a plant in Galveston to manufacture it. But Borden failed to persuade the U.S. Army and Navy even to try the product. Repeated attempts to market it to the public also failed. Borden finally made his fortune with the condensed milk that became a familiar sight in American households.

Pemmican nevertheless won worldwide fame when Admiral Robert Edwin Peary carried it on his Arctic expeditions, including his purported trip to the North Pole in 1909. "Too much cannot be said of the importance of pemmican to a polar expedition," Peary wrote. "It is an absolute *sine qua non*. Without it a sledge-party cannot compact its supplies within a limit of weight to make a serious polar journey successful."[4]

Still, the development of railways and highways in the twentieth century made pemmican less necessary. Food could be transported economically throughout much of North America. Condensed and dehydrated foods met the needs of many wilderness travelers. Furthermore, nutritionists declared that a mostly or all-meat product by itself could not keep people healthy.

The U.S. Armed Forces experimented with pemmican at the time of World War II and found it wanting in flavor and nutrition. Stefansson says they prepared the food incorrectly, and he argues that they ignored the experience of countless outdoorsmen who thrived months at a time on a pemmican-only diet.

Today pemmican has lost much of the standing it once enjoyed. One camping book claims: "If you've never eaten it before, a diet of pemmican can be quite a shock to your stomach. But nowhere near as much as to your nostrils." The author particularly condemns pemmican made with "beaver fat." *The L.L. Bean Guide to the Outdoors* and many similar books recommend that backpackers make their own gorp (from "good old raisins and peanuts") as trail food. The GoodMark Foods Company of Raleigh, North Carolina, manufactures a line of tasty meat products under the Pemmican label in packages displaying an Indian chief medallion, but the contents are really beef jerky, smoked turkey breast, and the like.[5]

Even in Canada, considered the home of pemmican, the food seems to have faded into obscurity. Writing in *Forbes Magazine*, Stephen S. Johnson, a Canadian living south of the border, says that American friends asked him to name his country's national dish. Baffled, he appealed to the Canadian consulate. "How about pemmican?" suggested a media relations man there. Johnson didn't know what it was. "You've never heard of it?" the informant incredulously said. "It's part of your heritage; it's as well known as a hockey puck." But Johnson soon learned that none of his Canadian friends had heard of it either.[6]

According to Bernadette Hince, editor of the *Dictionary of Antarctic English*, pemmican continues to be eaten, at least in Antarctica. There she says one expeditioner claimed that it had "the appearance, the feel, the odor . . . of hardened shoe polish." The comment was just one more putdown for a food that generations of Indians and trappers found nutritious and palatable.[7]

FURBEARERS

As blasts of Arctic air bore down on much of North America, hunters ventured out clad in weatherproof coverings of animal hide. Native clothing in many other parts of the continent as well came largely from animals. Furs also draped the interiors of wigwams, tepees, and igloos. The many practical uses of hides placed them among the most valued traditional articles of trade among native peoples.

Almost immediately on their arrival, Europeans too sought animal hides. The furbearing animals of Europe had been thinned out by overhunting. Clothing manufacturers there needed beaver for the fur hats that fashionable people wore. Leather workers looked for buckskins to make riding breeches and other outdoor clothing. Tailors wanted fancier furs for the coats, muffs, and carriage blankets going to the rich.

European traders exchanged beads, tools, guns, and later rum for the hides. But, soon, impatient with the native suppliers, fur companies sent trappers and agents into the forests of North America. The famed Hudson's Bay Company and its competition established trading posts deep in the wilderness to obtain millions of hides for eager customers.

Benefits of the fur trade included new income, as well as useful European goods, for the native population. Individual Europeans made fortunes from the furs, and their countries prospered from their enterprise. Foreign governments learned much from the explorations hundreds of trappers conducted in poorly mapped terrain. Trading posts developed into settlements that became cities such as Detroit, St. Louis, and St. Paul.

But traders often dealt brutally with native dealers or plied them with rum. Native peoples found themselves caught up in wars between European powers over territories. And in some cases — most dramatically that of the buffalo — an exploited animal population dwindled or almost disappeared. The furbearing *moose, caribou,* and *wapiti* (elk) have been discussed in the previous section. Here we will examine the also Indian-named *muskrat, raccoon, opossum, skunk, carcajou* (wolverine), *woodchuck,* and *chipmunk.* Except for the two last, these have been and still are valued sources of fur.

MUSKRAT
'Marsh rabbits'

Outsiders may blanch, but many people along the swampier regions of the Detroit River enjoy dining on muskrat. During the trapping season, from late November through February, they look forward to steaming platters of the rodent said to taste like duck. At this time of the year, muskrat dinners become a favorite fundraising event for local churches and sports clubs.

Indians had been eating muskrat for thousands of years, so the French trappers who founded Detroit in 1701 naturally took to eating it during harsh winters when other game was scarce. A person could break into a muskrat house and secure enough meat to feed a family for several days. The appeal of muskrat grew with a belief popular among Roman Catholics that it could be counted as fish on meatless days — an assumption the Detroit archdiocese refuted. So entrenched a tradition is muskrat-eating that a move in 1987 to restrict the sale of the meat to state-approved sources brought a storm of protest from local residents. "I've never seen so many people upset over an issue," said their state representative.[1]

Muskrats are a plentiful resource throughout most of North America. They grow to be one to two feet long and have a ratlike tail about half as long as their fur-covered body. Partially webbed hind feet make muskrats good swimmers. They feed mainly at night on water plants and other aquatic life such as shellfish. Muskrat houses with underwater entrances reach five feet in height and are composed of plants such as cattails.

Naturalists find the house-building muskrat a constant source of fascination. Henry David Thoreau wrote in his journal that they reminded him that "if we have no gypsies, we have a more indigenous race of furry, quadrupedal men maintaining their ground in our midst still."[2]

In *Pilgrim at Tinker Creek,* Annie Dillard describes how she spent several years learning how to stalk muskrats. She finally started waiting on a little bridge over a stream, blending with the structure. Soon she was seeing the animals regularly as they swam by or stopped to feed along the banks. "His jaw was underslung," she reported after one sighting, "his black eyes close set and glistening, his small ears pointed and furred."[3]

The name *muskrat* is commonly thought to derive from *musk* and *rat.* In fact, it is originally an Algonquian word akin to Massachusett *musquash,* still an alternative form. Its spelling does reflect the musky odor and ratlike appearance of the animal. To improve the appeal of muskrat meat, stores selling it often use the label "marsh rabbit."[4]

Indians found muskrat tasty and easily obtainable. The Ojibwa and Dakota of Minnesota employed a special spear to hunt the animal. "When the ponds and rivers, where the muskrat harbours, are found, their houses are perforated with a strong and peculiarly shaped spear by which the victim is transpierced, and the animal brought out upon its point," wrote the painter Seth Eastman in the mid-nineteenth century.[5]

Until the 1970s, the Gwich'in Indians of Alaska spent three months of the year "ratting," setting up camps along good lakes in the spring. Then entire families passed sunlit days catching and skinning muskrats. According to a visiting anthropologist, Richard K. Nelson, the boiled or roasted meat "was very tender and taste[d] delicious."[6]

The muskrat's waterproof brown fur long served Indians for

the making of blankets and winter clothing. With the coming of the white fur trade, muskrat gained in commercial value. Trappers today, Indian and non-Indian, still take nearly ten million muskrats a year — mostly for their hides. Dealers sometimes market the fur under the trade name "Hudson seal."

The popularity of muskrat meat, on the other hand, seems to have declined. Still, a fondness for it persists not only among some Indians, but among others along the Detroit River and in other tradition-oriented parts of the United States. On the Eastern Shore of Maryland, for example, gourmets eagerly await the muskrat-trapping season. Trappers there catch up to one hundred muskrats a day apiece and sell their hides in a ready market. But it is the famed dinners at restaurants and social events that delight natives and visitors in a custom going back as far as anyone can remember. "Rats" are "cooked like chicken and served with gravy, bones included," said Paul Bedard in the *Washington Post*. People travel from as far away as Washington, D.C., to participate in these feasts.[7]

RACCOON
Survivor

A clatter of trash barrels shatters the night's stillness. But the family inside the house listens calmly, aware of what is happening. A raccoon that has learned how to pry open the barrel lids is enjoying what's left of their fried chicken supper. Going to the door and shouting does little good. Five minutes later, the animal with a masked face is impudently helping itself once again.

Raccoons have been called "possibly the most adaptable wild mammal in North America." (See **Opossum** for a rival in this respect.) That characterization includes the ability to move stealthily among city dwellers at night. In the 1980s, at least eight thousand raccoons were estimated to be prowling the District of Columbia alone.

The raccoon lives in all forty-eight lower states and southern Canada. It is a native of North America and has been there for at least a million years. As each wave of immigrants, starting with the Indians, moved down or reached the continent, raccoons were around to greet them and forage in their garbage or become food themselves.

The North American raccoon grows to a husky twenty to forty pounds and to two to about three feet long. (Several other raccoon species inhabit Central and South America.) It has a coat of grayish fur, a pointed nose and black mask at one end, and a bushy tail with four to six black rings at the other — good camouflage in a woodland setting. Raccoons travel mostly at night, often live in hollow trees or rock dens, and sleep through much of the winter (though without truly hibernating).

Not picky about their food, raccoons eat almost anything — frogs, fish, crickets, mice, grasshoppers, birds' eggs, grapes, apples, nuts, corn, and carrion. The famed habit of washing food arises not from a desire for cleanliness, but apparently from a fondness for handling and rubbing objects with sensitive paws, which moistness seems to aid.

Owners of pet raccoons and biologists who have studied the animals agree on their high intelligence. Tame raccoons with the run of a house quickly learn how to remove the tops of boxes, work hook-and-eye latches, and open refrigerator doors. Studies indicate that raccoons may be more intelligent than any nonhuman species except the higher monkeys and apes.

Numerous Indian legends celebrate the raccoon's almost uncanny intelligence and skills. A Plains Ojibwa tale, paralleled in many tribes, tells how a raccoon cleverly caught crayfish by playing dead at the water's edge and snatching the animals as they inquisitively approached. Others, including the Caddo, described how a dead person once strayed from the long trail west to sample persimmons (which see) in trees along the way. The Great Spirit transformed him into a four-legged animal as punishment, but mercifully allowed him keen senses and paws with human dexterity as compensation. The Chawi Pawnee regarded the raccoon as holy and included its skin and a fork made of its bone in a sacred bundle.

Indians sought the plentiful raccoon as one of their most useful game animals. Its flesh tasted good (like beef, chicken, or lamb, according to various modern tasters), and the fat was used to flavor other food. Its thick pelt covered with coarse fur made warm matchcoats (an Indian mantle or other loose coat) or bedding. Ringed tails became a handsome ornament to be worn or to be displayed in a dwelling. The Yurok of California made a quiver out of raccoon skin, the head stuffed with moss as a base and the tail dangling from above. Raccoon bones could also be fashioned into tools, with the animal's curving penis bone oddly used to clean tobacco pipes. The fat, when not eaten, made a salve that soothed sprains and tired muscles.

Settlers, too, found the raccoon complex and useful. They wore the raccoon, with a special preference for the coonskin cap — tail hanging in back. Coonskins, when not converted directly into clothing or coverlets, could be bartered like buckskins. The settlers baked or boiled the meat and saved its fat for cooking with other foods, as the Indians did. Frontiersmen even converted the animal's penis bone Indianstyle into pipe cleaners.

After being captured by warriors of the Virginia leader Powhatan in 1608, John Smith introduced *raccoon* into English when he described the furs surrounding that dignitary:

> Arriving at Werawocomoco, their Emperour proudly lying uppon a Bedstead a foote high upon tenne or twelve Mattes, richly hung with manie Chaynes of great Pearles about his necke, and covered with a great Covering of Rahaughcums [one of Smith's various spellings of *raccoon*].[1]

Virginia Algonquian *raugroughcum* or *arocoun* was once often translated as "He scratches with the hands," or the like. Now dictionaries have abandoned this etymology.

A frontiersman who enjoyed fame for his skill at hunting game, including raccoons, was Davy Crockett (1786–1836), soldier and congressman. One legend described how he treed a raccoon. The animal, recognizing him, cried: "Don't shoot, Colonel. I'll come down. I know I'm a gone coon."

The hunting of raccoons became a national rite, especially in the rural South. Coon hunters might gather after dusk for a convivial chat and then release a pack of specially trained coonhounds. The dogs followed the scent left by raccoons in their rambling quest for food. Sometimes the trail went for miles through swamps, thickets, densely wooded forest, and other rough terrain. While in pursuit, each dog bayed in its own voice to create a wild chorus. When it was at last run down, the raccoon would commonly take refuge in a tree. There it would be shot or sometimes dislodged and captured alive. A raccoon was usually more than a match for a single dog, so it took a pack to handle one on the ground.

Coonhounds were and are the soul of coon hunts, with a keen nose and high stamina. Owners bred and trained them carefully because a man's standing as a hunter depended on his hounds. In 1945, the American Kennel Club finally classified the Black and Tan Coonhound as a standard breed. It is a trail-and-tree hound, with the ability to work in all kinds of weather and track a raccoon or other animal such as the opossum with accuracy. Its coloration is specified as "coal black with rich tan markings above eyes, on sides of muzzle, chest, legs, and breeching, with black pencil marks on toes."[2]

The usefulness and picturesque appearance of the raccoon has helped cause its name, usually shortened to *coon,* to be associated with various activities and objects. The importance of *coonskin* has already been noted. To *coon,* especially in the South, means to crawl or creep along like a raccoon. To be *coony* is to be crafty or cunning like the animal. A *Maine coon,* or *coon cat,* is a breed of large long-haired cats with a full tail. A *coon's age* means a long time, although raccoons in the wild rarely reach the age of two. A *raccoon grape* refers to the fox grape.

The raccoon became a symbol of the Whig political party in the 1830s, and specifically of William Henry Harrison in his "Log Cabin Campaign" of 1840. It was part of a successful attempt to nickname Harrison "Old Coon" and portray him as a frontiersman, although he had grown up on a Southern plantation and lived a life of gentility. Senator Estes Kefauver from Tennessee donned a coonskin cap in his unsuccessful campaign as the Democratic vice-presidential nominee in 1956. Political observers found the senator's headgear ironic, since he was generally perceived as a sophisticated "egghead," or intellectual. The familiar emblem became controversial in 1966 when President Lyndon Johnson addressed U.S. servicemen while in South Vietnam: "I salute you. Come home with that coonskin on the wall." Critics felt that Johnson's figure of speech showed a frontiersman's attitude that was all wrong.[3]

As the lore surrounding the raccoon has endured, so has its economic value. During the 1920s, raccoon coats became a fad among college students. Each coat represented about fifteen skins, and the raccoon population declined in some regions because of heavy trapping. The fad died out during the Great Depression, as had the earlier fashion of using raccoon for coachmen's capes and carriage rugs.

The Davy Crockett fad of 1955, however, sent the demand for coonskins skyrocketing again. Millions of young Americans from about five to fifteen years of age saw the actor Fess Parker, dressed in coonskin cap and buckskins, portray Crockett on television. They thrilled at "The Ballad of Davy Crockett," which became the nation's top-selling recording for five consecutive weeks. Admirers rushed to stores to buy items associated with the frontiersman, especially coonskin caps. The wholesale price of raccoon skins rose from twenty-five cents a pound to eight dollars a pound. (For dyed animal skin substitutes, see **Skunk**.) Then the fad collapsed, ending the acute demand for coonskins.

Yet raccoon-skin coats had never lost their allure among women. Furriers required from a million to about three million pelts a year in the decades after World War II. Most raccoon pelts in the late 1990s were going to Russia and China, to become hats and coats for export.

Meanwhile, some people continue the Indian custom of keeping raccoons as pets. They are entertaining and affectionate but require much care to prevent them from becoming destructive. Wildlife rehabilitators, on the other hand, rescue hurt or orphaned raccoons and focus their treatment on enabling the animals to return to the woods.

Such a one is Debra Gode, a raccoon rehabilitator in Haddam, Connecticut. Part of her task is to monitor raccoons for rabies, which became epidemic among raccoons in the Northeast in the 1980s. Working in the mid-1990s, Ms. Gode was releasing about four hundred raccoons a year back into the wild. "People may believe in letting nature take its course," she said, "but it's not nature that's causing the problem." She asserted that people are mainly at fault as they steadily encroach on the raccoon's habitat.[4]

Yet nationwide, the raccoon is not endangered. It has, furthermore, expanded northward in Canada and been introduced into Europe. Today the raccoon shows every sign of enduring many years more, a source of fascination and usefulness to the inhabitants of North America from the beginning.

OPOSSUM
The animal with nineteen lives

"An Opassom hath an head like a Swine, and a taile like a Rat, and is of the bignes of a Cat," wrote Captain John Smith in 1612. "Under her belly she hath a bagge, wherein shee lodgeth, carrieth, and sucketh her young."[1]

Smith did more than offer a pithy account of this native of North America. He called it by

opossum

its appropriate name — from Virginia Algonquian *apasoum*, meaning "white animal." Anyone who meets an opossum face to face will be struck by its white, pointed head on a body covered with grayish-white fur.

Early English explorers regarded the opossum with astonishment: It was the first marsupial, or pouch-bearing mammal, they had ever seen and an odd creature in other respects. About eighty-five species of opossum live in South America and Central America, but the ancestor of the common or Virginia opossum diverged from the other species in a migration north that made it North America's only opossum.

The opossum is a walking — or to be more exact, *waddling* — paradox. Even admirers admit that it is stupid, with a brain only one-third the size of a raccoon's. It looks raffishly old at two years and rarely lives beyond that age. During its brief life, family ties are limited to the mother's rearing of her young. The gory and mangled remains of opossums, commonly seen on highways in the spring, afford most people their only view of this nocturnal animal.

The opossum, nevertheless, is a survivor, with traits that have enabled it to persist since the time of the last of the dinosaurs. "If a Cat has nine lives, this Creature surely has nineteen," wrote John Lawson, surveyor-general of North Carolina in the early eighteenth century.[2] Its most famous trick (apparently involuntary) is "playing possum," feigning death until a predator may lose interest. A study of opossum skeletons shows that many survived bone-breaking mishaps that would have killed other animals. The opossum is willing to eat almost anything, from a rotting deer carcass to grubs or a rattlesnake, whose venom it is immune to.

But the opossum's secret weapon is breeding. It does this often, "with males and females controlling their mutual antipathy only for as long as it takes to get the job done," says an expert.[3] A female can breed about every hundred days and bears an average of eighteen young a year, carrying them at first in her pouch and later on her back. Thus the opossum keeps producing new recruits to replace the tremendous losses in its battle for survival.

"Archaeological excavations clearly indicate that opossums were a staple of Indian diet throughout the Americas," states the authority Steven N. Austad.[4] Yet opinions about the quality of opossum meat varied among Indians, as they would among settlers. Early explorers reported that some native West Indian peoples abhorred opossums and killed them simply to forestall their raids on papayas and other fruits. Writing in 1737, a surveyor in the Carolinas after Lawson called opossum meat "fat, white and well tasted." He said various people ate opossums, "especially the *Indians* and *Negroes,* who prefer them before *Pork,* but their ugly tails are enough to put one out of conceipt of them."[5]

Lawson reported that among Indians the rough opossum fur was "not esteem'd." But he noted that they braided the long fur from the animal's belly into cords for belts and straps.[6] Settlers do not seem to have esteemed opossum hides either, except possibly as decoration.

Although still hunted for food, fur, or sport, the Virginia opossum has greatly expanded its range in modern times. It now can be found five hundred miles north of its colonial habitat in the eastern United States, and in at least forty-two states. One can sometimes spot it incongruously heaving through New England snowdrifts, for example, though the toll in winter among these venturesome animals is high. Early in the twentieth century, wild opossums made their appearance in California — apparently introduced as pets. Now the animal thrives on the West Coast to the point of sometimes being a pest.

Improvements in the dressing and dyeing of opossum pelts have made them more desirable in modern times than they once were. About a million opossum skins a year were entering the U.S. fur market in the late 1980s.

The number of opossums that Americans eat today is hard to calculate. In Southern states, the hunting and consuming of opossum constitute a much-honored tradition. Poor people found opossums relatively easy to catch and, when properly prepared, tasty. "'Possum and taters" (sweet potatoes) is a dish that still graces the tables of gentry. Specific recipes vary from locality to locality, and regional additions such as sassafras or chestnuts enhance the basic dish. A platter of hot corn bread often comes on the side.

Yet the popularity of 'possum and taters has not kept pace with the opossum's physical advance. A non-Southerner coming across an opossum near a forest path or even on a street corner late at night may regard it less as a prospective meal than as a white-faced apparition from another time and place.

SKUNK
Beast of offense

During a tour of the West in the early 1830s, Washington Irving laughed heartily when his French-Osage hunter killed a skunk. Members of Irving's party advised the hunter to wear the skunk's scalp "as the only trophy of his prowess." But, to Irving's disgust, the hunter dressed the animal's carcass and tied it behind his saddle "like a fat sucking-pig" to be roasted for supper that night. Irving got hold of the skunk later in the day and threw it into the river.[1]

In fact, Indians of North America commonly ate skunks. Archaeologists on Long Island often find skunk bones mingled with those of muskrat, raccoon, deer, and other game animals. Josiah Gregg, a Santa Fe trader in the early nineteenth century, confirmed Irving's report of skunk as a Plains Indian food. Gregg added that non-Indian travelers "who have tasted the flesh of this animal have pronounced it fine, and of exquisite relish." He goes on to quote a white member of another expedition as calling skunk a "remarkably rich and delicate food."[2]

Yet skunks made a mostly bad impression on early colonists. "The beasts of offense be skunks, ferrets, foxes, whose impudence sometimes drives them to the goodwives' hen roost to fill their paunch," wrote William Wood in 1643, giving *skunk* its first printed appearance. "Some of these be black; their fur is of much esteem."[3] The Massachusett name *squnck* is thought to have come originally from the Proto-Algonquian words for "urinate" and "foxlike animal."

The skunk, a member of the weasel family, can be found throughout the continental United States and southern Canada. About the size of a small cat, with a bushy tail, it is often called a "wood pussy." The markings of skunks differ among the five different kinds in the United States and are usually black with stripes or spots in different patterns. The striped skunk is the most common species. It can hardly be mistaken, sporting a narrow white stripe that starts at its head and divides from the shoulder into two broad stripes down its back. Yet skunks are rarely seen except as roadkill, since they feed and move about mostly at night.

The skunk's first line of defense and best-known trait is its scent. When it feels threatened, it will typically give a warning by lifting its tail or stamping its feet. Then it will let fly with a pungent spray that can reach a target ten to fifteen feet away. The scent squirts out of two grape-sized glands in its rear end. People unlucky enough to be hit find the smell extremely hard to wash away, and sometimes just bury the clothes they were wearing. But the skunk is not an aggressive animal. It feeds quietly and furtively on a variety of plants and small animals such as grubs, beetles, snakes, and mice. Its only serious threat to people is as a carrier of rabies, and it is reportedly the leading carrier of that disease.

Indians not only ate skunks, they also wore them. In *Dress Clothing of the Plains Indians,* Ronald P. Koch says skunk was one of the skins commonly used by tribes of the northern Plains and the Plateau. A strip of skunk fur worn at the heels of a Mandan warrior, he notes, signified war honors. Comanche warriors, too, sometimes wore skunk tails attached to the back of their moccasins.[4]

The Hopi used skunk skins for symbolic displays. Sometimes they hung the skins from a bow used as a religious emblem. For example, a bow might hold skins of the "weasel for the Northwest, skunk for the Above, and raccoon for the Below." As "evil smellers," they were suspended in this fashion over the entrance to a kiva (the ceremonial chamber) to keep evil influences away.[5]

Skunk still makes money in the fur trade. During the 1983–84 trapping season, fur dealers handled about 175,000 striped and hooded skunk skins. Eastern spotted skunks are said to have the finest, silkiest, most valuable fur. In 1955, the Davy Crockett fad featuring "coonskin" caps exhausted the ready supply of raccoon fur, and dyed skunk became one of the substitutes worn by unsuspecting children. By the late 1990s, the use of skunk fur was usually confined to collars, cuffs, and trim.

Skunks are put to some odd uses. The clinging quality that causes their scent to linger has made it valuable to perfume manufacturers. They refine the golden-colored secretion for use as a fixative. And de-scented skunks are said to make affectionate and playful pets.

But skunks continue to get the largely undeserved bad press they have had since colonial times. A "skunk," figuratively, is a low-down person. A team that "skunks" another wins overwhelmingly, often without allowing the loser to score. Skunk cabbage and skunkweed are both foul-smelling swamp plants.

Still, the skunk has received a backhanded compliment in recent years. *Skunk works* refers to an inconspicuous department in a company (often one doing engineering research) allowed to operate with little supervision. This got its name from the "Li'l Abner" comic strip drawn by Al Capp. His imaginary town of Dogpatch included the Skonk Works, where moonshiners distilled Kickapoo Joy Juice out of old shoes and dead skunks. Staff at the Lockheed Advanced Development Company, creators of the U-2 spy plane and the F-117 Stealth Fighter, adopted the name informally, and it spread from there. From a skunk's point of view, the name's origin is appropriate — skunks shun attention and maintain a potent defense against any threats.

CARCAJOU, QUICKHATCH
'His tracks go on and on'

The headline of a *New York Times* sports story reads:

Wolverines' Defense Holds Down Gophers

Translated, that means the University of Michigan defeated the University of Minnesota in football. The wolverine, often called *carcajou,* is Michigan's official state animal and its university mascot. But the mysterious animal no longer inhabits the state, if it ever did.

Present or absent, the wolverine awed many Native American peoples. They knew it by various names. *Wolverine* is the European term and comes from *wolf,* an animal often regarded as an equal in strength and cunning. Its alternative name, *carcajou,* derives from Montagnais *kuàkuàtsheu* through Canadian French. *Quickhatch,* a related name, comes from East Cree. The eighteenth-century naturalist Comte de Buffon misleadingly gave the name *kinkajou,* cognate with *carcajou,* to a long-tailed mammal of Central and South America related to the raccoon.

At up to about three feet in length and forty to fifty pounds in weight, wolverines are the largest members of the weasel family in North America. With dark brown fur, they sport yellowish bands along their sides and a streak across their foreheads. Few people see them in the wild, even within their shrunken range.

Biologists express astonishment at the distances the solitary wolverine may travel. "It's just never ceased to amaze me how far these animals go in a short period of time," says one who tracked radio-collared specimens. "The hallmark of the wolverine is probably its insatiable need to be on the move."[1] Appetite drives the wolverine. It eats carrion by preference, but it will kill animals as big as snowbound moose or wapiti (elk). In its quest for food, a wolverine may lope fifteen miles in a day. A typical wolverine range covers hundreds of square miles of snowfields, bleak northern forests, and mountain ranges.

Native peoples felt ambivalent about the wolverine. "His tracks go on and on, back to the time before people were living here," said a storyteller of the Dene Dháa (Slavey) of northern Canada deferentially. This people regards the wolverine as a trickster and a spoiler of traps, though also a source of supernatural wisdom. A powerful twentieth-century Dene Dháa prophet bore the name of his inspirer, *Nógha*, or Wolverine.[2]

The Koyukon regard wolverines as the most spiritual of predators. When one is killed, it is hailed as "the great one, the chief of animals." Its carcass is dressed in finery and propped up in a place of honor, where it is offered food. Afterward, the Koyukon burn the skinned carcass along with more food to nourish its spirit.

A Blackfoot legend tells how a young warrior whose medicine power came from Wolverine wished to avenge three brothers slain by a powerful member of another tribe. The warrior fasted for many days on the prairie. At last Wolverine appeared in a dream and helped him transform himself into a pretty young woman. So disguised, he deluded and killed the culprit.

But native peoples and others often had to cope with mischief from flesh-and-blood wolverines. A wolverine would spring traps, sometimes apparently for amusement. It might travel along twenty miles of traps, adroitly removing the bait without getting caught. In nineteenth-century Alaska, a trapper set a kind of trap that connected bait to the trigger of a gun. The wily wolverines rendered the traps useless by gnawing through the lines that held the guns in place or the lines attaching the bait to the triggers. Even if they got caught, they often struggled free or dragged a trap for miles.

Trappers hated the wolverine because of its role as spoiler, and sought to kill it more for that reason than for its pelt. (Wolverine flesh often became dog food.) "Indians and trappers nearly always torture a wolverine when caught, very often roasting him alive over the fire," wrote an American traveling in the Canadian wilds during the nineteenth century.[3]

However, wolverine fur is famous in the north country as the ideal lining for parka hoods. Oils in the fur prevent frost from forming around the hoods — a danger in severe cold. Among the Koyukon, wolverine fur is used for men's parkas and boot trim, but only as a ruff and trim on women's parkas. Scarcity has reduced the once-great commercial importance of wolverine fur in the broader fur market.

The wolverine populations of northern Europe and Russia have declined in the twentieth century. Predator-control programs and trapper killing had reduced numbers among North American wolverines sharply by 1900. At the end of the century, the northern Rockies were thought to be the last main stronghold of the wolverine in the lower forty-eight states.

No one knows for sure how many wolverines remain; biologists are hard put to estimate its numbers. During the 1990s, the U.S. Forest Service and Idaho Fish and Game Department attached radio transmitters to about a dozen wolverines and tracked them in an attempt to assess their behavior and range. But three years into the study, funding dried up.

Wildlife groups such as the Western Carnivore Committee, made up of university and government biologists and researchers from conservation groups, have urged the government to declare wolverines threatened or endangered in some areas. But the inability to determine the animal's numbers has foiled efforts to document these warnings. All that experts can say for sure is that, despite a shrinking range, an unknown number of wolverines, or carcajous, still roam the deepest wildernesses of North America.

WOODCHUCK

The wildness of the woodchuck

Henry David Thoreau encountered the woodchuck, or groundhog, often. One ate a quarter-acre of his bean patch at Walden. He killed and ate another caught in a similar misdeed, finding its flavor "musky." And he once immobilized a woodchuck by continually cutting off its line of retreat in order to study it closely and sympathetically. Yet woodchucks still mystified him. In *Walden,* Thoreau recalled:

> As I came home through the woods with my string of fish, trailing my pole, it being now quite dark, I caught a glimpse of a woodchuck stealing across my path, and felt a strange thrill of savage delight, and was strongly tempted to seize and devour him raw; not that I was hungry then, except for that wildness which he represented.[1]

In its Anglo-Saxon guise, the word *woodchuck* preserves that "wildness." It is Algonquian, akin to Narragansett *ockqutchaun,* woodchuck. Settlers tried to familiarize the animal by making its name sound English.

The woodchuck is a ground squirrel of the marmot family found in northern and eastern North America. Typically about two feet long, it has small ears and stubby legs. Its lengthy burrows contain living quarters as well as a bathroom alcove (which it cleans periodically) and inconspicuous lookout holes. It hibernates in these quarters after fattening up during the fall. "Groundhog Day," February 2, is a European invention. The woodchuck does in fact tend to emerge from its burrow in late winter in Pennsylvania, but it does so earlier in its southern range and later in its northern range.

The *rockchuck* is a closely related member of the marmot family found in the West. In 1995 an archaeologist from Brigham Young University discovered the ongoing importance of that woodchuck cousin among Indians when he showed Rick

Pikyavit, a Paiute, some ancient ash pits excavated at Fish Lake National Forest, Utah. "We still use pits like that to roast rockchuck," Pikyavit declared. Local Indians subsequently gathered at Fish Lake with archaeologists and students to relate traditional stories, play American Indian games, and dine on the same roasted rockchuck that Indians had been enjoying for at least six centuries.[3]

In much of North America, Indians have eaten woodchuck. They have also worn its hide. Settlers and their descendants found woodchucks similarly useful. Thoreau saw one boy wearing a cap made from a woodchuck pelt and chatted with a man who was having mittens made of woodchucks caught raiding his fields. Into the twentieth century, Eskimo and northern Indians were turning woodchuck pelts into lightweight and cold-defying parkas.

Fewer people now seem to eat woodchuck, tasty though wild-game fanciers say it is. Farmers and gardeners are more concerned with what the *woodchuck* eats. Although some may pillage crops and leave troublesome holes and mounds, biologists say these depredations cannot justify the slaughter some hunters inflict on the typically harmless animals. Furthermore, woodchucks actually improve land by turning over topsoil — an estimated 1.6 million tons a year in New York State alone.

One reason for the woodchuck's low repute is that it has multiplied since the arrival of Europeans in North America. Settlers cleared woodlands, opening up the glades and meadows that woodchucks love to frequent. The thinning out of woodchuck enemies such as bears, wolves, and mountain lions further encouraged a woodchuck population explosion. Among the settlers, the woodchuck came to be regarded as a pest — a reputation that lingers.

Still, Groundhog Day has done much to enhance the rodent's reputation. Since 1887, top-hatted officials of the Punxsutawney Groundhog Club have gathered at a park in their Delaware Indian-named town each February. As if by magic, a woodchuck named Punxsutawney Phil appears. A handler picks the animal up to see whether the sight of its own shadow frightens it back underground — a sign that winter will continue six weeks more. If no shadow can be seen, winter will soon be over. Depending on the amount of solid news, the report goes out to the nation, conferring a rare moment of glory on an otherwise humble animal.

CHIPMUNK
'Tail-in-air'

The chipmunk's dainty size has kept it from being a target of either early Indian hunters or modern trappers. It is true that a 1735 painting portrays Tishcohan, a Lenape chief, with a chipmunk-skin tobacco pouch hanging around his neck. And in 1793, a book on natural history stated that chipmunk skins were "sometimes brought over [to England] to line cloaks." But at about three ounces and four inches (excluding tail), the exquisitely striped animal does not carry enough meat or wear a large enough hide to make catching it worth the trouble.[1]

Related to squirrels, chipmunks are sometimes called "ground squirrels." The sixteen or more species dart, hop, and burrow throughout much of North America. They are native only to that continent and Asia, from which they may have migrated along the same routes followed by the ancestors of Native Americans.

Today chipmunks can commonly be seen on forest floors and along patios or sometimes in trees. They search for nuts as well as seeds, fruit, birds' eggs, and insects — and the cheeks of foraging chipmunks often bulge comically with provender. (A mother was recently heard to admonish her hungry toddler at mealtime, "Now, don't chipmunk that food!") Chipmunk burrows may extend to twelve feet, furnished with nest, sleeping chamber, and storage areas. There chipmunks spend winters in a drowsy, though not fully hibernating, state. Thoreau notes that the chipmunk's first cries were considered by many to be a harbinger of spring.

The Ojibwa called the little animal *acitmo·n?*, which may mean "headfirst" (from its manner of descending a tree) or "red squirrel" (from its near cousin). Henry Wadsworth Longfellow opted for a version of the first derivation when he had Hiawatha say:

> 'Take the thanks of Hiawatha,
> And the name which now he gives you;
> For hereafter and forever
> Boys shall call you Adjidauma.
> Tail-in-air the boys shall call you!'[2]

Early writers transcribed the Ojibwa name as *chetamon* and then *chitmunk*. Probably influenced by the animal's cry, interpreted as "chip, chip, chip," popular usage modified the name to *chipmunk*.

The myths and legends of Indian peoples reveal close observation of — and admiration for — the animal. "Never kill a chipmunk," say the Navajo, who believe that a chipmunk will lead a lost person to food and water. They reportedly make prayer sticks in honor of the chipmunk, striped black and topped with feathers. When someone upsets a chipmunk, it will cause that person's nose to tickle, therefore Navajo children who scratch their noses may be suspected of having teased the animal, according to B. A. and H. K. Henisch in *Chipmunk Portrait*. A rare negative chipmunk story accuses one of filching a tobacco pouch during a famine for a lump of fat inside, a tale that curiously echoes the Lenape use of chipmunk hide mentioned earlier.[3]

The outsized power of the small chipmunk is described in an Iroquois legend. In early days, an animal council debated whether Earth should always remain in day or in night. Bear argued for perpetual night, but Chipmunk kept chattering for alternate night and day until dawn broke and resolved the argument. Bear angrily raked Chipmunk's back with its claws, leaving indelible stripes on the animal.

The Cherokee have a slightly different view of how the

chipmunk got its stripes. They say that the animals once held a council in which it was proposed that each wish a disease on men for hunting them. Chipmunk refused to join in because it wasn't among the hunted. The other animals angrily attacked the little animal, and Bear left permanent claw marks on it. The Navajo, on the other hand, hold that the chipmunk was allowed to streak its face and back with the blood of a monster whose death it had been brave enough to verify.

Today mythical chipmunks often appear in children's stories. They can be seen in Walt Disney's "Chip 'n' Dale" books and in TV cartoons. The musical group "Alvin and the Chipmunks" chirps a highly popular Christmas tune, "The Chipmunk Song," that millions of American children have been brought up on.

More lastingly, "The Chipmunk," by the English poet Ted Hughes, assures a place for the animal in twentieth-century literature. It begins:

> A rippling, bobbing wood-elf, the chipmunk came
> Under the Cape Cod conifers, over roots,
> A first scout of the continent's wild game,
> Midget aboriginal American.[4]

DOMESTICATED ANIMALS

Native Americans commonly felt close to animals as part of nature, regarding them as representatives of the supernatural powers that pervade the world. They sometimes chose certain animals as totems, or revered emblems of clan or family. (See **Totem**.) Yet they domesticated few.

The anthropologist Clark Wissler does note that Pueblo Indians bred turkeys for eggs and feathers, the Narragansett trained hawks to guard their fields, and Carolina Indians may have bred cranes. The Mogollon of the Southwest kept macaws in pens and traded their feathers.[1]

The dog, though, was the chief domestic animal of native peoples before the Europeans arrived. Often dogs in the West carried packs during journeys. Indians such as the Assiniboine, Hidatsa, and Blackfoot also hitched their dogs to the travois — a V-shaped contrivance of poles for dragging luggage. Some Siouan peoples ate dogs, though most North American tribes (unlike those of Mexico) did not. The Choctaw and others sometimes sacrificed a dog to supply a deceased person with a companion after death.

The kinds of dogs discussed in this section — the *Eskimo dog, husky,* and *malamute* — are superb working dogs that originated in the Arctic. Today they enjoy popularity throughout the United States as pets and sled-race dogs.

Horses, the second principal domesticated animal of the Indians, have a curious history in North America. They roamed the continent before becoming extinct about eight thousand years ago. After the Spanish reintroduced horses around 1600, Indians handled them as if born to ride. The horses gave Indian owners a mobility that increased the range of their travels and their ability to hunt game, notably the buffalo.

Various types of wild horses such as the bronco and mustang arose on the continent. This section deals with the *cayuse* and *Appaloosa*, which tribes of the Northwest not only bred but utilized to win power and wealth.

ESKIMO
Arctic working dogs

"The type of Eskimo we're enlisting today doesn't have the survival skills of the older Eskimos," said Alaska Adj. Gen. John Schaeffer in 1989. He huddled with a group of trainees beside a spruce fire one hundred miles north of the Arctic Circle. Schaeffer was a skilled Arctic outdoorsman who didn't need the training, but the assorted military personnel (Eskimo and non-Eskimo) at the Alaska Army National Guard school probably would have died if left on their own in the minus-forty-degree weather. Now they were learning how to build a spruce shelter, catch fish and bag rabbits, and even kill and butcher a caribou. Schaeffer was keeping them company to show his commitment to the program.[1]

The Eskimo experienced massive culture shock in the twentieth century. White influence led them to replace the kayak and oar-propelled boat with the gasoline-powered boat, the spear with the rifle, the dogsled with the snowmobile, the seal-oil lamp with electricity. Of course, modern technology has also opened up a life richer in possessions and formal education. In Canada, Eskimo (Inuit) further came into control of a region of the Northwest Territories larger than Alaska and California combined. But drastic transitions have taken a social toll on traditional Eskimo culture.

The stress of change can be seen in the sensitivity of some Eskimo about their ethnic name. "In the 1970s in Canada the name Inuit all but replaced Eskimo in governmental and scientific publications and the mass media, largely in response to demands from Eskimo political associations," reports the Smithsonian's book *Arctic*.[2]

These demands were influenced by the mistaken belief that *Eskimo* originally meant "eater of raw meat." Montagnais *aiachkimeou,* source of the name, actually means "Micmac," perhaps literally "snowshoe netter." Now *Eskimo* and *Inuit* ("people" in Eskimo) are used interchangeably, with the first preferred in the United States and the second in Canada.

Much of the world retains a traditional view of Eskimo culture. The *Eskimo dog* is a part of that heritage prized far beyond the northern regions from which it emerged. Eskimo developed this sturdy working dog with pointed ears and a plumed tail over thousands of years. It can haul sledges long distances in the winter, carry heavy packs in the summer, and track down wild game, including bears. Eskimo dogs are hardy enough to sleep outdoors, unsheltered, in the bitterest cold. One of their uncanny traits is their howl. "The dogs often give voice in a chorus of strangely woven tones, and this is one of the thrilling sounds of the Arctic," says a Canadian observer.[3]

Now Eskimo dogs are bred and enjoyed internationally for use in sled-dog races and as pets. Leading examples of these remarkable dogs are the husky and the malamute (both of which see).

HUSKY
Hero of the Iditarod

What today is commonly considered the world's toughest sled-dog race began with the exploits of the Siberian husky in a race to save lives. In January 1925, two Eskimo children died of diphtheria in Nome, high up on Alaska's coast. Lacking antitoxin serum, the city's only doctor feared the disease would spread to hundreds of other unvaccinated children. Anchorage, more than a thousand miles to the southeast, had a supply of the serum, but getting it to Nome in time to save lives looked almost impossible. Nome was snowbound — with frozen rivers and coast, constant blizzards, and temperatures that sank as low as minus seventy degrees Fahrenheit. No ships could reach the city, and the available airplanes were not capable of flying through Arctic storms. Alaska's governor, Scott Bone, pleaded for volunteer sled-dog drivers to rush the serum to Nome.

A train carried the serum close to Fairbanks in east-central Alaska. Then relays of sled-dog teams passed the package along the Iditarod Trail, a mail and supply route named after an Athabaskan village, Haiditarod. A Norwegian immigrant and skilled driver, Leonhard Seppala, set out from Nome with a team of twenty selected Siberian huskies to receive the serum and help carry it on the last part of the trip. Dogs of this breed originated in northeast Siberia and were brought to Alaska in the early twentieth century, where they became a favorite sled dog. Part of Seppala's harrowing nonstop run took him on a shortcut across a frozen bay. The serum reached Nome in less than six days, quickly enough to prevent further deaths. Seppala and his Siberian huskies became famous for their share in this feat.

Participants in that race to Nome were presented with medals, a presidential certificate of appreciation, and other honors. Seppala and his dogs went on a publicity tour in the United States. The Siberian husky's well-publicized accomplishments in Alaska attracted dog lovers. Some adopted the dog and established it as a breed that won American Kennel Club recognition in 1930. "The Siberian husky is a medium-size working dog, quick and light on his feet and free and graceful in action," states the AKC official standard. "His moderately compact and well furred body, erect ears and brush tail suggest his Northern heritage."[1]

The term husky — from huskemaw, a variant of Eskimo — had long been loosely applied to any heavy-coated working dog of the North American Arctic. Ancestors of the ordinary Alaskan husky, a mutt in the eyes of many dog fanciers, hauled heavy sleds for Eskimo long before the arrival of their Siberian cousin. But the outside world had paid little attention to these native huskies.

The Iditarod Sled Dog Race, established in 1973 to commemorate the delivery of antitoxin serum to Nome, helped change public attitudes. This yearly race follows the Iditarod Trail of about eleven hundred miles from Anchorage to Nome. Competitors face hurricane-force blizzards, treacherous drifts, and sometimes moose attacks. Because of unusual demands placed on the racing dogs, veterinarians check them throughout the race.

The Alaskan husky, lighter and faster than the Siberian husky, dominates the Iditarod. Reflecting mixed ancestry, it comes in a variety of shapes, though some breeders keep pedigrees. It can run at up to twenty miles an hour for stretches of twenty or thirty miles. It thrives in the cold and appears to enjoy racing over arctic terrain.

Huskies no longer play a vital role in much of the Far North. But the Iditarod and similar races draw on, and embody, the Eskimo-husky tradition that goes back thousands of years.

MALAMUTE
Call of the wild

On the coast of northern Alaska, nineteenth-century traders watched eagerly as dog sleds hurtled into view. The sleds, more than ten feet long, were piled high with furs. Guiding the sleds were drivers tall for Eskimo, with labrets (lip plugs) protruding below the corners of their mouths. A scientist of the era pronounced them "very finely proportioned and athletic."[1] These impressive men — famed for their ability to drive a hard bargain — were the Malimiut, who lived around Kotzebue Sound north of the Bering Strait.

The dogs that the Malimiut drove also came in for high praise. They are "powerful looking, have thick dense double coats called weather coats, magnificently bushy tails [and] have remarkable endurance and fortitude," according to a modern description.[2]

malamute

From the Malimiut breeders comes the name of this remarkable dog — the *malamute*.

Miners in the Klondike gold rushes of 1897–98 bought all the malamutes they could for their rugged trek to the goldfields. When the supply of native dogs ran out, the miners imported others such as St. Bernards. The new dogs crossbred with malamutes, leading to a "decay" of the breed.

A vogue for sled-dog racing in the United States in the 1920s revived interest in the Arctic original. Several breeders devoted themselves to the restoration of what they called the *Alaskan Malamute*. In 1935, the American Kennel Club (AKC) recognized this dog as an official breed. The AKC standards require that the breed's character be preserved: "In judging Alaskan Malamutes, their function as a sledge dog for heavy freighting must be given consideration above all else."[3] Compared to the Siberian husky, today's malamute is a bigger dog, though with relatively smaller ears and a heavier muzzle.

The dog Buck in Jack London's *Call of the Wild* is said to have probably been largely malamute. Malamutes were part of Adm. Richard E. Byrd's expeditions to the Antarctic in the 1920s and 1930s, and they did their job well. They also served during World War II as pack and search-and-rescue dogs.

In the early 1990s, more than five thousand Alaskan Malamutes a year were being registered with the AKC. Although many live far from their Arctic origin, they may still run in sport-sled events, and they serve as excellent pets.

APPALOOSA
The spotted horse

> *How they find death in a dramatic flare:*
> *Trying to ride the apaloochy mare.*

So wrote the poet Mary Carolyn Davies in 1924 of cowboys on an unbroken Appaloosa.[1] This saddle horse, typically with a spotted rump, may go back two centuries among Indians of the American West. The historian Francis Haines traces it back even further, to ancient Africa and Asia.

In North America, the Appaloosa seems to have emerged among the Nez Perce. This tribe of the Northwest was famed for its horsemanship. "Their horses appear to be an excellent race," wrote Meriwether Lewis of the Lewis and Clark expedition in 1805. "They are lofty, elegantly formed, active and durable; in short many of them look like fine English coursers and would make a figure in any country."[2]

Authorities, nevertheless, dispute the exact origin of the Appaloosa and its name. The historian Alvin M. Josephy, Jr., is not convinced that the Nez Perce bred the Appaloosa as such, though he notes early references to spotted horses among the tribe.[3] Some dictionaries regard the etymology of *Appaloosa* as unknown. But historians of the horse, along with other authorities, trace the name to the 140-mile-long Palouse River of Idaho and Washington that bordered Nez Perce lands. This river was named after the Palouse Indians, also superb horsemen. The region was ideal for horse breeding, with sheltered valleys for winter pasture and highlands for summer grazing.

The Nez Perce came to grief when the settler population started pressing upon their reservation in the 1860s. In 1877, Chief Joseph tried to negotiate a government order that the tribe move to a reservation in Idaho. An inevitable clash broke out, and Joseph led his people in a brilliant retreat from U.S. troops a thousand miles through Idaho, Washington, and Montana. At last forced to surrender, he made his famous vow that: "From here where the sun now stands I will fight no more forever."

Among the losses of the defeated Nez Perce were eleven hundred horses that had survived the war. These were sold and dispersed throughout the West as a way of confining the tribe to its reservation. "The loss of horses was like the loss of a good friend," said a Nez Perce in the 1990s. "It's similar to taking away our braids, our strength."[4]

Partly because of their distinctive markings, Appaloosas became a favorite in circuses and Wild West shows. But mixed breeding diluted their characteristics, including the famed spots. In 1937, however, interest in the breed began reviving. The following year saw the establishment of the Appaloosa Horse Club, devoted to the keeping of records and to standardizing the breed. In the 1990s, club membership had risen to thirty thousand.

Meanwhile, the Nez Perce looked back to their days as leading horse breeders. The Department of Health and Human Services began a program of "culturally appropriate" development among reservations across the country. Aided by a private organization, it financed the crossing of Appaloosas with the akhal-teke of central Asia. "The idea is to blend the Appaloosa's blocky, muscular traits as well as the distinctive 'blanket' — spots on the rump — to the slim and elegant akhal-teke horse of Turkmenistan," wrote Jim Robbins of the *New York Times* in 1996. The latter horse is believed to resemble those that the Spanish brought to North America and that migrated northward to give rise to the early Appaloosa. The resulting modern cross is called the Nez Perce horse. A Young Horseman's program trains Nez Perce youth aged thirteen to twenty-one in horse tradition and the skills needed for cattle roundups and tourist trail rides.

The word *appaloosa* has been applied to other than horses. The appaloosa bean can be bought in supermarkets as well as at specialty seed suppliers. This bean goes well with chili and makes a delicious bean soup. Its name apparently comes from the black and brown mottling it exhibits.[5]

CAYUSE
'A rough-haired, uncouth brute'

Hundreds of whites excitedly joined the Cayuse Indians of northeast Oregon for a high-stakes horse race in the spring of 1867. The racecourse ran two and a half miles through the Umatilla Reservation, where the Cayuse lived, parallel to a range of grassy hills. On the appointed day, people arrived on horseback and in carriages, buggies, and wagons. Indians wore their finery, with feathers and red blankets. White males milled around in dress coats, vests, and porkpie hats.

The two competing horses were a steed belonging to Cayuse chief Howlish Wampo and a thoroughbred brought in for the occasion. Large bets of twenty-dollar gold pieces, horses, and hardware such as pistols and saddles heavily favored the thoroughbred. Indians apparently had to be goaded into risking bets on the local horse. One look at the thoroughbred told why:

Cayuse
a cayuse horse and Spokane Indian rider

His thin nostrils, pointed ears, and arched neck, sleek coat, and polished limbs, that touched the ground with burnished steel, disdaining to stand still; while his gayly-dressed rider, with white pants tucked into boots embellished with silver-plated spurs, on his head a blue cap, and with crimson jacket, was being mounted, requiring two or three experts to assist, so restless was this fine thoroughbred.

Meanwhile the Cayuse horse "stood with head down, a rough-haired, uncouth brute, that appeared to be a cross between ox and horse." A hair rope served as his bridle. His rider was a gaunt, half-naked Indian youth with close-cropped head.[1]

Furthermore, Joe Crabb, the thoroughbred's owner, had furtively taken what appeared to be the Cayuse horse on a test gallop the night before. He wanted to confirm that he was betting on a sure thing. But Crabb didn't know that Howlish Wampo had placed the half-brother of the horse — like him in every respect except speed — where he suspected that Crabb would have someone go to "borrow" him.

At the call of "Ready-Go!" the competing horses tore down the track, the crowd yelling and screaming encouragement. The Cayuse horse lunged to a twenty-foot head start, lengthened his lead steadily, and ten minutes later pounded back down the homestretch well ahead.

Howlish Wampo took his victory imperturbably. He gave Crabb back the saddle horse he had won from him, as well as money to travel on. Then he added a warning about riding a competitor's horse on the sly. "You did not know how to make my horse run," the chief drily observed. "Cla-hoy-um, Crabb." (Goodbye, Crabb.)[2]

The tough Western range horse called the *cayuse* inherited its name from the Indians whose fate for a century was linked to the animal. The Cayuse originally called themselves *Waiilatpu,* "Superior People." French traders, however, referred to them as *Cailloux,* "People of the Rocks," because of the terrain in which they lived. The nickname evolved in pronunciation and spelling to its present form.

The Cayuse acquired horses sometime before 1750. The tribe had been living obscurely near the John Day River, a tributary of the Columbia, fishing, hunting, and gathering edible plants. Horses changed that. The tribesmen began thundering out of their native lands to dominate peoples living north of them along the Columbia River. They soon controlled trade in the bountiful region between the Cascades and the Rocky Mountains. They launched raids as far away as northern California, seeking women and children as slaves and looking for still more horses to enlarge their herds.

Their mount, its name shortened from "Cayuse Indian horse," was descended from Spanish horses introduced to Indians around 1600. These horses had gradually spread from tribe to tribe over much of North America. In many cases the animals revolutionized Indian life, especially among the Plains Indians, where horses fostered nomadic living and the efficient hunting of buffalo. A representative of that stock, the cayuse looked unprepossessing — often small and of varying color. But it was fast and hardy enough to stand up under the rigorous demands of Indian owners.

Status among the Cayuse depended on the number of horses owned. Tribal leaders kept as many as two thousand cayuse apiece. It was not unusual for an individual to own fifteen or twenty. Their upkeep was not costly: as range animals, they were turned loose at night to graze in the lush meadows of Cayuse country. The owners regarded their horses with pride, trained them with kindness, and rarely sold a favorite. The horses sometimes became so tame that they could be trusted to carry little children gently, and they liked to be petted.

The migration of whites into the Northwest, however, proved disastrous for rider and then horse. Trouble first broke out over the work of the Reverend Marcus Whitman. An epidemic of measles that began among Indian children at a mission school he ran apparently made the Cayuse deeply suspicious. In 1847, some tribesmen slew Whitman, his wife, and a dozen others. White militia retaliated, killing innocent Indians. An uneasy peace descended after the alleged killers of the Whitmans were hanged. But continuing hostilities led to further defeats of the Cayuse, and the government opened up their lands to white settlement. Surviving Cayuse (also ravaged by white diseases) scattered, a number settling with the Umatilla tribe and eventually losing their unique language.

The Cayuse Indians by Robert H. Ruby and John A. Brown describes the accompanying decline of the Cayuse horse, which was less useful on the spreading farms than was the American workhorse. A cayuse that had sold for thirty to sixty dollars in the early 1860s was worth only five dollars in 1875. Some of the horses were slaughtered for dog food; others were shipped to Chicago, where they hauled streetcars. Only a dwindling remnant lingered in the shrinking rangelands of the West.[3]

Yet their legend endures. "Seldom has the name of a people so numerically small contributed so much to a regional or national lexicon," note Ruby and Brown of the Cayuse Indians. *Cayuse* names a town in Oregon, a cold east wind blowing along the Columbia River, a pass in the Cascade Mountains, a rodeo in the Northwest, and a helicopter in the Vietnam War. But it is the horse called cayuse that most truly represents the spirit and tragic history of the "imperial tribesmen of old Oregon."[4]

ARTIFACTS

For many Indians, no tool carried more symbolic weight than the Algonquian-named *tomahawk*. A number of tribes displayed or sent around a tomahawk when threatening to go on the warpath; and they literally buried the tomahawk ("buried the hatchet") as a sign of peace. *Wampum,* with a Massachusett name, could be fashioned into belts that symbolized friendship or peace. Both are examined in this section, which covers artifacts often regarded as emblematic of Native Americans.

Another tradition-laden Indian artifact is the canoe, with a name from the Arawak people of the West Indies — the first Indians Columbus encountered. They hollowed out dugouts large enough to convey fifty people up rivers and along the coastline. Other large ocean-going dugouts carried Indians of the Pacific Northwest on their fishing and trading expeditions. Smaller dugouts appeared elsewhere in Indian North America.

"The canoe is really the closest thing Canada has to a national symbol," claims John Jennings of the Canadian Canoe Museum in Peterborough, Ontario. North American Indians paddled birch-bark canoes that carried as many as thirty people throughout the continent's innumerable rivers and streams. Later, trappers and explorers adopted the light but durable boat for expeditions that opened the continent for settlers.[1]

This section will examine the *kayak*, the canoe devised and named by the Eskimo. Kayaks were once a survival tool of people in the Far North. Today the boat enjoys worldwide popularity for recreation and sport. Millions of outdoors enthusiasts use kayaks to enjoy the natural beauty of inland waters and the sea coast.

The *toboggan* is another Native American artifact still bearing its original name. It has become a sport vehicle widely enjoyed in North America and abroad. And the bobsled, an offshoot, is featured in an Olympic sport.

TOMAHAWK
From ax to missile

The tomahawk was a major tool and weapon among Indians of the East coast and much of the West. Its name is often cited as derived from Virginia Algonquian *tamahaac,* although forms of the name occur in a number of Algonquian languages. The original root has been conjectured to be from early Algonquian *temah-,* "to cut off by tool."

By the time Europeans arrived, the tomahawk had taken a variety of forms. All employed a handle, which greatly improved their effectiveness over a primitive hand ax or unmounted stone tool with a sharpened edge. Some had a head of deer antler or rounded stone (the latter called a *pogamoggan*). Others, more hatchetlike, had a bladed stone head. This blade required a substantial effort to fashion — hours or days, compared to the minutes needed to make an arrowhead or spear point. The artisan first selected a piece of dense rock such as basalt (traprock) of approximately the desired form. He then painstakingly used a hammer stone to peck the rock into shape, polishing and sharpening it as desired.

The hatchets that Europeans brought with them partially replaced traditional tomahawks. Whites also started producing metal-headed tomahawks that had more cutting (though less crushing) power. One that was especially prized was the pipe tomahawk, with a hollow handle and a pipe bowl at the head opposite the blade. This dual-purpose tomahawk became a popular trade item.

Whites pushing westward encountered a variety of tomahawks and war clubs, some obviously obtained through trade. During his expedition through North Dakota in the 1830s, Prince

Maximilian of Wied found a considerable assortment among the Mandan and Hidatsa. He noted the pogamoggan, small iron types, a large club with a broad iron point, and a wooden club with knots like barbs. When the artist George Catlin was a boy in early nineteenth-century Pennsylvania, he saw an Indian demonstrate the hurling of a tomahawk. The Indian sent the weapon revolving through the air into a distant tree. He repeated this feat more than twenty times, never missing his target.[1]

In battle, the tomahawk inspired dread. Warriors could sometimes dodge an arrow, and a wound from one was rarely fatal. A blow from a tomahawk, however — wielded or thrown — tended to be devastating.

The effectiveness of the tomahawk as a weapon gave weight to its ceremonial and symbolic associations. The Delaware held a special dance before going to war in which warriors brandished their weapons. A chief led the dance, singing of his and his ancestors' warlike deeds. As he finished each telling, he smashed his tomahawk into a post. Each of the other warriors did their singing and hacked the post with *their* tomahawks. Among the Shawnee, a tribe that decided on war invited other tribes to join it by sending out a tomahawk painted with red clay.

But if raising the tomahawk could mean war, burying it meant the opposite. In 1680, fear of renewed Indian attacks after King Philip's War (1675–76) prompted negotiations between a Massachusetts major and a Mohawk chief to keep Mohawk war parties from venturing east of the Hudson River. We are told that "meeting wth ye Sachem the[y] came to an agree^t and buried two axes in ye Ground; one for English and another for y^{m}selves: which ceremony to them is more significant than all Articles of Peace the Hatchet being a principal weapon with y^m." This widespread custom led to the enduring expression "to bury the hatchet."[2]

In late Stone-Age Europe, the ax had similar deep significance. "The stone axe, symbol of life and death, was central to the activities," according to Aubrey Burl, the authority on megalithic Europe. Builders of ancient European stone circles buried actual ax heads, of volcanic rock and sometimes jade, at key points of their structures. They carved the sacred ax on their circles, and several of these carvings can be seen at Stonehenge.[3]

Today the tomahawk persists in altered forms. In the 1990s, promoters of the Atlanta Braves baseball team cast about for an item that would help fans express their loyalty to the team. They came up with a foam-rubber tomahawk that the fans could wave at games. More than one hundred thousand were quickly sold in the Atlanta area at a price of five to seven dollars. These were used in the "Tomahawk Chop," a gesture in which as many as fifty thousand people flourished the toys during games.

Not everyone was entertained by the gesture. Aaron Two Elk, a regional director of the American Indian Movement, characterized the Chop as "dehumanizing, derogatory, and very unethical." A spokesperson of the Concerned American Indian Parents said: "It hurts to see these white boys in the bleachers singing and chanting like that." Indians protested outside the Atlanta stadium, but the Chop went on.[4]

A more serious recasting of the tomahawk has been as the Tomahawk cruise missile. This weapon costs $1.1 million and is about twenty feet long. It can fly a programmed route of 800 miles, precisely avoiding objects such as oil-well platforms and populated islands, before demolishing a target. The missile played a powerful role in the Persian Gulf War of 1991, against Iraq in 1996 and 1998, and against Yugoslavia in 1999 — a high-tech weapon with the name of one far older, but just as fearsome in its day.

WAMPUM
Beaded archives

In 1989, the state of New York agreed to return twelve wampum belts to the Onondaga Nation. The belts of purple-and-white shell beads represented a treasure beyond price to the Onondaga. "These belts are our archives," said tribal spokesman Raymond Gonyea. "That's why we have been trying to get them back."

The Hiawatha Belt, named after the famed messenger of peace who lived in the 1500s, is considered the most important. It measures eleven inches wide by twenty-five inches long. Its design shows a white tree flanked by two white squares on either side against a purple background — representing the Iroquois Confederacy. "The negative background is trying to say we must think of the dark times before the Peace Maker [Deganawida] came, times of war, death, and suffering," explained Mr. Gonyea. "The tree in the middle represents the Onondagas and peace. The two white squares on each side represent geographically from left to right the Seneca, Cayuga, Oneida, and Mohawk, tied together by white beads. It shows they are independent but tied together, just like the Federal Government of the United States and the states," he said. "It's the same tradition, but we had it first."[1]

Indians in far-flung parts of North America made artifacts of mollusk shell beads, but those of the Atlantic coast and from around the Great Lakes were the leading makers of wampum. The word comes from Massachusett *wampan*, white + *api*, string + *-ag* (plural suffix). William Bradford of Plymouth Colony first recorded it in 1628. He commented: "But that which turned most to their [the Dutch] profite, in time, was an entrance into the trade of Wampampeake."[2] Subsequently, the word was often shortened to *wampum* or *peag* (also *peage*).

Two colors of shells went into the making of wampum. The white came from periwinkles or whelks. The dark, usually twice as valuable as the white, came from the purple spot in quahogs (which see). The hard work of fashioning the beads seems to have fallen to women. They broke up the shells into small pieces. Then they ground them into shape by rubbing them against a stone, with sand as an abrasive. Using a pointed stone or a stick, they painstakingly drilled a hole through each bead. A final polishing gave wampum its gloss.

Indians used wampum for adornment. They made armlets and necklaces out of it. Women twined strings of wampum about their hair. Wampum was threaded into robes and caps. The most luxurious and significant use of wampum came in the belts — first made in the early seventeenth century — reserved for high officials. These were worn around the waist or draped over the shoulder. A belt commonly included twelve rows of 180 beads each, but the largest belts sometimes included up to ten thousand beads. Often such a belt would consist of alternating white or purple rows, but a belt might display a complex array of symbolic figures and designs. According to Benjamin Church, a captain in King Philip's War, one of Philip's royal belts was "nine inches broad, wrought with black [dark purple] and white *Wompom,* in various figures and flowers, and pictures of many birds and beasts."[3]

As with the Hiawatha Belt, wampum could convey a message. In the simplest form, a string of wampum beads attached to a stick might be sent from village to village inviting sachems to a council. Notches on the stick indicated the number of days before the event. Special belts accompanied religious ceremonies or affirmed pledges and treaties. The Penn Treaty Belt, given to William Penn by the Delaware Indians in about 1682, displays two people holding hands in confirmation of lasting friendship between Indians and whites.

Not the least important role of wampum was as tribal archives. Sachems kept wampum belts to help recollect a tribe's history. Younger members of the tribe were schooled in the belts' meanings so that they too could pass on their traditions. Such wampum was invaluable: Loss of these beaded archives could mean loss of the past.

Before the arrival of settlers, Indians sometimes used surplus wampum in barter. Coastal tribes, with an unlimited supply of shells, traded wampum to inland peoples for animal hides and the like. Upon their arrival in New York, the Dutch seized on wampum as a means of exchange — a kind of money. In this, they were encouraged by the amount of wampum available on shell-rich Long Island.

The Dutch traded European goods to the Indians for wampum, then used it to buy furs from other Indians. To increase wampum output, the Dutch provided the Indians with metal drills and other labor-saving tools. Plymouth and Massachusetts followed the example of the Dutch in adopting wampum to boost trade with Indians. Starting in the 1630s, William Pynchon of Springfield, Massachusetts, acquired large stores of wampum beads and set up a shop where women and children strung the beads. In six years, he had bought and sold nine thousand beaver skins, to amass the largest fortune in his part of the Connecticut Valley.

Short of hard currency, Massachusetts made wampum legal tender in 1637 for sums under twelve pence. Connecticut did the same for any amount. Authorities soon had to crack down on dealers who tried to circulate beads of wood or inferior shells or crudely fashioned strands of wampum. The decrease in the number of beaver in the Northeast, together with new supplies of coins, led to the end of wampum as official currency in Massachusetts in 1661 and in other colonies soon after. Yet backwoods settlers continued using wampum among themselves long afterward.

An outgrowth of wampum money was the rise of several factories with machines to produce shell beads. Campbell's wampum factory opened for business in Pascack, New Jersey, in 1735. Some of its product would go to the Continental Army, but Campbell wampum went mainly to fur traders and U.S. Army forces in the West. The factory's shells came from Long Island and Fulton's Fish Market, as well as from trading ships that used West Indian shells for ballast. This curious enterprise survived until the end of the nineteenth century.

The fragility of strung beads and the dispersal of Indian treasures have made examples of early wampum rare. Only a few Indian groups, such as the Onondagas, retain their hereditary wampum belts. The word *wampum* is now also commonly used in the sense it acquired after the Europeans arrived — as a synonym for money.

KAYAK
Eskimo boat

Jonathan Waterman and his wife felt bored with their comfortable lives, so they decided to remove themselves "so far from the refrigerator and the couch and the television that we will surprise ourselves with the verity of nerve endings and remnant instincts . . . to find adventure without guides, and in a place where we might glimpse the world not only as the world used to be, but as the world should remain." So Waterman recalled in *Kayaking the Vermilion Sea* (1995). The voyage of a million paddle strokes (their count) along the sparkling coast of Baja California did turn into an adventure such as kayakers throughout the world are enjoying today.[1]

For the Eskimo, the kayak was a necessary tool for surviving in the Far North. The traditional kayak (Eskimo *qajaq*) consisted of a light, skin-covered wooden frame about twenty feet long and less than two feet wide. Delicate in appearance, it could endure rough weather, including gales. Some Eskimo, such as the Copper Inuit, navigated kayaks through inland waterways, but most used kayaks to venture into the sea to hunt animals such as seals, sea lions, and even whales. For a man's family, his skill at handling a kayak and hunting from it made the crucial difference between hunger and sufficiency. An accomplished kayak hunter enjoyed high prestige. The people of Kodiak Island, for example, had an elite secret society of successful whalers.

A burial cave in the Aleutian Islands excavated in 1990 yielded the remains of a kayak probably more than nine hundred years old and its pilot, who had two paddles wrapped with him. But experts on the kayak believe that the vessel was developed over thousands of years. Its basic design prevailed across much of the

Arctic, although with interesting variations, such as the needle-nose prow of the Copper Inuit kayak and the split prow of the Aleut craft. Another skin-covered Eskimo and Aleut boat was the umiak (Eskimo *umiaq*), an open boat.

Eskimo and Aleut boys learned early to handle kayaks. (In the case of a shortage of males, girls might also be taught.) A young East Greenland boy began by hunting animals on land and ice. At twelve, he received a kayak and started training to hunt at sea — a complex activity that required maneuvering the craft, making a kill, and recovering the prey.

The hazards of sea kayaking were many and often fatal. Not the least of these was capsizing. Kayakers of West Alaska and Greenland learned the "Eskimo roll," in which an overturned person used his paddle to revolve to an upright position. This was made possible by a waterproof parka secured around the face and wrists and buttoned to the manhole rim, joining man and boat into "a single waterproof unit," says one authority. Loss of a paddle also could bring death to the lone kayaker. It is no wonder that kayakers in Greenland sometimes developed what has been called "kayak angst." The onset of this phobia would come on a calm day as the kayaker gazed into a glassy sea that reflected the sky and allowed the kayak's shadow to appear in the water. A victim would become disoriented, lose control of himself, panic, and feel nauseated. Failure to overcome this malaise would force the hunter to abandon kayaking and accept a demeaning role in his community as a fisher or shellfish gatherer.[2]

Europeans learned of the kayak in the late Middle Ages. Starting in the 1420s, several reports describe little men washed onto the coasts of Scotland and Norway with their skin boats. Some of the boats were preserved in churches and public halls as curiosities. But not until 1865 did John MacGregor build his kayak *Rob Roy*, which he called a canoe, a usage still common in Great Britain. MacGregor toured Europe's waterways in his craft and inspired others to build their own. Soon kayak races began being held regularly in Europe. Non-Eskimo Americans adopted the kayak, using it to explore the streams and rivers of North America as well as its coastline. In 1936, kayak racing won world recognition as an Olympic event.

Improved technology has made the kayak available to greater numbers of enthusiasts. The Germans invented a collapsible kayak with a rubberized fabric skin. Fiberglass-hulled kayaks became available in the 1950s. Polyethylene plastic hulls were another breakthrough for the production of sturdy, affordable kayaks. Kevlar, the synthetic fiber used in bullet-proof vests, added another dimension to kayak construction.

The result has been a sharp rise in kayaking, especially in North America. Some enthusiasts run races in slalom kayaks. Others ply lakes and rivers in recreational touring boats. The more daring seek turbulent rapids of the West to test wildwater kayaks. Some among the most expert have traveled the entire navigable length of the Mississippi as well as the Nile and the Danube.

Sea kayaking is easier, say some, and more popular. Between 1989 and 1991 the sale of sea kayaks doubled in the United States. In 1995, the executive director of the Trade Association of Sea Kayaking (TASK) reported that he was hearing from five to ten new companies every month involved with sea-kayak equipment, training, or tours.

How do the modern kayaks compare with the Eskimo originals? European explorers have said that Aleut kayaks (also called by the Russian name *baidarka*) could maintain a speed of ten miles per hour, a rate modern kayaks reach only in sprints. George Dyson, world-renowned kayak expert, believes that ancient makers of the vessels might have evolved kayak designs that could be adapted to improve modern versions. Dyson wonders whether the subtle curvature of the traditional hull might facilitate waterflow in a way superior to that of modern hulls. The traditional flexible skin covering, Dyson also notes, might increase speed and cause less drag than the more rigid skins of the modern craft.

Ironically, the Eskimo use of kayaks has declined sharply as people elsewhere have adopted the craft. Greenland seems to be the last stronghold of the traditional hunter's kayak. There Eskimo find that a silent kayak does not scare away seals as a motorboat does.

TOBOGGAN

Down the chute!

During the Great Depression, the inhabitants of Camden, Maine, sought to boost the economy of their coastal town — rich in scenery but poor in dollars. They decided to put snow, a natural resource of which they had plenty in winter, to work. Town leaders in 1936 called for volunteers to make Camden the winter sports capital of New England. They advertised:

> Thin men, fat men, young or old,
> Weak men, strong men, timid or bold,
> Are earnestly asked. Bring ax and respond
> To a brush clearing bee, Sunday, at Hosmer Pond.

More than a hundred people labored for twenty Sundays in a row to create the Camden Snow Bowl. They not only cleared brush but hauled tons of wood and stone to build a ski lodge and skating house. The centerpiece of their efforts was a 440-foot toboggan chute — New England's longest. Events offered the following year included figure skating, ski races, and, of course, tobogganing.

toboggan

Gradually, over the years, the chute fell into disrepair. But in 1990, a call went out once again for volunteers to restore the monumental slide. The next year, thousands of tobogganers were hurtling down it at thirty miles an hour or more, screaming with terror and delight. Today the Camden Snow Bowl is host of the annual U.S. National Toboggan Championships.[1]

The tobogganers ride one of North America's most ancient vehicles (though sleds of various sorts had been developed earlier in the world's northern regions). *Toboggan* comes through Canadian French from an Algonquian word akin to Micmac *tobâgun,* meaning drag made of skin. The Micmac toboggan measured six to eight feet long and a foot and a half to two feet wide. It was usually made of a thin rock-maple or beech slab curled up in front. A missionary who lived with the Micmac in the nineteenth century described its performance:

> The whole forms a light, convenient, yielding, yet strong sledge for a conveyance through the woods. Such sledges are especially adapted for hunting on snow-shoes, as they readily yield to the uneven surface, slipping over the snow and windfalls; and even if they capsize, they sustain no injury, — the load, being bound on, can be readily righted.[2]

Not until modern times, however, did some other northern Indians acquire the toboggan. The Kutchin Indians of Alaska traditionally used sleds, turned up at both ends, to haul gear and game. Then the Hudson's Bay Company brought in the toboggan around the beginning of the nineteenth century. This more efficient vehicle replaced the sled. Today the Kutchin traverse forests with toboggans pulled by dogs — or "iron-dog" snowmobiles.

Toboggans proved valuable to early Euroamerican settlers, trappers, traders, and others. In the early nineteenth century, the vehicles became popular for sport as well. An English visitor to Quebec during the 1840s described a toboggan party, complete with a picnic of sandwiches and champagne served while the party sat on buffalo robes. Everyone, he said, was "in high glee" despite subzero weather.[3]

Writing in 1902, the scholar Alexander F. Chamberlain noted the popularity of tobogganing and the development of expressions associated with the sport:

> Since *tobogganing* has come so much into favor as a winter
> sport, *toboggan*-clubs with their *toboggan*-slides (artificial hills)
> exist over all suitable regions of Canada and the United States,
> while the *tobogganist* in his quaint costume, smacking of the
> *voyageur* and the Indian, is a common figure at social events of
> the winter season.[4]

Sport tobogganing remained in vogue until the 1930s, when
skiing came to the forefront. Many village chutes — once the
scene of youthful merriment — rotted away amid invading trees.
Still the toboggan continued, to a lesser extent, to be ridden for
sport, and it never ceased to serve as a utility vehicle at ski resorts
and the like.

Over this period, though, an offshoot of the toboggan was also
gaining favor. In the late nineteenth century, some tobogganers
joined two sleds together and fixed runners under them to make
the bobsled, or bobsleigh. The turns of runs were banked to increase the sled's speed. The new vehicle was first launched in Al-
bany, New York, or St. Moritz, Switzerland, depending on the authority one consults. In any case, organized bobsled competition
began in Switzerland around 1900. The new sport grew steadily.
Today two- and four-person bobsledding is an Olympic sport. In
the four-person event, helmeted crew members act as a highly
synchronized team: They rush their massive sled forward, then
pile aboard as it gains momentum. They lean together, or bob, on
turns as they hurtle downward.

A bobsled must be fast enough to challenge its streamlined
competition yet rugged enough to withstand violent twisting on
icy tracks. Made of steel, aluminum, and high-tech materials,
a competition bobsled can cost $750,000 or more. Speeds of
close to 100 miles an hour make bobsledding both exciting and
dangerous.

The traditional toboggan, still useful and a source of winter
fun in its basically original form, has also spawned modern sports
that technology is pushing to ever more breathtaking speeds.

NORTHWEST COAST

Several words already examined come from the spectacularly beautiful region reaching from northern California to southeastern Alaska. Among them are the names of several kinds of salmon and shellfish. (See Section 7, **Fish and Seafood.**) Not surprisingly in an area so varied in geography and so rich in wildlife, enterprising native people there contributed a number of additional words to English.

The *Chinook Jargon,* a trade language that developed in the area around the mouth of the Columbia River, has been especially fertile in its verbal contributions. *Chinook* itself designates a licoricelike plant and numerous places and commercial products — along with chinook salmon (which see) and *Chinook wind,* covered in this section. English is further indebted to the jargon for *potlatch* and *high-muck-a-muck,* examined here, and other words.

On a darker note, this section will also discuss *hooch,* from the Tlingit language.

CHINOOK
Money talks

"Chinook Jargon Project" read the sign on an office door in the early 1990s at British Columbia's University of Victoria. Inside, the linguist Barbara Harris was examining files that included dictionaries compiled by nineteenth-century traders, yellowed newspapers, a letter from a convict seeking a pen pal, and assorted papers of families who lived in the region. She learned that the

Pacific Northwest trade language she was studying still showed some vitality, and that a few people continued to use it. This was in addition to about thirty borrowed Chinook Jargon words that have become a living part of the English language.

Chinook Jargon is the language that developed around the great trading mart where the Columbia River meets the Pacific Ocean. The dominant people in that region for centuries were the Chinook (Lower Chinook, to be specific). Their location cast them in the role of middlemen among inland tribes, coastal peoples, and traders from overseas. Their name comes from the Salishan village name *ts'inúk*. In 1805, members of the Lewis and Clark Expedition discovered them living in spacious cedar houses with plank floors and bunklike cubicles along the walls, which were also decorated with large, masklike sculptures.

The explorers were put off by the sloping foreheads of some Chinook, deformed to show high status. But this peculiarity did not lessen the skill native traders showed in driving hard bargains with the many people who came to trade with them. In 1792, several British and American ships had opened up international connections for the Chinook that would radically change the lives of a people numbering less than a thousand. (About 16,000 people at the time are estimated to have been Chinookan *speakers*.)

The Chinook had initially prospered from the runs up the Columbia that millions of salmon undertook several times a year. The fish included chinook, sockeye, coho (silver), and chum (dog) salmon. Chinook traded their surplus fish, typically dried and in sacks, to other tribes. A further valuable item they offered was the tapering dentalium shell harvested from the sea, a prized ornament and the leading medium of exchange on the Northwest coast.

This trade attracted a cornucopia of products from far-flung regions. Nearer inland tribes, says the geographer James R. Gibson, brought "mountain sheep horn, buffalo robes, rabbitskin robes, jade celts, obsidian blades, native tobacco, baskets, horses, and slaves." More remote tribes sent skins of moose, deer, and ermine. California Indians furnished abalone shell, obsidian blades, and more slaves.[1] The Europeans and Euroamericans added iron tools, copper kettles, guns, bolts of cloth, blankets, clothing, buttons, and strings of beads.

In the late 1820s, the overseas traders brought with them something less welcome. It was called the "Cold Sick," and it gave its victims fever, chills, and stomach upsets before usually killing them. Besides this plague came venereal diseases, smallpox, and other exotic diseases introduced by outsiders. Alcohol took a deadly toll as well. By about mid-century, the number of Chinook had dropped to fewer than a hundred survivors.

Meanwhile, traders cut deals with them in a language they all shared. Chinook Jargon is actually a pidgin — a simplified tongue with vocabulary derived from several languages. It lacked verb tenses and noun cases and employed only one preposition. The approximately two thousand Chinook Jargon words mostly originated from Nootka (an Indian language of Washington and British Columbia), Chinook, French, and English. Added to them were onomatopoetic words such as *hehe* for "laugh" or "ridicule" and *tumtum* for "heart." Despite its primitive look, the Chinook Jargon facilitated business transactions and became an all-purpose means of communication for about one hundred thousand people.

From their pidgin and native languages, the Chinook have contributed a surprisingly large number of words to English. Among them are several for edible plants: *camas* (member of the lily family), *salal* (a small shrub with purple berries), and *wapatoo* (a marsh plant with egg-sized tubers). Among the names for edible fish are *chum salmon* (also known as *dog salmon*) and *eulachon* (also called *candlefish*).

The cultural impact of the Chinook is further evidenced by the canoe, licoricelike plant, Army helicopter, towns and other places, and business enterprises that bear their name.

CHINOOK WIND
Snow eater

The warm wind, or *chinook*, that blows eastward from the Rocky Mountains is the stuff legends are made of. One tells of a cowboy in the nineteenth century who reached Calgary, Canada, during a blizzard. He hitched his horse to a post and went into a bar for a drink that stretched into several more. As the tale goes, when he at last came out, he was amazed to see that the snow had melted, his hitching post turned out to be a church steeple, and his horse was dangling from it.

Another legend has it that in the distant past a maiden strayed from her Sarsi tribe into the Rocky Mountains. She wanders still, and the chinook is said to be her warm breath as she searches endlessly for her family.

The literal truth about one of the two winds called chinook is practically as strange as the legends it has inspired. The first chinook is a warm, moist wind that flows northward along the Oregon coast — and is so named because it seems to arise where the Chinook Indians live. (See **Chinook** for the background of those Indians.) At some point, apparently, another, more spectacular wind became confused with it.

This second chinook produces the startling effects that the legends imply. It is caused by Pacific winds blowing over the Rocky Mountains and losing much of their moisture through condensation as they do. This process warms them, and they become still warmer and drier through compression while descending the eastern slopes. The resulting chinook is a kind of *foehn*, named after the winds blowing over the Alps and carrying blasts of hot, dry air into parts of southern Europe.

The chinook from the Rocky Mountains brings a respite from the numbing cold and blizzards that winter northers send cascading onto the Great Plains. On January 22, 1843, the temperature at Spearfish, South Dakota, soared from minus four degrees Fahrenheit at 7:30 A.M. to (plus) forty-five degrees Fahrenheit at

7:32 A.M. In the winter, such rapid increases in temperature melt snow so abruptly that the chinook is widely known as the "snow eater." Sometimes the snow disappears by a process known as sublimation — passing from a solid directly into vapor.

Chinooks may blast the eastern Rocky Mountain landscape at any time of the year, but their primarily winter appearances are the most memorable. It is said that around Calgary, for example, there are about twenty to twenty-five chinook days between November and February. Those days raise Calgary's mean winter temperature well above "chinookless" cities of similar latitude.

The impact of this wind on the Indians can be gauged from a Blackfoot (Siksika) legend, "The Bear Who Stole the Chinook." It seems that the Indians waited and waited one winter for a chinook to relieve them of constant blizzards that drove away game so that hunters returned home empty-handed. Everyone was hungry, and little children cried for food. A poor orphan boy befriended by animals decided to do something about the calamity. He heard that a great bear had captured the chinook to keep itself warm, so the boy and his animal friends went into the mountains and finally located the bear's den. They put the bear to sleep with medicine smoke and opened up its huge elkskin bag to release the chinook. The story concludes:

> The Bear woke up, and came roaring out of his lodge, and the friends fled. But the bear could never recapture the Chinook, and, ever since then, bears have slept all winter. . . . [T]he snow can be deep, and the cold bitter, but, in a short while, the Chinook will come blowing over the mountains, and everyone is happy again.[1]

The career of Charles M. Russell, cowboy and painter, helps illustrate the modern impact of this peculiar wind. In the winter of 1886, Russell was herding cattle for a company in Montana when the region experienced the worst snowstorm in its history. Many cattle died, and Russell's employers asked for an explanation. In reply, he painted a picture of a gaunt steer surrounded by wolves, some on their haunches and others circling impatiently. He called the painting *Waiting for a Chinook*, with the subtitle "The Last of 5000." Russell's powerful painting made him famous, and he became known as the "cowboy artist" for his renderings of the Old West in paintings and sculptures.

Chinooks have saved the lives of countless numbers of cattle and thereby the livelihood of their owners. Range animals facing death from hunger and crippling cold may enjoy an astonishing recovery under the "snow eater's" influence. Early in the twentieth century, a cowboy in Kip, Montana, observed great herds of cattle stumbling pathetically over the range in search of food and shelter during a harsh winter. Then he saw a characteristic wall of dark clouds gather over the mountains. In his words:

> First, a puff of heat, summer-like in comparison with what had existed for two weeks, and we run to our instrument shelter to observe the temperature. Up goes the mercury, thirty-four degrees in seven minutes. Now the wind has come with a 25-mile velocity. Now the cattle stop traveling, and with muzzles turned toward the wind, low with satisfaction. Weary with two weeks standing on their feet they lie down in the snow, for they know their salvation has come.[2]

The foehn occurs in various parts of the world, but the wind with the Indian name is more powerful and widespread than any other.

POTLATCH
The ultimate party

"Potlatch is one of the top ten terms in anthropology," says a leading anthropologist. This celebration among Indians of the Pacific Northwest marks major events such as a wedding, the naming of a child, the transfer of a rank or privilege, or the mourning of a death. The traditional potlatch is a lavish feast accompanied by the donning of masks and the performance of

potlatch
c. 1895 photograph of potlatch participants, Chilkat, Alaska

dances and other rituals. A sponsor showers guests with gifts that may be worth thousands of dollars, leaving him empty-handed. But he receives in return what has been described as "a mountain of wealth in what people think of him and his family: He has status and prestige."[1]

Central though the potlatch is to much Northwest Indian culture, white contact heightened the ceremony's size and importance. Traders who came for the region's furs, salmon, and timber built trading posts that attracted native settlement. Fort Rupert, established by the Hudson's Bay Company on Vancouver Island in 1849, became the leading Kwakiutl village. Indians of the region enjoyed new prosperity by selling fish and other products to the whites or by working in canneries. These Indians already followed traditions of gift giving on special occasions. Now they had the means to do so on an epic scale — with the famed Hudson's Bay Company blankets as one of the main articles bestowed. Whites started calling the ceremony a *potlatch*, from the Chinook Jargon *patlač*, gift or giving. The word originally came from the Nootka language, where it also meant gift or giving, but not necessarily in a potlatch. Although native groups had their own names for the potlatch, they adopted white usage when talking to outsiders.

The extravagance of the expanded potlatch began alarming Canadian authorities. Some potlatches were two-month festivals during which participants moved from village to village and lived in makeshift shelters, causing people to fall sick and children to miss school. Native women, it was charged, sometimes prostituted themselves to raise the funds needed for the lavish get-togethers. And worst of all from the authorities' point of view, it looked like a wholesale waste of time and money. Canada banned the potlatch in 1885.

Yet the Kwakiutl and others found ways to continue practicing a ceremony basic to their societies and their sense of self-worth. Indians in more remote areas carried on as before, merely keeping a lower profile. Other Indians did their potlatching under the guise of celebrating Christmas and similar holidays. Still others conducted "disjointed potlatches" — dancing in one place, giving gifts in another, and so forth. Authorities enforced the law where they could and turned a blind eye where they couldn't.

Some cases just couldn't be ignored. Dan Cranmer, a Kwakiutl of Alert Bay, British Columbia, threw a potlatch in 1921 that caused a stir at the time and still evokes admiration. During this five-day event, he gave away goods he had received through marriage as well as additional property from his own and from his wife's family. About three hundred guests attended. The larger gifts included twenty-four canoes and four gasoline boats. Cranmer gave the women dresses and shawls, and the young people sweaters and shirts. He threw showers of coins to the little children. There followed stacks of sewing machines, gramophones, gas lights, violins, guitars, household furnishings, and three hundred oak trunks. On the concluding day, he distributed hundreds of three-dollar sacks of flour.

This magnificent gesture won Cranmer fame among his people, but also the critical attention of the Canadian government. Authorities slapped fifty-one of those present with criminal charges. Twenty-two spent two months behind bars, and others received suspended sentences. All had to forswear potlatching and to surrender "potlatch paraphernalia" to the government. Much of the superb artwork given up went to Canadian and U.S. museums, which paid sums the Kwakiutl regarded as inadequate.

Despite native persistence, the potlatch declined during the first half of the twentieth century. The law discouraged some Indians; Christianity emptied the potlatch of meaning for others. Then fishing by outsiders in the 1920s and the depression of the 1930s hurt the region's economy and the ability of Indians to afford large-scale gift giving.

But a 1951 revision of Canada's Indian Act reinvigorated the potlatch. The new law made potlatches legal. Perhaps more important, it encouraged a revival of enthusiasm among Indians for traditional ways. They openly resumed the potlatch as a proud and colorful expression of their heritage. "The potlatch is our central constitution," said Robert Joseph, a chief of the Kwakiutl. "It emphasizes our ties to the spirit world."[2]

Today's potlatch is still evolving. As a concession to jobholders, the event now often takes place on weekends. Although the ceremonies are typically shorter than in earlier times, participants still don outsize masks (some borrowed from museums) and engage in the old songs and bestowing of gifts. Gloria Cranmer, daughter of the famed Dan Cranmer, believes that her ancestors would feel "that under the circumstances, we are not doing too badly."[3]

And the potlatch continues to fascinate non-Indian Canadians and Americans — the general public as well as anthropologists. In the Northwest especially, *potlatch* has come to be a tradition-laden term for any special event or celebration.

HIGH-MUCK-A-MUCK, MUCK-A-MUCK, MUCKETY-MUCK
Big shot

> Our Indians shouted joyfully, "Hi yu salmon! Hi yu muck-a-muck!" while the water about the canoe and beneath the canoe was churned by thousands of fins into silver fire.

So wrote the naturalist John Muir, on an Alaskan expedition in 1880, about salmon swarming upstream to their spawning grounds, The Indians were not calling out a greeting to the fish. They were exclaiming at the abundance of succulent food around them.[1]

Their Chinook Jargon expression, now commonly joined as *high-muck-a-muck,* comes from the Nootka Indian *hayo* ("ten" or "plenty") plus Nootka *mak(a)mak* (the part of whale meat between blubber and flesh). By itself, *muck-a-muck* commonly meant "eat" or "food." Altogether, *high-muck-a-muck* meant "plenty to eat."

For some reason, the word's English meaning shifted to "big shot" or "self-important person." One dictionary suggests that the new meaning may have arisen from the potlatch (which see). To outsiders, this event could have looked simply like bragging.

Mark Twain adopted the extended meaning. Although Twain modestly expressed doubt that he had ever coined words that became part of the English vocabulary, he was a master of the vernacular who gave currency to scores of words and phrases that might otherwise have remained obscure. He used a version of *high-muck-a-muck* in an 1866 letter. Then in *A Connecticut Yankee in King Arthur's Court* (1889), Twain's hero decides to best his enemy Merlin by predicting an eclipse. He exults:

> I want you to get word to the king that I am a magician myself — and the Supreme Grand High-yu-Mucka-muck and head of the tribe, at that.

During the twentieth century, *high-muck-a-muck* has been used freely to put down pompous politicians, but they are not the only ones to feel the sting of the word or one of its variations. On CBS-TV's *Mayflower Madam* in 1987, one heard: "You bust a mucky-muck, you get noticed." In the *New Yorker* (1988), we learned of "an assistant director who's a shameless . . . groveller when the high-muck-a-mucks are in the vicinity."[2]

The unusual look of *high-muck-a-muck* has led to several variant spellings. Rudyard Kipling shortened the word in his *Songs from Books* (1912): "Shaman, Ju-ju or Angekok, Minister, Muk-a-muk." (*Angakok* is the Eskimo word for shaman.) Other variants include: *high-muckety-muck, muckety-muck, muckey-muck,* and *high-monkey-muck.*

HOOCH
Howling drunk

In the 1870s, the naturalist John Muir visited a thriving Hutsnuwu-Tlingit town in southeastern Alaska. He reported that he had never felt more at home than among the kindly people who welcomed him. The next day he canoed to Angoon, an associated Hutsnuwu town. While Muir was half a mile away from the town, he heard howling, yelling, and screaming, accompanied by grunts and groans. The alarmed Muir wanted to turn back, but his guides assured him that the townspeople were only drunk. He cautiously climbed a hill to view a row of houses that had become "a chain of alcoholic volcanoes." After surveying the riotous scene, Muir retreated to his canoe and paddled away with his guides. Later he said he had learned there, at last, the true meaning of "howling drunk."[1]

The spirits that made the Hutsnuwu so intoxicated became widely known by the people's traditional name — commonly rendered *hoochinoo,* from *xucnu·wú* brown bear's fort" in Tlingit. This would later be condensed to *hooch.* The Hutsnuwu had traded furs for imported alcohol until, even more disastrously, they learned to brew their own.

In his short story "To the Man on Trail" (1898), Jack London describes the essence of hooch and its impact. Men preparing Christmas punch in an isolated cabin reminisce:

> "Hain't fergot the *hooch* we-uns made on the Tanana, hev yeh?"
>
> "Well, I guess yes. Boys, it would have done your hearts good to see that whole tribe fighting drunk — and all because of a glorious ferment of sugar and sour dough."[2]

Russians had introduced liquor to Alaska well before these nineteenth-century vignettes. They gave an Aleut a sip of brandy in 1741, which he spat out in disgust. He was typical of other Indians, who at first spurned alcohol — disliking both its taste and its effect. Later Russians tried to limit the alcohol they ladled out to native fur traders — who had acquired a craving for it — so as to keep them under control. Then around 1800, American trading ships began bringing in huge shipments of rum to make quick profits. Traders felt that they could drive harder bargains if the natives were drunk and eager to lay in supplies for further binges.

With the U.S. acquisition of Alaska in 1867, alcohol became a bigger issue in the territory. The United States officially prohibited drinking among Alaskan natives — extending to them laws against Indian drinking in the states. Only the U.S. military was legally allowed to handle alcohol.

Prohibition worked no better in nineteenth-century Alaska than it would in the United States during the 1920s and 1930s. Soldiers supplied liquor freely not only to natives but to others flocking into the territory. In addition, some soldiers taught natives how to make hoochinoo. The dubious honor for this instruction is sometimes given to a soldier named Brown who married a woman of Angoon and settled there with her. No one knows for sure.

The formula for hoochinoo required a few simple pieces of equipment and some readily obtainable ingredients. The still consisted of a vat such as a five-gallon coal-oil can and a six- or seven-foot worm (condensing tube). Ingredients included fermentable matter such as dried fruit, berries, or the liquid that rises to the top of sourdough, plus yeast. To this one added sucrose in the form of candy, sugar, or molasses — the latter being a favorite when available. Fermentation turned the sucrose into alcohol. Boiling condensed the resulting alcoholic liquid into a potent concoction.

An 1879 government report describing the consequences of the brew rose to a level of passion unusual in such writings:

> This is about the most infernal decoction ever invented, producing intoxication, debauchery, insanity, and death. The smell is abominable and the taste atrocious . . . . When the Indians become crazed with this devilish drink, they lose all reason and become raving maniacs, carouse, indulge in the most lascivious and disgusting immoralities, frequently ending in death, murder, and suicide.[3]

It was not only the Indians in Alaska who drank deeply. The drinking of imported liquors as well as hoochinoo was a pastime among all nationalities drawn to the territory for wealth or simply work. Capt. Joseph B. Campbell, U.S. Indian agent who arrived in Sitka in 1874, described the town as a "pandemonium of drunkenness." Miners and others, when not toiling under brutally harsh conditions, found oblivion in saloons. Drunken whites at loose ends were often just as guilty of starting brawls as natives in the same condition.[4]

Foiled in their attempt to end the bootlegging of alcoholic beverages, government officials tried to limit the ingredients that went into hoochinoo. In one three-month period during the 1870s, nearly five thousand gallons of molasses had poured into Sitka. (One gallon of molasses would contribute to the making of three-fourths of a gallon of hoochinoo.) Obviously the great bulk of the sweetener was headed for illicit stills. Officials urged Washington to set curbs on the importation of molasses and sugar, but the attorney general felt that such regulations would not be enforceable. Alcohol, to a large extent hoochinoo, continued to be a rankling problem in the territory.

By 1900 the fame of *hooch* — the word's abbreviated form — had spread well beyond Alaska, and it had become a slang term for any illicitly distilled whiskey. The beginning of Prohibition in 1919 gave still greater currency to the word as Americans began frequenting speakeasies that served bootlegged liquor, or made "bathtub gin" in their homes. "Believe me, we got more houses and hootch-parlors an' all kinds o' dives than any burg in the state," brags George F. Babbitt about his city in Sinclair Lewis's novel *Babbitt* (1922).[5]

Today *hooch* seems to have secured an enduring place in American slang for an inferior or illicit alcoholic beverage — a reminder of the distillers, and their victims, a century ago.

MISCELLANEOUS

Half the thousand borrowed native words come from those Indians speaking Algonquian languages on the East Coast. Many settlers, knowing these Indians first and most familiarly, misapplied their words to more remote Indian peoples. This section begins with several borrowed native words whose acquired meanings would have puzzled the original speakers.

The Algonquian *squaw,* now disreputable, and *papoose* came to be used also of Western Indians with other cultures and languages. *Sachem* and *sagamore,* however, usually (but not always) referred to leaders of the Algonquian speakers with whom the titles originated. The specialized meanings and connotations acquired by *Tammany* and *mugwump* arose in curious ways that say more about the historical times of their adoption than about the Indians themselves. *Kinnikinnick* stays close to its original meaning, with a specialized reference to the bearberry that is a common ingredient in the smoking mixture.

This section concludes with names of two natural watery places of unplumbed mystery — the *bayou* and *muskeg* — in the continent's extreme south and north, respectively. Certain natural places in North America are so majestic or mysterious that Indians and settlers alike viewed them with awe. Their presence dazzled foreign visitors and won the sites international fame. In several cases, their native names became part of the English vocabulary as well. Indians frequented bayous and muskegs with care, celebrated them in legend, and harvested food and raw materials from both. Today their recognized value to the ecology of all North America has heightened the fascination they have long inspired.

SACHEM, SAGAMORE
Chief

"In his person he is a very lusty man, in his best years, (of) an able body, grave of countenance, and spare of speech." So wrote an Englishman in 1622 after meeting Massasoit, the Wampanoag sachem, or chief.[1] The courteous leader wore "a great chain of white bone beads about his neck" but was otherwise dressed in deerskin much like his followers. Massasoit aided the Pilgrims during their time of starvation, attended the first Thanksgiving, and honored his peace treaty with the settlers. The Pilgrims enjoyed similar friendly relations with female Indian leaders known as *Squa Sachems*.

Sachem and the related word *sagamore* (usually a lower-ranking chief) have long occupied an illustrious place in American history. The titles are Algonquian in origin, but they were applied to Indian dignitaries generally in the Northeast. Later, and loosely, they referred to Indian leaders elsewhere in the country.

A sachem typically inherited the title but ruled with the advice of a council and the consensus of tribal members. In *Native People of Southern New England, 1500–1650*, Kathleen J. Bragdon describes the sachem's duties, which included:

> ➤ distributing land and land rights;
> ➤ dealing with representatives of other peoples, native or foreign;
> ➤ dispensing justice, sometimes personally conducting executions;
> ➤ serving as a unifying figure and ceremonial leader.

In return for their services, sachems received many perquisites. Tribute to them included stores of food, quantities of animal hides, properties such as wigwams, and rights to windfalls such as beached whales and drowned deer. Many sachems kept several wives.[2]

The Iroquois government was based on a complex system that sachems administered. A Great Council of the Confederacy met each autumn around a council fire among the Onondaga, attended by fifty sachems from the five original members of the confederacy. These sachems — each appointed by a clan matron from among suitable families — maintained peace and unity in the league. Their skin was supposed to be seven spans (a span equals about nine inches) thick to endure gossip or idle criticism from their constituents. Any league sachems who failed in their duties risked being deposed.

In proposing a union of the American colonies in 1754, Benjamin Franklin cited the Iroquois league (though in a partly demeaning way):

> It would be a strange thing if Six Nations of ignorant savages should be capable of forming a scheme for such an union, and be able to execute it in such a manner as that it has subsisted ages and appears indissoluble; and yet that a like union should be impracticable for ten or a dozen English colonies, to whom it is more necessary and must be more advantageous, and who cannot be supposed to want an equal understanding of their interests.[3]

Euroamericans came to use *sachem* in a figurative way. "The patricians, the sachems, the nabobs, call them by what name you please, sigh, and groan, and fret," John Adams fretted in 1776.[4] Later, the title would be applied ironically to various American political leaders.

The head of each state's "tribe" in the Tammany Society, which adopted Indian terminology, proudly bore the title of Sachem (see **Tammany**). The society exalted the president of the United States as honorary Great Grand Sachem. A Sagamore presided at such important ceremonies as the induction of new members, or braves.

Apart from their original and historical contexts, *sachem* and *sagamore* persist widely as place names. Thus one finds Sachem

Head, Connecticut, on Long Island Sound. This community received its name because Uncas, the Mohegan sachem, slew a Pequot sachem in 1637 and lodged his head in the fork of an oak there. Sagamore Hill, Theodore Roosevelt's home at Oyster Bay, Long Island, is preserved as a national historic site; it was named after Sagamore Mohannis, who had signed away land on which the estate is located. Towns called Sagamore or including that word occur in Massachusetts, Pennsylvania, and Ohio — reminders of the personal and responsive Indian leadership that long prevailed throughout the Northeast.

SQUAW
Politically incorrect?

Lake County, Minnesota, made national news in 1996 when it challenged a state law ordering counties to change place names that included the word *Squaw*. Indian leaders had protested that the word was highly offensive to them, but they asked that the law apply only to topographical features, to avoid dividing Indians and non-Indians living in villages with names such as Squaw Lake.

Lake County contained Squaw Creek and Squaw Bay, both topographical features. County officials asserted that those names were generations old and implied no insult to anyone. Defiantly, they offered to change the names to Politically Correct Creek and Politically Correct Bay. The geographic name keeper of the Minnesota Department of Natural Resources spurned the idea. "They're trying to bill this as political correctness," he said, "but it's a matter of civility."

"If (he) is right, then the United States has a lot of places known by an offensive word," wrote *New York Times* reporter Eric Schmitt in an account of the controversy. "There are 1,050 natural or manmade locales around the country whose names include 'squaw,' according to the United States Geological Survey's Board on Geographic Names."[1]

That many Indians found *squaw* repugnant was reflected in a comment in 1997 by Judy Knight Frank, chairwoman of the Ute Mountain Ute tribe of Colorado. The presence of the rare Colorado squawfish in a nearby river was complicating plans for diversion of river waters to the tribe's semi-desert reservation. "That squawfish — and I take offense at that name — seems to have more of a right to live than I do," she complained.[2]

Some Indians claimed that *squaw* arose from a Mohawk word meaning vagina. The word was worse than demeaning, they said — it was obscene. But Ives Goddard, the authority on American Indian languages at the Smithsonian Institution, explains that this interpretation is not correct:

> It is as certain as any historical fact can be that the word *squaw* that the English settlers in Massachusetts used for 'Indian woman' in the early 1600s was adopted by them from the word *squa* that their Massachusett-speaking neighbors used in their own language to mean 'female, younger woman' and not from Mohawk. . . .[3]

The early settlers had good reason to use the Indian word for woman respectfully. They had to deal with a person they knew as the "Squa Sachim, or Massachusetts Queene." She deeded the Mystic River Valley, north of Boston, to the settlers. Captain Benjamin Church later persuaded Awashonks, another squaw sachem, to withdraw her Sakonnet tribe's support from King Philip's warriors — an act that helped save the settlers during the uprising of 1675–76.

But sensitivity about the word *squaw* partly reflects a long-standing dispute over the role of women among native peoples. Early English settlers gave mixed reports. "The men employ their time wholly in hunting and other exercises of the bow except that they sometimes take some pains at fishing," scoffed Governor Edward Winslow of Plymouth in the 1600s. "The women live a most slavish life: they carry all their burdens, set and dress their corn, gather it in, and seek out for much of their food, beat and make ready the corn to eat and have all household care lying upon them."[4] From a European standpoint, the Indian men enjoyed all the glory, while the women appeared to be burdened with most of the drudgery.

Many early writers, however, testify to the mutual respect and loving cooperation between Indian men and women. With some exceptions, this kind of relationship prevailed among Native American groups. "[Women] were esteemed mistresses of the soil," said an Oneida sachem in 1788. "Who brings us into being? Who cultivate our lands, kindle our fires, and boil our pots but the women?" Women often played a key role not only in practical matters but also in the spiritual life of their tribes. Ojibwa women presided over their wigwams and directed the distribution of the game their husbands brought back. Women among the Blackfoot of Canada were in charge of their tribe's sacred medicine bundles. One could cite innumerable other examples of the dignity Indian women commonly enjoyed.[5]

With the westward drive of white settlement in the nineteenth century, *squaw* was misapplied to some Indians who didn't even speak an Algonquian language. To make matters worse, all Indians — including women — tended to be disparaged during the Indian Wars. The *Oxford English Dictionary* offers no citations until after 1800 indicating a low status for *squaw;* then slurring references start to appear. Now dictionaries typically categorize the word as disparaging.

Understandably, the word *squaw* has largely fallen into disrepute except in a historical sense. It is still too early to tell whether the same fate will befall terms from natural history such as *old-squaw* (a common sea duck), *squawberry* (deer berry or partridge-berry), *squawbush* (a kind of sumac), *squaw cabbage* (Indian lettuce, etc.), *squawfish, squawflower* (purple trillium), *squaw mint* (pennyroyal), and others.

PAPOOSE
Complete freedom

> Unhappily in these lands the young have no respect for the old,
> nor are children obedient to their parents, and moreover there
> is no [corporal] punishment for any fault. For this reason every-
> body lives in complete freedom and does what he thinks fit. . . .
> This is conduct too shocking and smacks of nothing less than
> the brute beast.

So grumbled the Franciscan priest Gabriel Sagard about the
Huron in the early 1600s.[1]

Europeans found the Indian rearing of children baffling in its
mixture of severity and tenderness. This seemingly contradictory
treatment began at birth. In many eastern and northern tribes
such as the Micmac, a mother gave her newborn a dip in the river,
followed by a dose of animal oil, as from seal or bear. After the
doubly cleansing experience, a baby was gently swaddled in
downy materials covered with animal hide.

Papoose, the name whites eventually gave Indian babies in
much of America, comes from the Narragansett *papoòs* or the
Massachusett *pappouse*. Settlers carried the word to the Far West,
and it even appeared in some versions of the Chinook Jargon
(which see).

Tribal names for "baby" differed, but many Indians shared key
customs in their treatment of the young. After the initial dunking,
native mothers commonly secured their babies on a cradleboard,
or *papoose board*. The framework consisted of a flat board or other
backing such as branches lashed together. A block at the bottom
sometimes supported the baby's feet. The lining consisted of soft
material — dry moss, rotted cedar, and milkweed floss in the case
of the Ojibwa. Such material could easily be replaced as the need
arose. Over it would be hide such as beaver skin. At the top was a
small hoop, protecting the baby's head in case of a spill.

The proud mother adorned her cradleboard with decorations such as beadwork, porcupine quills, toy bows and arrows, and the like. A nineteenth-century traveler saw an Ojibwa woman who had covered her cradleboard with "sky-blue cloth on which glistened a couple of pounds of pearl beads"; the cloth had cost her ten dollars, or half her yearly income.[2] Some early cradleboards are museum pieces today.

The arrangement benefited both mother and baby. She could wear the baby strapped to her back while she did chores. At other times, she would prop the board against a tree or suspend it from a branch to swing in the breeze. The babies did not seem to mind the confinement, and Indians felt that it made young bodies straight and prevented feet from turning outward (bad for threading narrow trails).

At the age of nearly a year, a child would be released from the cradleboard. Then it remained close to its mother while she was at home, working in the fields, or walking about. A mother fostered hardiness in her children through cold-water baths and dressing them in scant clothing in all but the severest weather, and sometimes then as well. But both parents refrained from chastising a small child who acted up, believing that discipline at a tender age would break the spirit.

As soon as children could walk, parents gently began introducing them to the occupations they would follow as adults. Boys came to track animals, hunt squirrels with little bows and arrows, or play war games. Girls helped their mothers cook, tend crops, mind babies, and make clothes. Both learned by example and mild admonishment. Grandparents and other elders joined in pointing out the path that their young heirs were to follow. In certain tribes, such as some in Michigan, extremely unruly children might receive a dash of water in the face — a correction so unusual as to be deeply felt.

As children matured, their parents and elders expected them to behave in a more accomplished way. Boys, for example, might begin hunting bigger game. Among the Delaware, a boy bringing home his first deer offered a doe to an old woman or a buck to an old man. The recipient prayed for the boy's continued success at hunting. Although the accomplishments of girls tended to be less spectacular, their domestic skills earned them praise and status in the village.

Often a youth had to go through a ceremony in order to achieve formal adulthood. Adolescent boys typically underwent an ordeal. In Virginia, the process was called a *huskanaw* — during which their elders shut several candidates together for two or three weeks in an enclosure outside the village and gave them an herbal beverage supposed to blot out memories of the past. The Iroquois, Plains Indians, and other peoples practiced what came to be known as a *vision quest*. In this exercise, adolescent boys left their village for several days of fasting to acquire spiritual insight or connection with a supernatural guardian.

For girls, the menarche — or start of menstruation — marked the beginning of womanhood. Iroquois girls withdrew to a hut in the woods upon this event to avoid contaminating others with the new power they had attained. Among the Illinois, some abstained from food and water during their isolation. At the end of this time, a girl might be honored with a puberty dance. She was then marriageable.

The starkly contrastive Indian experience — of restriction during the first year of life, followed by easy-going indulgence during the rest of youth — left a mark on the character of those who underwent it. They tended to acquire a lifelong fear of constraint or dependency, combined with self-reliance and a love of independence. Describing the Iroquois in 1657, a Jesuit observer wrote:

> There is nothing for which these peoples have a greater horror than restraint. The very children cannot endure it, and live as they please in the houses of their parents.[3]

The resourceful, self-sufficient Indian became an all-American archetype — long accepted as a model for the country's youth. "Trust thyself: every heart vibrates to that iron string," said Ralph Waldo Emerson in "Self-Reliance," exhorting readers to rely on themselves rather than merely follow conventions.[4] It is a message only slightly dimmed a century and a half later.

The word *papoose,* however — except in a historical sense — has not held up as well. Today it can have a condescending ring, especially when applied to children whose tribal languages designate them by another name.

Papooseroot, or blue cohosh, was so named because women used the herb to assist in childbirth; it was also valued as a diuretic. In medical situations, to *papoose* a child has come to mean immobilizing it with velcro wrappings during treatment.

KINNIKINNICK
Sacred weeds

In the 1830s, the painter and Indian chronicler George Catlin was finishing a sumptuous meal provided by a Mandan chief in his tepee. The chief prepared to honor his guest with a ceremonial smoking of *kinnikinnick,* one of various herbal substances enjoyed like tobacco and sometimes including it. Catlin described the steps leading to the event:

> For this ceremony I observed he was making unusual preparation, and I observed as I ate, that after he had taken enough of the k'nick-k'neck or bark of the red willow, from his pouch, he rolled out of it also a piece of the "*castor*" [an extract from beaver glands], which it is customary amongst these folks to carry in their tobacco-sack to give it a flavour; and shaving off a small quantity of it, mixed it with the bark, with which he charged his pipe. This done, he drew also from his sack a small parcel containing a fine powder, which was made of dried buffalo dung, a little of which he spread over the top, (according also to custom,) which was like tinder, having no other effect than that of lighting the pipe with ease and satisfaction. My appetite sati-

ated, I straightened up, and with a whiff the pipe was lit, and we enjoyed together for a quarter of an hour the most delightful exchange of good feelings, amid clouds of smoke and pantomimic signs and gesticulations.

When Catlin rose to leave, the chief presented him the pipe and the buffalo robe on which Catlin had sat.[1]

For more than two thousand years, American Indians have gathered to offer tobacco or kinnikinnick at social and sacred ceremonies. Fragrant smoke put them in touch with the spirits, or manitous (which see). It sanctified key activities such as hunting expeditions. A "peace pipe," or calumet, circling among participants, sealed agreements.

The style of pipe, its contents, and the way smokers handled it spoke to participants. The pipe stem channeled smoke to the spirit world, and its rounded bowl mirrored the cosmos. Indians chose red pipestone (a clayey material that hardens after being quarried) from the Upper Missouri River region for some of their most highly prized bowls, its color symbolizing the life force.

Pipe smoking followed hallowed rules, though with variations according to different ceremonies. A pipe ceremony among the Oglala Sioux required that prayer and song accompany each stage of it. The pipe bundle had to be opened, the bowl and stem formally fitted together, and the bowl filled. Once the pipe had been lighted and presented, it was passed sunwise (clockwise) around the participants. Each greeted the pipe in turn and puffed on it.

Numerous tribes still follow the pipe ceremony, and it has been prominent at intertribal gatherings. Some Christian churches on reservations incorporate the pipe in their services and altar furnishings.

For tobacco, eastern Indians traditionally used *Nicotiana rustica,* one of several dozen species, in their worship. Western Indians used other kinds. After Columbus's discovery of *Nicotiana tabacum* in the West Indies, Europeans introduced that species to continental North America. Now dominant in the United States, it produces a mild tobacco widely considered the most smokable — though many Indians regard their traditional species as the truly sacred kind.

But not all pipe ceremonies require actual tobacco. Participants sometimes smoke kinnikinnick, as Catlin had. Its Algonquian name means "item for mixing in." Dried leaves and bark of various plants, and sometimes tobacco itself, go into this blend. Some Indians smoke kinnikinnick as a substitute for tobacco; others smoke kinnikinnick by preference. Edward S. Rutsch's study of Iroquois smoking technology lists ingredients used by several Indian groups: leaves or bark of red-osier dogwood, arrowroot, red sumac, laurel, ironwood, wahoo (burning bush), squaw huckleberry, "Indian tobacco," Jamestown weed, black birch, cherry bark, corn, mullein; along with muskrat glands or oil, and other animal oil or rendered fat.

Kinnikinnick also specifically means bearberry, with leaves that are a favorite ingredient in the herbal smoking mixtures. Bearberry is a trailing evergreen shrub that grows in the northern United States and Canada. The English name arose from the bear's relish for the plant's cranberry-type red berries. Indians have also used extracts of the plant as an astringent medicine and a treatment for kidney and skin diseases. Well into the twentieth century, pharmacies of of the United States and Great Britain carried it.

The word *kinnikinnick* may look and sound unusual. Without the *c,* a variant form, it is the longest English word spelled the same forward and backward. But its significance lies in its survival as a living part of traditional American culture. Besides kinnikinnick's common use as a synonym for bearberry, some Indians apply the word to sacred tobacco in general. And it appears in several U.S. place-names (usually for bodies of water) in eight states — two examples being Kinnikinnick, Ohio, and the creek that town was named after.

TAMMANY
Chief Tamanend and the tiger

A candidate for membership in the Society of Saint Tammany waits behind a curtain in the wigwam, or hall, for his initiation. The sagamore questions him about his citizenship, honorable intentions, and love of freedom. Each time, the candidate replies affirmatively in an Indian dialect: "Etho!" Then he is led through a gauntlet of braves to the far end of the wigwam, threatened (though not harmed) by a tomahawk. After some more stern questioning by the Father of the Council, the former paleface is declared a Son of Tammany and a member of the Columbian Order.

Such, in brief, was the initiation into the Society of Tammany, founded in about 1789. Each of the thirteen original states boasted its own tribe. These tribes all affected Indian and pseudo-Indian terminology and customs. The president of the United States was the honorary Great Grand Sachem and the head of each tribe a Grand Sachem. The master of ceremonies was a Sagamore and the door-keeper a Wiskinkie ("his eye" in an Algonquian language). Members were braves. On special occasions, these braves paraded through the streets carrying bows, arrows, and tomahawks. They gathered at a wigwam where they listened to speeches, witnessed "Indian" dances, and smoked the calumet of peace and friendship. The society even divided the year of twelve "moons" into

Tammany
1871 political cartoon entitled "The Brains" by Thomas Nast

Indian-sounding seasons — Snows, Blossoms, Fruits, Hunting, and so forth.

Tammany traces its origins to Tamanend, a chief of the Lenni Lenape (Delaware) Indians. He had reputedly joined in welcoming William Penn to America in 1682. Twelve years later, minutes of a conference between the Provincial Council of Pennsylvania and Indian delegates record Tamanend as expressing warm friendship for the whites. Writing in the early nineteenth century, the theologian John Heckewelder commented that his name was still "held in the highest veneration among the Indians" of Pennsylvania.[1] Few other details are available about the life of this clearly charismatic leader, whose name is said to mean "affable."

With the Revolutionary War, the legend of Tamanend grew among Americans seeking a heritage that would help free them from oppressive British influence. Loyalists belonged to European-oriented societies such as those of Saint George (English), Saint Andrew (Scottish), and Saint David (Welsh). Patriots responded by transforming a Loyalist American group, the Sons of King Tammany, into the homegrown and patriotic Sons of Saint Tammany. Added impetus for the organization came from fears that the newly formed Society of the Cincinnati, for former officers of the Continental Army, would side with the privileged against the common people.

In 1790, New York's young Tammany Society made a venture into the real world of Indians. The Creek of Georgia and Florida had been a constant source of anxiety to the new Republic because of their refusal to sign a peace treaty. President George Washington, taking Tammany at face value, called on the organization to use its influence for a settlement. A delegation of twenty-eight Creek under their chief, Alexander McGillivray, accepted an invitation to confer with their ostensible Indian brothers in New York. Incredibly, the meeting turned out to be a success. Tammany members treated the Creek to banquets, tours of the city, and visits to the theater. The two groups regaled each other with songs and speeches. At week's end, a beguiled Chief McGillivray signed the treaty.

This accomplishment seems to have whetted the appetite of New York Tammany leaders for political activity in their own city. They saw that loyal members could constitute an election-winning bloc. Aaron Burr, a political comer in New York State and a Tammany member, used his extraordinary talents to convert the society into a political powerhouse. He started a drive for new members, kept records profiling recruits, raised campaign funds, and sparked rallies and organizational meetings throughout the city. Tammany carried New York City for the Republicans in the election of 1800 and helped that party win the state, making Thomas Jefferson the president and Burr himself vice president.

Tammany societies in other states withered away, but for the next century and a half, New York's Tammany Hall (as the politicized society was known after its headquarters) loomed large in the politics of the city and state — and, several times, the nation. Although the organization did much good, as in the help it traditionally offered recent immigrants, its skill in manipulating members led to paternalism and then corruption. By the middle of the nineteenth century, Tammany Hall operatives were helping themselves to a large share of the graft rampant in New York City politics. William Marcy ("Boss") Tweed outdid all the rest. Tweed took over Tammany Hall in 1863, led an expansion of Tammany's influence in the city and state, and created a system that netted him and his henchmen untold millions. The appearance of a tiger as Tammany Hall's emblem at the time may have been inspired by the tiger-decorated truck Tweed had manned in his earlier days as a fireman (though the various Tammany tribes had shared a tradition of animal totems). This emblem proved to be a boon to Thomas Nast in his cartoons that excoriated Tweed.

Finally Tweed's operation became too blatant even for cynical New Yorkers. In the 1870s, he was thrown into prison, where he died several years later. Still, Tammany continued as a political force — sometimes benign, sometimes not — in New York City.

Until about the middle of the twentieth century, it remained one of the city's notable and seemingly indestructible institutions.

Television and high-rises helped make Tammany Hall obsolete. Ward heelers no longer could comfortably keep tabs on tenement dwellers and frequenters of neighborhood saloons. Oliver E. Allen in *The Tiger,* his history of Tammany Hall, puts the demise of the organization at about 1961 — when voters resoundingly defeated the machine's irrelevant slate of candidates. By that time, Tammany's Indian theme had long since faded to a quaint reminder of the past. *Tammany* and *Tammany Hall* — originally commemorating an idealized Indian leader — would ironically survive as synonyms for big-city bossism and political corruption.

MUGWUMP

From duke to maverick

Widespread dissatisfaction with political parties has led many Americans to regard themselves as independents. Mugwumps, they used to be called, and sometimes still are. The history behind this name reflects some of the political turbulence that has roiled the United States during the past century.

mugwump
1884 political cartoon by C. J. Taylor

The Reverend John Eliot (1604–90), the person ultimately responsible for *mugwump's* introduction into English, won fame as the "Apostle to the Indians." Educated at Cambridge University, he crossed the Atlantic to become a popular minister in Massachusetts. Gradually Eliot felt called to preach to the Indians, who were commonly regarded in the colony with both fear and condescension. His half century of ministering to the Indians and founding the colony's Indian "Praying Towns" bear witness to his piety and energy.

But Eliot's most extraordinary accomplishment has to be his translation of the Bible into an Algonquian dialect: *Mamusse Wunneetupanatamwe Up-Biblum God* (The-whole Holy his-Bible God). Eliot toiled on this mammoth project for fourteen years. To complete it, he had to transcribe the Algonquian tongue spoken by the Indians of Massachusetts, construct a grammar for it, and then translate the complex language of Christianity into that of a totally different culture. *Up-Biblum* was published in 1663 by the Cambridge Press, located at the Indian College in Harvard Yard. Eliot hoped that it would be a powerful tool to convert and redeem the Indians. One historian observes that his project was "the first Bible printed in America, the earliest example in history of the translation and printing of the entire Bible as a means of evangelization."[1]

Mugwump occurs in Eliot's Bible as a translation of *duke* in the King James Version, used in Genesis chapter 36 for the title of the chiefs of Edom. The word comes from *mugquomp,* a syncopated form of *muggumquomp,* meaning "war leader." And it might have remained in its Algonquian context if it had not caught the fancy of colonial New Englanders. For years, *mugwump* was used along parts of the Massachusetts and Connecticut coast in the sense of "a person of importance" or "a man who does not think small beer of himself."

During the early nineteenth century, *mugwump* again found its way into print as a gibe at a self-important person. It took the James B. Blain–Grover Cleveland presidential campaign of 1884 to give the word its specifically political meaning. Republican leaders dubbed Blaine "the plumed knight," but critics within the party joined Democrats in blasting Blaine's record of abusing his congressional authority to aid railroad interests. On June 15, the *New York Sun* sneered that Republican waverers were "mugwumps." Less than a week later, the *New York Post* countered that Blaine supporters were defaming Republican independents as "pharisees, hypocrites, dudes, mugwumps, transcendentalists, or something of that sort."

These "mugwumps" included a number of distinguished and principled people such as president Charles W. Eliot of Harvard. They felt no embarrassment in opposing a tarnished candidate, and they embraced the nickname with pride. One, William Everett, declared on September 13: "I am an independent — a *mugwump*. I beg to state that *mugwump* is the best American [language] . . . ; it means a great man."[2]

Cynics disagreed. An oft-repeated quip had it that a mugwump was a bird with his *mug* on one side of the political fence and his *wump* on the other. A year after Cleveland's election, the poet Eugene Field wrote:

> *Oh, what has become of the Mugwump-bird*
> *In this weather of wind and snow,*
> *And does he roost as high as we heard*
> *He roosted a year ago?*
> *A year ago and his plumes were red*
> *As the deepest of cardinal hues,*
> *But in the year they've changed, 'tis said*
> *To the bluest of bilious blues!*[3]

Now *mugwump* is nearly always used in a complimentary way. A 1961 book, *The Day of the Mugwump* by Lorin Peterson, describes such a person as an activist who judges "political issues in terms of morality. The mugwump always asks first: Is this thing right or is it wrong?" Peterson holds that mugwumps have been a saving force in U.S. municipal politics.[4]

An editorial in the *Boston Globe* on November 1, 1994, praised Massachusetts as "the Mugwump state" and explained that the term had reversed its historical role in the elections that were current there:

In politics, with or without irony, Mugwump means independent. The New Mugwumps are the mirror image of the originals. . . . Today's Mugwumps are traditional Democrats who
have broken ranks to support the Republicans.[5]

Thus *mugwump* survives in U.S. political lingo, a curious
(though not unworthy) relic of John Eliot's great Algonquian Bible.

BAYOU
Mysterious waterways

> They, too, swerved from their course; and entering the Bayou of
>   Plaquemine,
> Soon were lost in a maze of sluggish and devious waters,
> Which, like a network of steel, extended in every direction.
> Over their heads the towering and tenebrous boughs of the cypress
> Met in a dusky arch, and trailing mosses in mid-air
> Waved like banners that hang on the walls of ancient cathedrals.[1]

So wrote Henry Wadsworth Longfellow in *Evangeline* about
his heroine's journey down a Louisiana *bayou* while vainly searching for her exiled sweetheart. In general, a bayou is a creek or sluggish, meandering stream. But the word refers most aptly to the
network of waterways through the vast delta at the mouth of the
Mississippi River and including New Orleans. The French borrowed the word from *bayuk* from the Choctaw, many of whom
lived in Louisiana and knew its creeks intimately.

Louisiana bayous teem with lush plants and varied wildlife.
The Spanish moss-draped cypresses Longfellow mentions cast
their shade over leafy banks dotted with wildflowers. Water lilies
and purple water hyacinths fleck the channels, sometimes clog-
ging them. Snow-white egrets poise on branches overhead or on
tree stumps; great blue herons wade in the shallows. During warm
weather, alligators drift in the water, today snapping up thrown
marshmallows or chicken proffered to them on long sticks from

bayou
bald cypress trees in the Atchafalaya Basin Bayou, Louisiana

tour boats. Lurking in the oozy undergrowth are swamp animals such as beavers, mink, muskrats, otters, and raccoons.

To the earliest whites, the bayous were bewildering. A wrong turn could mean days of wandering, and sometimes death. Local Indians — including Houma, Tunica, and Choctaw — guided these settlers over the safest routes in dugout canoes that evolved into the French pirogue. They demonstrated how to kill an alligator by thrusting a sharp stick down its throat and turning it over to expose the vulnerable underbelly.

Settlers learned from Indians how to live off the land. Indian women taught the wives of early French settlers how to prepare and cook the local foods. They feasted on the fish, game animals, and edible plants that abounded in the waterways. Some Indian delicacies helped to create the world-famous Creole cuisine. For example, the distinctive taste of filé gumbo derives from the Choctaw practice of adding powdered sassafras leaves to thicken it and impart a delicate flavor somewhat like thyme.

Spanish moss, often regarded as an emblem of the bayous,

proved useful for settlers, as it was for Indians. The flowering plant is neither moss nor a parasite; it lives on airborne water and dust. Indian legend holds that it arose from the hair of a girl killed on her wedding day, rising to the branches of an oak tree at her gravesite. It spread from tree to tree, turning gray but enduring as a memorial to lost love. The Indians used the substance to clothe their babies and to cover the sick. Settlers stuffed upholstery with it.

Eventually the crowding in of outsiders — French, Spanish, and others — doomed many native inhabitants through disease or warfare, and forced others deeper into the bayous or finally out of the region altogether. The French traveler Victor Tixier glimpsed this result when he encountered a small band of Choctaw in 1839 about twenty miles outside New Orleans. The men were helping to support their families by hunting while the women wove baskets for sale. They had traveled from a large village on the Red River between Texas and the territory of Missouri to winter in their previous homes. Tixier was surprised when "these former masters of the country" addressed him in good French.

The main reason for the Choctaw band's excursion appears to have been to visit their ancestral burying ground. Local settlers felt a superstitious awe at the Indians' ability to understand events that had taken place during their absence. Someone had thrown a stone idol from among the graves into a lake; afterward the Choctaw unerringly retrieved the idol and placed a fatal curse on the perpetrator. A few months later, Tixier viewed the Choctaw campsite somberly — although he did not hesitate to rifle one of the nearby graves that was pointed out to him.[1]

Today what happens in Louisiana's 2300 square miles of marshlands, including the bayous, resonates throughout the nation's ecology and economy. Millions of ducks and geese travel the Mississippi flyway to winter there, and the region is home to the largest number of shorebirds outside of Florida. It is a leading source of wild furs. A fifth of America's shellfish and commercial fish come from its waters. And the lands themselves help buffer New Orleans and other cities against hurricanes rising out of the Gulf of Mexico.

The bayous depend for their renewal on the rich sediment that the Mississippi washes down from the nation's heartland. Yet levees and other projects designed to channelize the river's flow are flushing more of the sediment out to sea rather than spreading it throughout the river's delta. Furthermore, oil and gas companies have cut networks of channels through the marshes, thereby sealing off outlets or letting in seawater. The Gulf of Mexico is steadily swallowing the Louisiana coast.

These modern-day threats have focused national attention on the once-obscure bayous so rich in wildlife and in the heritage of Indians and other peoples. By 1999, the federal government had launched scores of projects to protect the coast. The Audubon Society chose the region's vast Atchafalaya Basin as the first project of its Wetlands for Wildlife program, which emphasizes land acquisition and ecotourism. At the century's end, the future of the bayous looked more hopeful than it had for years.

MUSKEG
"Mud, mosquitoes, and muskeg"

Viewing proposals for the Alaska (Alcan) Highway early in World War II, critics laughed. One called the idea an "engineering monstrosity" and an "economic absurdity." But a highway into Alaska was needed urgently, the U.S. government felt, because of Japanese threats in the Aleutians and along the Pacific coast. On March 2, 1942, crews began surveying a route through northern British Columbia. By summer, ten thousand American troops were building a track across the rugged wilderness. They struggled through clouds of giant mosquitoes in the summer and temperatures as low as minus seventy degrees Fahrenheit in the winter. Cutting down forest was fairly easy; laying the 1442-mile roadway proved much more formidable.[1]

Permafrost — permanently frozen subsoil — made road builders curse, but the bog with the Indian name *muskeg* (from Cree *maske·k*) proved especially devilish. During winter, crews spread gravel over frozen muskeg, and in summer, the muskeg thawed and turned into quagmire. Bulldozers sank out of sight in the worst areas. It took thousands of trees laid side by side across the bogs to form corduroy roads that held up in warm weather. Often engineers curved the course of the road near or over drier hills. When asked why the road zigzagged so much, locals later quipped that the purpose had been to confuse Japanese warplanes on strafing runs. The real rea-

muskeg
an area of muskeg near British Columbia's Chilko River, Canada

son, of course, was to avoid boggy soil. In summing up the challenges of the eight-month project, a standard description was some version of "mud, mosquitoes, and muskeg."[2]

The bogs called muskeg brim with *sphagnum*, an absorbent moss, and are dense with *peat*, partially decayed plant matter. The muskegs of North America display what might strike some observers as a primeval look, and appropriately. Many began with the ice that once mantled the northern half of the continent. Glaciers retreating ten thousand or so years ago left behind a scattering of huge ice blocks. These finally melted, leaving depressions, or "kettles," that filled up with waterlogged plants and sphagnum. Canada is the most muskeg-pocked country, with forty percent of the earth's peat lands. The United States, with seven percent, stands third behind Russia.

Indians not only named the muskeg but gleaned useful plants from its peaty soil. In autumn, the Koyukon still gather tart cranberries and blueberries that grow in it. The cranberry bush also yields them pliant stems for reinforcing the rims of birch-bark baskets. Many Indians also used the highly absorbent sphagnum moss for diapers. Among the healing plants Indians found in bogs were the pitcher plant for kidney and lung ailments, leatherleaf for fever and inflammation, bog goldenrod for boils, and sheep laurel for headache and backache.

Bogs, including muskeg, supply contemporary Americans with peat moss — dried sphagnum used for mulch and plant food. Farmers utilize peat fertilizer, and many farms have been established on the rich soil of drained peat land. Further, bogs form a key part of the nation's ecology, providing habitat for many forms of plant and animal life.

Besides their practical uses, bogs offer recreation to hunters, birders, hikers, and nature lovers. Approaching a muskeg in Connecticut's Mohawk State Forest, Robert Winkler described its eerie effect:

> Suddenly, the forest emits a supernatural aura. On the right, a hemlock's gnarled roots grip a boulder, and a pink glow surrounds the branchless trunks of a group of red pines. The trail dips, and ahead the canopy opens slightly. A lumpy carpet of moss and a twisting boardwalk mark the beginning of the bog.[3]

Now the spread of human settlement endangers bogs, and laws in the United States are intended to protect them and other wetlands. Canada too is working to preserve wilderness lands, including muskeg. A 1997 Canadian law bans development of 2.5 million acres in northeastern British Columbia and limits development in 8 million acres of buffer land. This includes a stretch of the Alaska Highway in muskeg country — regarded not long ago as mainly an obstacle to progress.

Canada's position as the world's leading host to muskeg may be seen in the number of mainly Canadian expressions including that word: *muskeg grass* or *hay, school, soil, swamp, tea, vehicle, water,* and others.

SPIRIT

"There are so many Native American religions and their expressions are so varied," says the anthropologist Åke Hultkrantz, "that it is difficult to generalize upon all Native American religions." Yet Hultkrantz notes that most Indians believed in:

- ➤ a close affinity between people and animals;
- ➤ the idea that animals are spirits and thus mysterious;
- ➤ the supernaturalism of certain natural and man-made forces or objects;
- ➤ some kind of afterlife.[1]

How do Indians today feel about the trend among some "New Age" followers to adopt perceived Indian religious practices such as use of the sweat lodge? "We have a real problem [with the] ongoing abuse and sacrilege of what we hold sacred," says Raymond D. Apodaca, a Pueblo who is chairman of the religious and human rights committee of the National Congress of American Indians. But other Indians feel that society can only benefit from a spreading of Indian customs. "If we want the white man to change, we must teach him," asserts Ed McGaa, Oglala Sioux author of *Mother Earth Spirituality*.[2]

This section examines Native American legends, beliefs, and religious practices that influence mainstream American and Canadian culture: *Sasquatch, totem, kachina, inukshuk, powwow,* and *manitou*.

SASQUATCH
Mystery of the Northwest

The Sasquatch, or Bigfoot, strides across a clearing in the dusky forest. It is manlike but much bigger than a person, perhaps eight feet tall. Dark hair covers its body, except for face, palms, and soles. One can hear a whistling sound as it seems to call to companions. Then the giant slips back into the foliage, leaving behind a powerful, offensive body odor.

So goes a characteristic description of the rarely sighted creature that is reputed to have haunted the Pacific Northwest for as long as people can remember. From northern California into British Columbia, Sasquatch sightings have been reported over a range of forest-covered mountains about 125,000 square miles in area. Parts of this wilderness are so remote that a downed plane may go undiscovered for twenty years or more. Add to the difficult terrain the Sasquatch's traits of being shy and nocturnal (say the creature's advocates), and one should not be surprised that it is seldom seen. Most of the evidence offered for the Sasquatch's existence comes in the form of massive, five-toed footprints sixteen inches long or longer.

Indian legends describe dreaded encounters with Sasquatches, or Bigfeet. The Nisqually, a Salishan-speaking people of Puget Sound, Washington, call the creatures *Seatco*. They consider the Seatco to be a race of tall "wild" Indians. These beings, it is said, live in hollowed-out places like the dens of animals. During nightly wanderings, they play tricks on other Indians, such as stealing fish from their nets. Occasionally they have gone so far as to kidnap children to keep as slaves. If harmed, the Seatco relentlessly seek to injure or kill the offender. The anthropologist Claude Lévi-Strauss characterizes Sasquatches, along with the Dzonokwas reported by several Pacific Northwest groups, as supernatural creatures who dwell "far inside the woods" and who "are savage giantesses, also ogresses, who kidnap the Indians' children to eat them."[1]

Far to the north, among the Koyukon people, a strangely similar being called the Woodsman is said to live. This creature is covered with hair, like the Sasquatch, and has long arms, though it does not seem to be larger than human beings. Also like Sasquatch, it has a rank odor. Koyukon catch only glimpses of it but hear its whistle or maniacal laugh. It plagues people with petty thefts and, more seriously, the kidnapping of children to raise as its own. The Koyukon theorize that Woodsmen developed from people forced by hunger to commit cannibalism, who thus became unfit for human society.

Names for Sasquatch — and details of its appearance — differ from tribe to tribe throughout the Pacific Northwest. *Sasquatch* comes from *sesqɔc,* a word in a Salishan language of southwestern British Columbia meaning "wild men." Since the 1920s this name, together with *Bigfoot,* has become the most common public designation.

Reports of Sasquatch or a Sasquatchlike creature, however, have been current among white settlers for almost two centuries. In 1810, the explorer David Thompson reported seeing footprints fourteen inches long and eight inches wide in the Canadian Rockies belonging, said Indians, to a huge creature. In 1884, miners in British Columbia captured a hairy animal four feet seven inches tall that might (it has been suggested) have been a young Sasquatch. Other miners near Mount Saint Helens claimed in 1924 to have shot a "huge creature at least seven feet tall and covered with long black hair," but it disappeared into a canyon.[2]

Reports of that kind continued to be made sporadically up to the middle of the twentieth century. But only since about 1960 have Sasquatch observations become as widespread among whites as they traditionally have been among the Indians.

It is not clear why the number of Sasquatch sightings appears to have increased in recent decades. If the Sasquatch exists, the spread of human settlement may be encroaching on its habitat. Alternatively, a heightened interest in ecology may be producing more and better observations of the natural world. If the

Sasquatch does not objectively exist, some say the reports may reflect a longing to recover a closeness to nature believed lost in modern societies.

In any case, scientists and explorers are working to determine whether Sasquatch is "an *idea* or an *animal*," as a biologist puts it.[3] In her book *Still Living?* the British anthropologist Myra Shackley points out a number of resemblances between Sasquatch and the Yeti, or Abominable Snowman, of Asia. These likenesses include furred bodies, large footprints, and nocturnal habits. She and other anthropologists speculate on a physical relationship between the two creatures and possibly others like them that reaches across continents. Some conjecture that the Yeti or a similar creature migrated to North America in the distant past.[4]

A leading theorist on Sasquatch is Grover Krantz, professor of anthropology at Washington State University. He has analyzed more than a hundred reputed Sasquatch tracks and possesses plaster casts of more than eighty tracks that fit criteria for those possibly left by the creature.[5] According to Krantz, the Sasquatch may be related to the giant fossil ape *Gigantopithecus blacki.* If the Sasquatch is found to belong to a different species of *Gigantopithecus,* he proposes naming it *G. canadensis.* Krantz shows considerable tenacity in the face of opposition to his theories. Some fellow anthropologists chide him for being credulous. Some Sasquatch buffs, on the other hand, complain of his willingness to allow a Sasquatch to be shot (it's not human, he emphasizes) if that is necessary to secure scientific proof of its existence.[6]

Peter Byrne, a former tiger hunter in Nepal, now actively searches for Sasquatches in the field. His Bigfoot Research Project operates out of The Dalles, a city in northern Oregon. Byrne stated in 1995 that his staff employed five vehicles — a Jeep, Toyota Land Cruiser, International Scout, large snowmobile, and van — called the Bigfoot Mobile Base. His scientific equipment included night-vision devices and pistols that shoot biopsy darts. He had two helicopters — one to transport his staff and another to carry equipment such as an infrared heat-sensitive device for tracking animals. Convinced that Sasquatch is real, Byrne believes that he can prove its existence without gunning one down.

These research efforts, regardless of outcome, have helped foster the Sasquatch legend on both a regional level (comparable to Paul Bunyan) and a national level in Canada and the United States. The publications of Sasquatch Books in Seattle are distributed well beyond the Pacific Northwest. Major writers such as Francine Prose (the book *Bigfoot Dreams*) and Margaret Atwood (the poem "Oratorio for Sasquatch, Man and Two Androids") address a North American audience. The Sasquatch has been further popularized by business enterprises, including that of a major pizza manufacturer.

Pending conclusive evidence, what is one to believe about Sasquatch? John Napier, former director of the Primate Biology Program at the Smithsonian Institution, chose to reserve judgment. "If we confine ourselves rigidly to what most scientists would regard as hard evidence, then the answer is heard loud and clear: *"Bigfoot does not exist,"* he said in his book *Bigfoot*. Yet he also pointed to "a certain amount of soft evidence" — eyewitness reports, footprints, and "a few supplementary items such as scalps, hairs, mummified hands, and droppings."[7] He found it hard to believe that all of this evidence was part of a hoax.

To those who regard the Sasquatch as significant but not necessarily a certifiable creature, proof is not all-important. "While Sasquatch-like creatures may inhabit the real world of the Indians," says the anthropologist Wayne Suttles, "this may not be relevant to the question of whether they inhabit the real world of Western science." The ecologist Robert Michael Pyle recounts his personal quest for Sasquatch in the illuminating book *Where Bigfoot Walks*. Pyle concludes that Sasquatch does walk, but he feels no need to define this mysterious creature in scientific terms.[8]

TOTEM
Emblem of the clan

"Quick, responsive, and resourceful, the eagle has long been an inspiration for us in the way we do business," reads a 1997 newspaper ad for the Eagle Bank, an institution with thirty branches in Connecticut. Graphically underscoring the bank's image, the ad displays a bald eagle logo with the slogan "Our Standards Are Higher."[1]

Animals and other objects long served as Indian clan and family emblems, or *totems,* which is from Ojibwa *oto·te·man,* "his totem." The significance of a totem varied from people to people. The Wyandot were originally divided into eight clans — Turtle, Bear, Beaver, Deer, Hawk, Porcupine, Wolf, and Snake. Membership came through the mother, and the members typically had to marry outside their clans. Often killing one's clan's totem animal was forbidden. Such arrangements were common not only among North American Indians but also among natives of South America and other continents.

totem
the top of a Haida mortuary totem pole with watchmen at the crown

"Totemism is . . . a complex of varied ideas and ways of behavior based on a world view drawn from nature," says one authority. The system placed members not only in their clans but also within the natural world that pervaded their lives. This relationship could be direct, or it could be more of a formality, as when a totem mainly governed the choice of a marriage partner.[2]

Sometimes, though not usually, says the anthropologist Åke Hultkrantz, Indian clan members might believe they were actually descended from a totemic animal. The Yuchi of the Southeast thought so, holding that they had assumed the identities of their animal ancestors. In any case, clan members and others might feel that they exhibited traits of their totem. Thus members of the Ojibwa Bear clan were believed to be "ill-tempered and fond of fighting," like bears.[3]

Henry David Thoreau remarked on the importance Indians attached to their totems:

> They are as proud of their origin from the tortoise, the turkey, & the wolf, as the nobles of Europe are of their descent from the feudal barons of ancient times, & when children spring from intermarriages between different tribes, their genealogy is carefully preserved by tradition in the family, that they may know to which tribe they belong.[4]

Totems, furthermore, had practical value. Among the Ojibwa, a totem was sometimes carved or drawn on a tree to show the membership of a traveling party. Wooden grave markers bore the totems of the deceased upside down, showing wayfaring clan members where to leave offerings of food. Indian leaders often signed treaties by sketching their totems on documents.

Emblems reminiscent of totems — usually without the breadth of meaning these have among Indians — are common in the modern world. Nations, athletic teams, fraternal groups, and corporations claim association with animals or other objects that inspire them. Thus the American eagle, British lion, and Russian bear commonly stand for their respective countries. And the Yale bulldog, the Loyal Order of Moose emblem, and the Prudential Insurance Company rock are part of American lore. In recent years, however, the once-common custom of depicting Indians as sports mascots — sometimes in an especially demeaning way — has come under fire. Many schools and colleges across the country have modified or ended this practice.

Today the word *totem* often refers to any emblem or revered symbol. One reads in the *New York Times*: "As totems go, a doctor's white coat is a real bargain ($22.95 in 1997)." A recent book review posits that "T.S. Eliot is an artist with a totemic presence in the cultural imagination." Such expressions sound distant echoes of the belief systems that shaped the lives of Native Americans and others.[5]

KACHINA
Spirit messengers

The masked *kachina* dancers file up to the kiva, an underground chamber used for religious services. They announce themselves and descend a ladder into a packed room. "Their presence is powerful, heightened by the closeness of the room and the sound of feet stamping in unison, by the body movements and guttural singing, by the sounds of many rattles and the beating rhythm of the big drum."[1] So goes one account of Hopi kachina dancers performing their Bean Dance on a chilly February night. The dance is part of a sixteen-day ceremony intended to help crops grow and bring blessings on the village.

Kachina dancers perform their world-famous rites in several pueblos of Arizona and New Mexico — villages of stacked, flat-roofed houses. Some of the dances take place in a kiva, others in a plaza. The entire village spends days preparing gifts, holiday finery, and treats such as corn pudding for the events. (Most of the details in this essay refer to the Hopi, whose kachina celebrations are the best known.)

The complex, colorful masks worn by dancers represent the spirits who visit villages during the first six months of the year. These spirits control the weather, always vital in a land with little water. The spirits further inspire the villagers and help them live in harmony with one another.

At intervals during the ceremonies, the dancers bestow gifts upon watching children. But they also chasten any people who need correction, even striking them with yucca-leaf whips. Thus they offer guidance directly and indirectly.

The word *kachina* comes from the Hopi *katsina*. It is now used in three senses:

- ➤ "Ancestors who act as messengers between the people and their gods," according to E. Charles Adams, archaeologist at the University of Arizona. "They are also rainmakers, coming as clouds to the villages to which they are annually summoned."[2]
- ➤ Masked dancers who, as noted above, impersonate the kachina spirits in religious ceremonies.
- ➤ Dolls (called *tihü* in Hopi) that represent kachina dancers.

Evidence of kachinas in the first sense appears to date back to about 1300. Around that time, peoples of small villages in the Southwest began gathering to form larger communities. The kachina religion helped unify the various groups and then sustain them through centuries of challenge and hardship.

Throughout the year, *kachina dolls* now dangle from the walls of Hopi homes. Kachina dancers bestow the dolls and other gifts on children during the dances. The dolls are traditionally carved from the dense roots of dead cottonwood trees (a kind of poplar) and painted. They are not an idol or object of worship but serve to educate Pueblo children and remind them of the kachina ceremonies.

Only in the past century and a half has the kachina doll become common. Outsiders coming to the Southwest helped spur new interest in the dolls. Anthropologists sought them out for what they reveal about Pueblo culture, and others began collecting the dolls as curios and works of art. Hopi disagree among themselves about the sale of dolls. Some argue that it profanes their religion; others find it a necessary source of income in their impoverished region. Cheap imitations mass-produced elsewhere are, of course, regarded as unacceptable.

Kachina ceremonies are regional, but the dolls springing from them have lent a national significance to the term *kachina*. Former Senator Barry Goldwater of Arizona and actor John Wayne built up large collections, now in museums. By 1984, it was estimated that more than ten thousand dolls a year were being produced. Today collectors and museums increasingly treasure the best of kachina dolls as works of art and precious relics of one of the continent's ancient religions.

INUKSHUK
Stone men from the Arctic

Arctic travelers and hunters once oriented themselves by inukshuks, rocks heaped up as high as about twelve feet. These signposts rising starkly out of snowy wastes guided Eskimo to their settlements. They directed hunters toward prey or served to bewilder the animals being pursued. Still standing, they are the northernmost monuments on Earth.

Modern Eskimo no longer need inukshuks, But the rough constructions have become a significant part of their heritage. And increasingly in Canada, one finds inukshuks treated as sculptures or portrayed as a symbol of the country's Eskimo, or Inuit, peoples.

The constructing of inukshuks goes back a thousand years or more. Their form ranges from that of a cairn, or mere heap of stones, to an abstract but recognizable human figure topped with a clump of turf for hair. *Inukshuk* in the Eskimo's language means "like a man."

Writing in the magazine *Natural History*, Fred Bruemmer tells of discovering a chain of inukshuks on Coats Island in northern Hudson Bay. He was dropped off by boat on the coast to observe some colonies of murres, a kind of auk, or diving sea bird.

Having concluded his observations, he hesitated — clambering back over the rocks would have been arduous. Then he began to notice cairns on ridges and at other strategic points. Following them, he discovered that they guided him efficiently back to his camp, the site of an old Eskimo settlement. Early Eskimo had used this means to mark their route to the murres, a source of meat and eggs.

inukshuk
1986 inukshuk sculpture by Alvin Kanak on the shores of English Bay, Vancouver, Canada

Rows of inukshuks were commonly used in the hunting of caribou. Hunters would stampede the animals between two rows of cairns. The caribou were terrified of the inukshuks, which often concealed women and children howling like wolves. At the end of this aisle of death, hunters in shallow pits waited to slaughter the prey running past them. These inukshuk rows resemble the lanes of cairns leading to the hundred or so prehistoric jumps on the North American plains, where thousands of harassed bison tumbled to their deaths. Some anthropologists speculate that both may be traced back to Paleolithic European hunting techniques.

By itself, an inukshuk could serve as a marker in an otherwise featureless location. Eskimo sometimes placed one on a headland to guide hunters out in kayaks and other boats. An inukshuk's distinctive shape, looming through the fog, would let a seafarer know his whereabouts. Or a solitary inukshuk might call attention to something such as an outcrop of soapstone, used in making bowls and oil lamps.

Inukshuks furnished more than practical benefits to Arctic

peoples. Travelers venturing out to sea sometimes raised one for luck. Eskimo made offerings to certain inukshuks as if they were a source of spiritual power. Lonely travelers still find comfort in seeing forms made by other human beings, introducing meaning into a landscape scoured by some of the world's fiercest storms. The Canadian author Farley Mowat described his awe on viewing a cluster of inukshuks near Hudson Bay:

> They are such puny monuments, these lone inhabitants of emptiness, it seems inevitable that they must topple into the anonymity of the rocky slopes from which they sprang. And yet they will not fall. They stand immutably, contemptuous of the winter gales and of the passing years, imbued with an essential quality that belies their faceless forms and gives to them more than a semblance of reality as men.[1]

With the introduction of rifles, snowmobiles, and other modern conveniences, Eskimo largely stopped building inukshuks. But in recent years, Canadians have been displaying inukshuks in public places and private gardens. National law protects antiquities, so corporations and others commission Eskimo (Inuit) artists to construct new ones. Toronto International Airport set an example in the early 1960s with three granite inukshuks that were first assembled on Baffin Island north of Hudson Bay and were then shipped to the airport for reassembly.

One of the most spectacular recent inukshuks is the six-and-a-half-ton "Spirit of the Land" in the lobby of Calgary's Stock Exchange Tower. The Inuvialuit artist Abraham Ruben developed the sculpture with two other artists. At its unveiling in 1995, Ruben indicated that the inukshuk "represents the transition made by the Inuvialuit of the western Arctic from a hunting society to an economy-based part of contemporary society." He described it as reflecting Inuvialuit beliefs "connecting the physical world to the invisible world."[2]

By then, nineteen-year-old Beth McEachen had already brought the inukshuk before the entire nation. She wanted to attend art school but didn't know how she could afford it. So she entered a competition for coin designs to celebrate Canada's 125th anniversary in 1992. Her rendition of an inukshuk to represent the Northwest Territories won first prize out of eleven thousand entries. The Royal Canadian Mint chose it because of its simple beauty and its value in teaching about the north. McEachen received $5000 toward her first year at the Ontario College of Art — and millions of pure-nickel quarters with an inukshuk design began circulating in Canada.

POWWOW

Circle of life

Eleven men are pounding a big drum at the powwow, singing, "Ah hey yah," at intervals during the beat. Dancers with bright shirts, feathered ornaments, jingling bells, and moccasined feet rhythmically shuffle by. They include young children and white-haired matrons, people who look traditionally Indian and others who don't — all united in the living, weaving ring some call the "circle of life."

During the second half of the twentieth century, the powwow has become a nationwide spectacle and event. An estimated two thousand powwows were held yearly across the United States and Canada toward the century's end, ranging from lavish productions with half a million dollars in prizes for dancers to modest get-togethers in the obscure outposts of Indian country. But opinions varied widely on the nature of what was taking place. Participants regarded the festivals as anything from a party to a way of renewing ancient traditions.

The powwow arises from age-old Indian lore. *Powwaw* in Narragansett and related languages first meant priest or shaman. It literally signified "one who has visions," from the shaman's practice of seeking wisdom through dreams and trances. The earliest occurrence of *powwow* in English conveys its primordial power. When the explorer George Waymouth visited the Maine coast in

1605, a member of his crew chanced to witness a ceremony of the local Indians. With *powwaw* transcribed as *Baugh, Waugh*, the Waymouth report stated:

> One among them (the eldest of the Company, as he judged), riseth right up, the other sitting still, and looking about suddenly cried out with a loud voice, *Baugh, Waugh*: then the women all fall downe, and lie upon the ground, and the men all together answering the same, fall a stamping round about the fire with both feet, as hard as they can, making the ground shake with sundry out-cries, and change of voice and sound.[1]

The emotional impact of this two-hour ceremony can be gauged by the reportedly shaking ground.

Settlers could make little sense of such proceedings. They extended the meaning of *powwow* from leader of sacred ceremonies to the ceremonies themselves. By the late eighteenth century, the word was coming to be used for meetings in general — its second principal meaning. The condescending tone of this usage can be discerned in an item from a Massachusetts newspaper of 1812: "The warriors of the Democratic Tribe will hold a powwow at Agawam on Tuesday next." Yet the entries in the Merriam-Webster dictionary of 1848 indicate that the original religious meaning persisted.

In fact, these early religious meanings of *powwow* persist today. "The combination of charms, incantation, magic, and 'laying on of hands' for avoiding or curing disease or injury, which survives to this day among the Pennsylvania Germans, is called 'powwowing' by those who use it," the scholar Virgil Vogel wrote in 1970.[2]

The third principal meaning of *powwow* gained currency early in the twentieth century. Still reeling from their military defeats, some American Indians called tribal and intertribal gatherings to celebrate their beleaguered cultures. These powwows have become widespread in the United States since World War II. To a lesser extent, powwows are also staged in Europe.

For many Indian participants, the modern powwow offers a cherished opportunity to keep in touch with fellow Indians. They renew friendships with scattered members of their own tribes and with those from a variety of other tribes. They exchange news about what is happening on the heavily traveled "powwow trail" throughout the United States. "I keep saying it," said Jimmy Boy Dial, a Lumbee and organizer of several East Coast powwows: "A powwow is like dancing to your heartbeat with all your friends."[3]

Beyond enjoying the fellowship of other Indians, participants in powwows (together with spectators) can reestablish — or become acquainted with — their links to traditional Indian culture. "These celebrations," said one attendee, "are how we maintain continuity in the face of incredible change."[4] The displays of handicrafts present a liberal amount of standardized souvenirs, travesties of artifacts. Yet one can glean from among them fine examples of Indian design and workmanship. The typical powwow also includes lively demonstrations of leatherwork, jewelry making, and flint knapping. Indian and non-Indian alike can view a way of life and an outlook that had once seemed about to disappear.

Then there is the dancing, the heart of the powwow. In 1987, powwow dancing led to creation of the American Indian Dance Theatre. This company brought together some of the finest singers and dancers of the nation's powwows. Among them were members of tribes such as the Apache, Assiniboine, Cherokee, Chippewa, Comanche, Cree, Hidatsa, Kiowa, Navajo, Northern Arapaho, Sioux, Yakima, and Zuni. The company performed throughout the United States and Europe as well as in Tokyo, the Persian Gulf states, and North Africa. "What the audience feels is something beyond the blazing bravura and decorative pattern on view," said a 1991 *New York Times* review of a performance. "Every image has its own power in this company, and if symbols sometimes go unexplained, the general meaning suggests a timeless rite common to mankind."[5]

MANITOU
Holy spirits

It rankled Michigan Indians to see a street in Flint named Manitou Avenue. The name, said the Genesee Valley Indian Association, was holy and shouldn't be profaned. In 1973, the Flint City Council responded by renaming the street. The change reflected a growing public sensitivity to the nuances of Indian culture.

Manitou, from the Ojibwa *manito,* originally meant a supernatural power that pervades the world. It is roughly equivalent to the Sioux *wakan* or the Iroquois *orenda,* also terms for supernatural power. The anthropologist Ruth Landes describes the wide range of specific manitous among the Ojibwa:

> The numerous manitos, of fairly equal rank, appeared as spirit prototypes of plants, birds, beasts, elemental forces, and life circumstances such as Poverty and Motherhood. They included useful trees like cedar and birch; certain roots, plants, and berries; [numerous animals]; and the sun, moon, thunder, lightning, meteoric stones, and winds of the cardinal points.[1]

Ranking above all these manitous was the Gitche (or Kitchi) Manitou, Great Spirit — regarded by at least some of the Great Lakes peoples as a hunter-gatherer chief who lived in the sky.

Human hunters had to be careful in their treatment of slain animals, which were considered to have allowed or offered themselves to be taken. As representative of a manitou, each animal had to be shown due honor and respect — often with elaborate ceremonies, as in the case of a bear. The penalty for not doing so could be failure in future hunting expeditions.

Powahs, or shamans, communicated directly with manitous by means of dreams or trances (see **Powwow**). Endowed with insight and power gained this way, the powahs healed the sick or enabled devotees to achieve success in hunting or other activites. In addition, the powahs could change the weather, predict the future, or perform various other supernatural feats.

Significantly, *manitou* seems to have been one of the first Indian words referred to directly in English. The explorer and scientist Thomas Harriot wrote of the Virginia Indians in 1588: "They beleeue that there are many Gods, which they call *Montóac,* but of different sortes and degrees."[2] Harriot's observations on Indian beliefs reflect the beginning of the English perception of Native American religions as a source of wonder, dread, and — ultimately — inspiration to Euroamericans.

Conversely, their association with settlers would lead to a shift in the way some Indians viewed manitou. For example, in the twentieth century New England Indians often referred to God as Manitou or the Great Spirit. This usage, the anthropologist William S. Simmons observes, "bridges Pan-Indian and mainstream American symbolism."[3]

North Americans today most commonly hear references to manitou in place-names. The United States has Manitou Springs, a town in Colorado; North and South Manitou Islands in Michigan; Manitowoc County in Wisconsin; and others. The name of Canada's province of Manitoba is believed to mean "strait of the Manitou" — from the mysterious roar of storm-driven pebbles against the narrows of Lake Manitoba. Several towns and other places in Canada also carry some form of the name manitou, presumably as relics of Indian awe or worship.

The *concept* of manitou exerts a wider influence than the word itself. Although they rejected Indian religion, settlers could not fail to be impressed by the close relationship native inhabitants enjoyed with their environment. By lesson and example the Indians showed settlers how to understand and live in the apparent wilderness of North America. Naturalists such as Henry David Thoreau and John Muir learned about nature directly from Indians. The native belief in manitou — the sacredness of nature — helped inspire the conservation and environmental movements of modern America.

∧∧∧∧∧∧∧∧∧∧∧∧∧∧∧∧∧∧∧∧∧∧∧∧∧

CONCLUSION

∨∨∨∨∨∨∨∨∨∨∨∨∨∨∨∨∨∨∨∨∨∨∨∨∨

The trail of words

From outcast to status symbol — that has been the route of many Native Americans in the second half of the twentieth century. According to one national poll, Americans think that fifteen percent of the population is of Native American descent. University of North Carolina pollsters estimate that twenty-eight percent of Americans believe that they themselves can boast American Indian ancestors. Yet the Census Bureau reports that less than one percent of the population is actually classifiable as Native American.

This book confirms that Native Americans exert an influence well beyond their numbers, and not just on public opinion. Loanwords from native tongues point to a cultural presence that pervades the United States. Some have become so familiar that few users recognize their origin. But most of the words reflect, in sound as well as meaning, native contributions to mainstream America.

Significantly, many of the loanwords refer to nature or outdoor living. Hundreds of plants and animals unique to North America keep native names. So do places and forces of nature such as bayou, muskeg, and Chinook wind. Walt Whitman spoke of Indian words imitating "sounds of rain and winds, calls as of birds and animals in the woods, syllabled to us for names."[1]

Thousands of place-names further mark the ancient connections of native peoples with the continent. Such links have become all the more important as modern developments obscure the visible past. In "Indian Names," the nineteenth-century poet

Lydia H. Sigourney reminded readers that Indians might have faded from common view,

> But their name is on your waters,
> Ye may not wash it out.
>
>   * * *
>
> Old Massachusetts wears it
>   Within her lordly crown,
> And broad Ohio bears it
>   Mid all her young renown;
> Connecticut hath wreathed it
>   Where her quiet foliage waves,
> And bold Kentucky breathed it hoarse
>   Through all her ancient caves.[2]

Still other kinds of words not discussed in this book reveal the Indian's influence. Indianisms — English words or phrases that translate expressions from the Indians — also enrich English vocabulary. Thus Americans may say that they *go on the warpath*, *bury the hatchet* (or *tomahawk*), or pay a *buck* (buckskin) for a purchase. Dozens of phrases containing *Indian* have arisen from Euroamerican association with native peoples. (But in 1999, the Crayola company abandoned "indian red" as a crayon color name.)

Hundreds of commercial brand names give evidence of Native American prestige with the American public today. For example, *Apache* identifies specific pharmaceutical preparations, analgesics, automotive parts and accessories, bicycles, boats, clocks, filters, floor coverings, food products, footwear, gates, insecticides, medical equipment, motorcycles, pet collars, shoes, sporting goods, insulators (thermal and acoustical), tires, wet mops, toys, and other products. More than a dozen products go out to the American public under the name *Tomahawk*.

Nor are the more than 1600 loanwords in English from the Latin American Indian languages examined here. They include *avocado, barbecue, cashew, chili, chocolate, cocaine, condor, hurricane, jaguar, maize, potato, quinine,* and *tapioca.* These reveal contributions to the United States from Indian peoples who are physically but not culturally remote.

How do native peoples feel about a relationship that has been so heavily weighted in favor of Euroamericans? The poet and teacher Joseph Bruchac expresses one point of view:

> As I look around me, seeing with Indian eyes, I do so with pride. I recognize how much of the world we live in has been shaped by Native American culture and Native American contributions. The equality of women, ideas of participatory democracy, foods that we eat, words that we speak, the names on the land around us all have roots that may be traced back to American Indian nations.[3]

The authoritative *Native American Voices* (1998) points to values that Native Americans have offered the United States. Among those, it says, are "protecting the environment, gender equality, grassroots democracy and a sense of community, respect for elders, family values." It asserts that the Native American heritage afforded the basis for numerous contributions from later immigrants. Beyond that, the book mentions the native stories and songs "that are intimately linked to the land."[4]

The psychiatrist Carl Jung commented on the Native American influence he discerned in the personalities of his American patients, leading him to believe that such influence is pervasive throughout American society:

> In everything on which the American has really set his heart we catch a glimpse of the Indian. His extraordinary concentration on a particular goal, his tenacity of purpose, his unflinching endurance of the greatest hardships — in all this the legendary virtues of the Indian find full expression.[5]

The notion is mere speculation, one may say, but it suggests the subtle way in which settlers became Indianized.

The loanwords examined in this book are an avenue to understanding the basic Native American cultural presence throughout American society. "We've always been a multicultural country, from the beginning," asserts the historian Arthur Schlesinger, Jr. Yet one people (or group of kindred peoples) came first in the settlement of North America. Words from their languages bear witness to the often disregarded native influence on later inhabitants of the continent, today as in the past.[6]

NOTES

SHELTER

The sources consulted for this section include: Breed; Carlisle; Catlin, *Letters*, vol. 1; Dow; "Farmstead" at Mashantucket Pequot Museum, Connecticut; Harrigan; Hauptman and Wherry; Hoxie; Huden; Laubin and Laubin, *Tipi*; Mallory and Ottar; Morrison and Germain; Nabokov and Easton; *New Yorker*, 16 March 1946; Nomadics Tipi Makers; Oswalt, *Eskimos*; Howard S. Russell; Skinner; Tomb; Winship.

TEPEE

1. Catlin, *Letters*, vol. 1, 44.
2. Laubin and Laubin, *Tipi*, 310.

IGLOO

1. Quoted in Oswalt, *Eskimos*, 170.
2. Morrison and Germain, 36.
3. Tombs, 44; Harrigan, 94–99.

WIGWAM

1. Quoted in Winship, 264.
2. Nabokov and Easton, 52; Skinner, 85.
3. Howard Russell, 55; Dow, 16–18.

QUONSET HUT

1. Hoxie, 346.
2. *New Yorker*, 16 March 1946, 21–22.
3. Quoted in Mallory and Ottar, 77.

CLOTHING

The sources consulted for this section include: *American Heritage Dictionary*, 4th ed.; Berton, vol. 1; Birket-Smith; Burch; Calloway, *Captives*; Cunningham and Lab; Demos; *Dictionary of Canadianisms*; Driver; C.C. Filson Co.; Flaherty; Hamilton; Hatcher; Havighurst, *Flags at the Straits*, "Three Flags"; Hemingway; Hodge, vol. 1; Kewanwytewa and Bartlett; Latorre and Latorre; Lescarbot; L.L. Bean, Inc., *1995 Fact Sheet, Spring Thaw 1996, Hunting &*

Outdoors 1997; Lowie; Mackinac Island Chamber of Commerce; Mathews; McKeown; McPhee; Montgomery; Murie; Edward Nelson; Richard K. Nelson, *Hunters; New York Times,* 6 August 1995; *New York Times Magazine,* 13 August 1995; Oswalt, *Eskimos, This Land;* Parker; Plog; Ray; Rochman; Safire, "Maneuvering"; Skinner; Vaught; Wissler, *Indians of the Plains.*

MOCCASIN

1. Lescarbot, 188–89.
2. Cunningham and Lab, 30–32.
3. *New York Times Magazine,* advertisement, 13 August 1995, 18.

MUKLUK

1. *Dictionary of Canadianisms.*
2. Richard K. Nelson, *Hunters,* 204–6.
3. McPhee, 307.

SHOEPAC, PAC BOOT

1. L.L.Bean, Inc.
2. Hamilton, vol. 1, 99.

PARKA, ANORAK

1. Vaught.
2. Safire, "Maneuvering."

MACKINAW

1. *Wisconsin Historical Society Coll.,* XX, 287, in Mathews, 1014.
2. Hatcher, 147–48.
3. Havighurst, *Flags at the Straits,* 114.
4. Hemingway, 535.

FOOD FROM PLANTS

The sources consulted for this section include: Abbey; *American Heritage Cookbook; American Heritage Dictionary,* 4th ed.; Baker; Bartlett; Boit; Bradbury; Bragdon; Burritt; Carlson; Catlin, *Letters,* vol. 1; Coe; Duke; Erath; Fussell; Hardeman; Hazen-Hammond; Heiser; Kidwell; Leonard, *American Cooking: New England;* Moerman; Morison; Native Seeds; Okie; Pilgrim Society; *Random House Unabridged Dictionary,* 2nd ed.; Raver; Rotstein; Safire, *New Language;* Amelia Simmons; John Smith, vol. 1; Stephen, part I; Terrell; Thoreau, *Walden;* Twain, *Huckleberry Finn;* Underhill, *Papago Indian Religion;* Will and Hyde; Roger Williams.

INTRODUCTION
1. Duke, preface; Moerman, 11.

HOMINY
1. Burritt.
2. Roger Williams, 101.
3. Hardeman, 143–44.
4. Fussell, 176.
5. Burritt.

CORN PONE
1. Bartlett, 626; Twain, *Huckleberry Finn* (1996 ed.), 49. The first of these quotations from Twain comes through the character of a slave who gave daily sermons.
2. *American Heritage Cookbook*, 449.
3. Quoted in Mathews, 873; Amelia Simmons, 34.
4. Thoreau, *Walden* (1951 ed.), 77.
5. Safire, *New Language*, 131.

SUCCOTASH
1. December 22 is the usual date, but the celebration in 1996 was postponed a day since the twenty-second fell on a Sunday.
2. Erath, 43.
3. Roger Williams, 100.
4. Kidwell, 204; Coe, 30.
5. Quoted in Will and Hyde, 153.
6. Fussell, 184.
7. Baker, 8.

SQUASH
1. Morison, 99.
2. Catlin, *Letters*, vol. 1, 121.
3. John Smith, vol. 1, 158.
4. Roger Williams, 172. Dictionaries used to claim that *squash* arose from an Algonquian word meaning "vegetables eaten green," but this etymology is now not commonly given. *Pumpkin* ultimately comes from Latin and Greek.

SAGUARO
1. Gary Naphan, *The Desert Smells Like Rain*, North Point, quoted in Raver.

2. *American Heritage Dictionary,* 4th ed.: "probably of Piman origin"; *Random House Unabridged Dictionary,* 2nd ed.: "said to be" from Opata (an extinct language that belongs to the Uto-Aztecan family, as does Piman).

3. Underhill, *Papago Indian Religion,* 44.

4. Ibid., 49.

5. Ibid., 59.

ADDITIONAL PLANTS

The sources consulted for this section include: *American Heritage Dictionary,* 4th ed.; Associated Press, 24 April 1987; Clampitt; Coon; Dykeman; Elbert; Gibbons, *Stalking the Wild;* Hodge, vol. 2; Jones; Klimas; Lacy; Martin; Mathews; Moerman; Rountree; John Smith, vol. 1; Stark; George Stewart; Thoreau, *Writings,* vol. 10; Vogel; Weiner.

INTRODUCTION

1. Vogel, 404, 405; Moerman, 11.

POKEWEED, PUCCOON

1. Jones, 133; Lacy.

2. Clampitt, 329.

3. Thomas Anburey, quoted in Mathews, 1273.

4. Gibbons, *Stalking the Wild,* 174–77.

5. Vogel, 354–56; Klimas, 10. *Poke* itself has several meanings in addition to *pokeweed.* In the sense of pushing or jabbing, it goes back to Middle English. But when derived from *poughkone,* it also means a kind of tobacco or kinnikinnick (which see): "He then wishing to smoke a pipe, searched the island for tobacco; but finding none, filled his pipe with poke a weed which the Ind. sometimes used as its substitute," wrote Henry David Thoreau. (Quoted in Vogel, above.)

PIPSISSEWA

1. Thoreau, *Writings,* vol. 10, 176.

FOOD FROM TREES

The sources consulted for this section include: *American Farmer;* Barbour; Bartram; Cannon and Brooks; Carlson; Clark; *Dairy Industries International;* Duke; Dupree; Gilmore; Hodge, vol. 2; *Houston Chronicle,* 4 April 1994; Manaster; *Merriam-Webster's Collegiate Dictionary,* 10th ed.; *New York Times,* 28 April 1997; Nichols, Doveton and Griswold; Parker; Payne; Peattie, *Eastern and Central, Western*; Preston; Proulx; Remini; Robertiello; Rogers; Rountree; Reich; Schrambling; Skinner; John Smith, vol. 1; Sokolov; Thwaites, vol. 14; VanDerBeets; Vogel; Weiner.

HICKORY

1. Peattie, *Eastern and Central*, 135.
2. Hanson in VanDerBeets, 142–43.

PECAN

1. Schrambling.
2. Peattie, *Eastern and Central*, 148–51; Nichols and Griswold, 143–45.
3. *Dairy Industries International*, June 1995, 43.

CHINQUAPIN

1. John Smith, vol. 1, 152.
2. Payne et al., 62.
3. Peattie, *Western*, 410.

PERSIMMON

1. John Smith, vol. 1, 152.
2. Sokolov, 24.
3. Proulx.
4. Sokolov, 28–29. However, in an article in the *New York Times* (28 April 1997), Lee Reich warns that "many wild persimmons never develop good flavor."

OTHER TREES

The sources consulted for this section include: *American Heritage Dictionary*, 4th ed.; Bartram; Braund; Brooke; Driver; Dykeman; Farquhar; Fenyesi; Frick and Streans; Gunsky; Robert F. Hall; Ketchum; Little; Longfellow, *Hiawatha*; Mathews; Melham; Mohlenbrock; Patterson; Peattie, *Eastern and Central*; Plimpton; Powers; Reader's Digest, *Our National Parks*; Richardson; Rudkin; Schlich and Schlich; Wetherell; Roger Williams.

INTRODUCTION

1. Ketchum, 54.

SEQUOIA

1. Quoted in Plimpton, 345.
2. Gunsky, 232, 242.
3. Richardson, 565; Melham, 91, 99.

CATALPA

1. Patterson.
2. Frick and Stearns, 19–21, 45–46.
3. Quoted in Mathews, 162.
4. Ibid.; Fenyesi.
5. Patterson.

TUPELO

1. Quoted in Mathews, 1779.
2. Bartram (1940), 42.

TAMARACK, HACKMATACK

1. Wetherell; Peattie, *Eastern and Central*, 34.
2. Quoted in Mathews, 1702.
3. Longfellow, *Hiawatha*, 92–93.

FISH AND SEAFOOD

The sources consulted for this section include: American Friends Service Committee; *Associated Press*; Barnhart; Beardsworth; Begley et al.; Boxberger; Dale Brown et al.; Calloway, *Indians*; Carlton; Carmichael; Casselman; Clayton; Ditmars; Dretzka; Dybas; Earle; Egan, 11 August 1988 and 9 September 1997; Feibleman et al.; Garber; German; Gibbons, *Stalking the Blue-Eyed*; Grimal; Haldane; Holbrook; Hooker; Hornblower; Huggler; Kenworthy and Pearlstein; Kipling, *From Sea to Sea* (in *Works*, vol. 16); Lane; Leonard et al., *The Great West*; Longfellow, *Hiawatha*; Marriott and Rachlin; Matthews; Maxwell; *National Fisherman*; *Merriam-Webster's Collegiate Dictionary*, 10th ed.; Obst; Jacqueline Peterson; Powers; Reiger and Reiger; Howard S. Russell; Simcoe; Skinner; Sokolov; Stern; Szkotak; Time-Life, *Cycles of Life* and *Indians of the Western Range*; Tooker; Trager; *Hartford Courant*, 10 March 1998; Trainer; United Press International, 13 July 1983 and 26 August 1984; Verhovek; Verrill; Walden; Walter et al.; *Washington Post*, 7 September 1995; Alexander Whitaker; Roger Williams; Wilson et al.

INTRODUCTION

1. Verhovek.

ABALONE

1. Haldane.
2. Verrill, 182.

3. Time-Life, *Indians of the Western Range*, 84–85.

4. Leonard et al., *The Great West*, 140.

QUAHOG

1. Szkotak.

2. Roger Williams, 182.

3. Lane.

GEODUCK, YAQUINA, UMPQUA

1. Gibbons, *Stalking the Blue-Eyed*, 182–85.

2. Egan, 9 September 1997.

3. Trainer.

4. Matthews, 93.

CHINOOK SALMON

1. Kipling, *From Sea to Sea*, in *Works*, vol. 16, 101.

2. Quoted in Dale Brown et al., 99.

SOCKEYE

1. Boxberger, 82.

2. Egan, 11 August 1988.

MUSKELLUNGE, MUSKIE, MASKINOGE

1. Huggler, 43.

2. Longfellow, *Hiawatha* (1863), 101–2.

3. Simcoe, 115–16.

TERRAPIN

1. Alexander Whitaker, 42; Ditmars, 377.

2. German, 323; Obst, 183; Hooker, 173.

GAME ANIMALS

The sources consulted for this section include: *American Heritage Dictionary*, 4th ed.; Barnhart; Bernton; Binder; Daniel B. Botkin; Brooks; Hannah Campbell; Colin; Arthur Davidson; Driver; Eliot; Gildart (Oct./Nov. 1997); Goldberg, 13 July 1997; Grinnell; Sarah James; Stephen S. Johnson; Krech; Kuralt; Langer; Lobo and Talbot; Mathews; McGillivray; Messiter; Mitchell; Nelson, *Make Prayers*; Randall; *Random House Dictionary*, 2nd ed.; Rayburn; Reader's Digest, *America's Fascinating*; Riviere; Robbins, 22 August 1996; Roosevelt et al.; Rosen; Rosier; Stefansson; Stevens; Stewart; David Taylor; Thoreau, "Walking," *The Maine Woods*; Thwaites; *U.S. Distribution Journal*; Marla Williams.

INTRODUCTION

1. Driver, 84.

MOOSE

1. Randall, 342, 409–10.

2. Rayburn, 151–55.

CARIBOU

1. Bass. Caribou are divided into several groups, partly according to their habitats and behavior. Woodland caribou (of which the Porcupine caribou are one example) are more common in Canada than in the United States, with up to five thousand in British Columbia. Barren Ground caribou inhabit the treeless plains of northern Canada and Greenland part of the year. Mountain caribou are the largest caribou, living from British Columbia to Alaska. Reindeer, smaller than caribou, are frequently tamed by people such as the Laplanders.

2. Sarah James.

3. Thoreau, "Walking," 422.

4. Marla Williams.

5. Goldberg; Gildart, "Hunting," 22, 24.

WAPITI

1. Roosevelt et al., 138.

2. Ibid., 135.

3. Quoted in Mathews, 1829.

4. Quoted in Thwaites, vol. 22, 369; vol. 23, 34.

5. Robbins.

6. Kuralt.

PEMMICAN

1. Stefansson, 194–96.

2. Messiter, 81.

3. Ibid., 74.

4. Stefansson, 256–58.

5. Langer, 85; Riviere, 140; *U.S. Distribution Journal.*

6. Stephen S. Johnson.

7. Brooks.

FURBEARERS

The sources consulted for this section include: *American Heritage Dictionary,* 4th ed.; American Kennel Club (1992); Austad; Bedard; Chapman and Feldhamer; "A Chipmunk Christmas" ©; Dillard; Driver; Ellis; Foster; Fraser; Gilbert; Hartman; Henisch and Henisch; Holden; Holmgren; Holusha; Hughes; Irving, vol. 6; James Alton James; Richard A. Johnson; Patricia Johnston; Koch; Krajick; Lawson; LeDuff; Longfellow, *Hiawatha* (1863); Mathews; *Merriam-Webster's Collegiate Dictionary*, 10th ed.; Messiter; Milewski; Moore and Wheelock; Murie; Nelson, *Make Prayers*; *New York Times*, 27 December 1992, 2 November 1997; Nowak, vol. 2; *David Petersen*; Stephen Powers; *The Random House Unabridged Dictionary*, 2nd ed.; Redford; Rich; Safire, *The New Language*; Seidensticker; Shea; John Smith, vol. 1; Stephen; Steubner; Stith; Tenney; Thompson; Thoreau, *Walden, Works*, vol. 9; Thwaites; Time-Life, *Algonquians*; Tunis; John Whitaker; William Wood.

MUSKRAT

1. Holusha.
2. Thoreau, *Writings*, vol. 12, 389.
3. Dillard, 193–205
4. Thomas Harriot, quoted in Mathews, 1104. The word may be among the very first North American Indian words recorded in English. "Saquenuckot & Maquo'woc; two kindes of small beastes greater than conies which are very good meat," he wrote in 1588 with a possible reference to muskrat.
5. Patricia Johnston, 49.
6. Nelson, *Make Prayers*, 262–70.
7. Bedard.

RACCOON

1. John Smith, vol. 1, 53.
2. American Kennel Club, 157–59.
3. Safire, *The New Language*, 130.
4. Milewski.

OPOSSUM

1. John Smith, vol. 1, 155.
2. Lawson, 120.
3. Seidensticker and Lumpkin, 112.
4. Austad, 98.
5. Quoted in Hartman, 150.
6. Lawson, 121.

SKUNK

1. Irving, 77–78, 80–81.
2. Quoted in Thwaites, vol. 20, 333–34.

3. Wood, 45.

4. Koch, 43; Gregg, quoted in Thwaites, vol. 20, 345.

5. Stephen, 690.

CARCAJOU, QUICKHATCH

1. Stuebner, 43.

2. Moore and Wheelock, ix.

3. Messiter, 52.

WOODCHUCK

1. Thoreau, *Walden,* 210.

2. Foster.

CHIPMUNK

1. Time-Life, *Algonquians,* 113; quoted in Henisch and Henisch, 20.

2. Longfellow, *Hiawatha,* 105.

3. Henisch and Henisch, 28–29.

4. Hughes, 62–63.

DOMESTICATED ANIMALS

The sources consulted for this section include: American Kennel Club; Bartley; Cheek; Crisman; Damas; Davies; Derr; Dolan; Haines, *Appaloosa, Horses in America;* Josephy; Le Kernec; Meacham; *Merriam-Webster's Collegiate Dictionary,* 10th ed.; Native Seeds; Edward W. Nelson; Plog; *Random House Unabridged Dictionary,* 2nd ed.; Robbins; Frank Roe; Ruby and Brown, *Cayuse;* Terrell; Wilcox and Walkowicz; Wissler, *American Indian.*

INTRODUCTION

1. Wissler, *American Indian,* 28; Plog, 174–75; Cheek, 98. The latter describes macaws as being raised in a Mesoamerican trading post in Mexico "grafted onto Mogollon roots."

ESKIMO

1. Bartley.

2. Damas, 7.

3. Wilcox and Walkowicz, 387.

HUSKY

1. American Kennel Club, 314.

MALAMUTE

1. Edward William Nelson, 29.
2. American Kennel Club, 237.
3. Ibid., 240.

APPALOOSA

1. Davies, 49.
2. Quoted in Haines, *Appaloosa,* 77.
3. Josephy, 29, 648.
4. Robbins.
5. Native Seeds.

CAYUSE

1. Meacham, 192–93.
2. Ibid., 198.
3. Ruby and Brown, *Cayuse,* 288.
4. Ibid., 294. The phrase forms the subtitle of the Ruby and Brown book.

ARTIFACTS

The sources consulted for this section include: *American Heritage Dictionary,* 1st ed.; Dave Anderson; Balf; Bradford; Bruemmer, *Arctic World*; Burl; Camden-Rockport-Lincolnville Chamber of Commerce; Catlin; Chamberlain; Church; Condon; De Palma; Evans; Faber; Gillette; Hodge, vol. 2; Linscott; Markoff; *Merriam-Webster's Collegiate Dictionary,* 10th ed.; Molloy; Morrison and Germain; Nelson, *Hunters; New England Historical and Genealogical Register*; Oswalt, *Eskimos*; Pazniokas; Robert Petersen; Polk; Rand; Reddish; Speck; Stuhaug; Sussman; Thwaites, vol. 23; Todhunter; Paul Wallace; Wallis and Wallis; Warburton; Weeden; Roger Williams.

INTRODUCTION

1. DePalma, "In a New Museum"; Weatherford, 238.

TOMAHAWK

1. Catlin, *Life,* 49–50.
2. Quoted in *New England Historical & Genealogical Register,* 120–21.
3. Burl, 179.
4. Anderson; Lipsyte.

WAMPUM

1. Faber.
2. Bradford, 281.
3. Church, 52.

KAYAK

1. Sussman.
2. Morrison and Germain, 130, 132; Oswalt, *Eskimos*, 96–97, 104–5.

TOBOGGAN

1. Balf, 64–69, 114–15; Camden-Rockport-Lincolnville Chamber of Commerce.
2. Wallis and Wallis, 51–52; Rand, 451.
3. Warburton, 68–69.
4. Chamberlain, 262.

NORTHWEST COAST

The sources consulted for this section include: Andersen; Batten; Slater Brown; Lyle Campbell; Cole and Chaikin; Fraser; Gibson; Gruening; Hidore and Oliver; Hodge, vol. 1; Jonaitis; Kipling, *Verse*; Kron; Sinclair Lewis; London, vol. 1; Lovell; *Merriam-Webster's Collegiate Dictionary*, 10th ed.; William Morris; Muir, *Travels in Alaska*; *Random House Unabridged Dictionary*, 2nd ed.; *Random House Historical Dictionary of American Slang*; Ruby and Brown, *Chinook, Guide*; Becky Smith; Sterngold; Thomas; Twain, *Connecticut Yankee*; Vansun; Verdi.

CHINOOK

1. Gibson, 376.

CHINOOK WIND

1. Fraser, 7–9.
2. Slater Brown, 75.

POTLATCH

1. Kron.
2. Sterngold.
3. Jonaitis, 248.

HIGH-MUCK-A-MUCK, MUCK-A-MUCK, MUCKETY-MUCK

1. Muir, 211.
2. *Random House Historical Dictionary of American Slang*, 606.

Hooch

1. Muir, 131–33. This chapter is indebted to *Alaska Hooch: The History of Alcohol in Early Alaska* by Thayne I. Andersen and to additional documents generously supplied by him.

2. London, vol. 1, 156.

3. Morris, 62.

4. Andersen, 148.

5. Sinclair Lewis, 175.

MISCELLANEOUS

The sources consulted for this section include: Allen; Arber; Axtell; Bragdon; James Brooke, "Battle"; Catlin, *Letters*, Vol. 1; Connable; DePalma, "Canada to Preserve"; *Dictionary of Canadianisms*; Dodge; Driver; Emerson, "Self-Reliance"; Feibleman et al., *American Cooking, Bayous*; Field; Fiske; Freiberg; Guynup; Heckewelder; Hodge; Hoxie; Hughes and Allen; Charles W. Johnson; Josephy, *Indian Heritage*; Klein and Ackerman; Kniffen et al.; Kohl; Kramer; Thomas H. Lewis; Longfellow, *Evangeline*; Malone; Mathews; Mencken, *American Language*; Richard K. Nelson, *Prayers*; *Newsletter*; *Oxford English Dictionary*, 2nd ed.; Ottawa Citizen, 1 August 1992; Paper; Lorin Peterson; *Random House Unabridged Dictionary*, 2nd ed.; Richter; Francis Russell; Howard S. Russell; Rutsch; Schmitt; Schueler, "Losing Louisiana," "That Sinking Feeling"; Mimi Sheraton; Tixier; Heath Twichell; U.S. Board on Geographic Names (telephone interview, 11 November 1998); Anthony F.C. Wallace; Warsh; Winkler; Winslow; Woodhead.

Sachem, Sagamore

1. George Morton, quoted in Arber, p. 458.

2. Bragdon, 140–54.

3. Josephy, *Indian Heritage,* 34–35.

4. Quoted in Mathews, 1439.

Squaw

1. Schmitt.

2. Brooke, "Battle."

3. Quoted in *Newsletter,* vol. 16, no. 2 (July 1996), 6.

4. Quoted in Howard S. Russell, 96.

5. Woodhead, 22, 78, 104; see also Klein and Ackerman, 245.

Papoose

1. Gabriel Sagard, quoted in Axtell, 7.

2. Kohl, 8.

3. Anthony F. C. Wallace, 38.

4. Emerson.

KINNIKINNICK

1. Catlin, *Letters and Notes*, vol. 1, 115.

TAMMANY

1. Heckewelder, 300.

MUGWUMP

1. Francis Russell; Winslow.

2. Mencken, 291.

3. Field, 495–96.

4. Lorin Peterson, 14.

5. Warsh, 39.

BAYOU

1. Longfellow, *Evangeline*, in *Writings*, vol. 4, 67.

MUSKEG

1. Tixier, 55–59, 81–83.

2. Ibid., 92, 316–17, 244.

3. Winkler.

SPIRIT

The sources consulted for this section include: Adams; *American Heritage Dictionary*, 4th ed.; Bruemmer, "Sentinels"; Burrage; Byrne; Cahill; Collison; Densmore; Dockstader, *Kachina*; Donahue; Fleck; Carey Goldberg, "Powwows"; Haekel; Harriot; *Hartford Courant*, 25 June 1997; Holmstrom; Hulktrantz, *Native Religions, Religions of the American Indians*; Jenkins; David Johnston; Kisselgoff; Krantz; Landes, *Ojibwa Religion, Ojibwa Sociology*; Lévi-Strauss; *Merriam-Webster's Collegiate Dictionary*, 10th ed.; Morrison and Germain; Mowat; Napier; Nelson, *Make Prayers*; *New York Times*, 10 March, 1973; Niebuhr; Nieves; Parfit; Pringle; Pyle; John Roe; Ruben; Shackley; William Simmons; Marian Smith; Teiwes; Time-Life, *People of the Lakes*; Trigger; *12,000 Words*; Underhill, *Red Man's Religion*; Vogel; Zuger.

INTRODUCTION

1. Hultkrantz, *Native Religions*, 20–34.

2. Niebuhr; David Johnston.

SASQUATCH

1. Lévi-Strauss, 59, 65.
2. Byrne, 36–51.
3. Napier, 197.
4. Shackley, 49, 167–68.
5. Krantz, 17–19.
6. Ibid., 191–94, 227, 257.
7. Napier, 197.
8. Pyle, 147, 319–20.

TOTEM

1. *Hartford Courant,* 25 June 1997, A6.
2. Haekel.
3. Hultkrantz, *Religions of the American Indians,* 68–69; Time-Life, *People of the Lakes,* 93.
4. Quoted in Fleck, 83.
5. Zuger; Jenkins.

KACHINA

1. Teiwes, 14.
2. Adams, 3.

INUKSHUK

1. Mowat, 237.
2. Collison. Quotes in the paragraph are directly from the article, indirectly from Ruben.

POWWOW

1. Burrage, 374.
2. Vogel, 126.
3. Nieves.
4. Parfit.
5. Kisselgoff.

MANITOU

1. Landes, *Ojibwa Religion,* 22.
2. Harriot, 372.
3. William Simmons, 269–70.

CONCLUSION

The sources consulted for this section include: Bruchac; Cutler; Herring; Jung; Lobo and Talbot; McLynn; Morin; Scancarelli; Schlesinger; Sigourney; "State of the Union"; Whitman, *Collected Poems*.

1. Whitman, 21.
2. Sigourney, 234–38.
3. Bruchac, 128.
4. Lobo and Talbot, 56–57.
5. Jung, 47–49; McLynn, 392–93.
6. Schlesinger.

BIBLIOGRAPHY

Abbey, Edward, and Editors of Time-Life Books. *Cactus Country.* New York: Time-Life Books, 1973.

Adams, E. Charles. *The Origin and Development of the Pueblo Katsina Cult.* Tucson: University of Arizona Press, 1991.

Allen, Oliver E. *The Tiger: The Rise and Fall of Tammany Hall.* Reading, Mass.: Addison-Wesley, 1993.

American Friends Service Committee. *Uncommon Controversy.* Seattle: University of Washington Press, 1970.

American Heritage. *American Heritage Cookbook.* New York: American Heritage, 1964.

American Heritage Dictionary of the English Language. Boston: Houghton Mifflin Co., 1969.

American Heritage Dictionary of the English Language, 4th ed. Boston: Houghton Mifflin Co., 2000.

American Kennel Club. *The Complete Dog Book.* 18th ed. New York: Howell, 1992.

Andersen, Thayne I. *Alaska Hooch: The History of Alcohol in Early Alaska.* Fairbanks: Hoo-Che-Noo, 1988.

Anderson, Dave. "The Braves' Tomahawk Phenomenon." *New York Times,* 13 October 1991.

Arber, Edward. *The Story of the Pilgrim Fathers.* Boston: Houghton Mifflin, 1897.

Associated Press. "Bright and Brief." 24 April 1987.

———. "Two Biologists Help Return an Oyster to the Coast." *New York Times,* 2 February 1997, 24.

Austad, Steven N. "The Adaptable Opossum." *Scientific American,* February 1988, 98–104.

Axtell, James, ed. *The Indian Peoples of Eastern America.* New York: Oxford University Press, 1981.

Baker, James W. "Feeding Pilgrim Memory: Plymouth Succotash and Forefathers' Day." *Plimoth Plantation Almanack,* September/October/November 1992, 8–9.

Balf, Todd. "The Louder You Scream, the Faster You Go." *Yankee,* January 1992, 64.

Barbour, Philip L. "The Earliest Reconnaissance of the Chesapeake Bay Area," Pt. 2. *Virginia Magazine of History and Biography* 80 (1972): 21–51.

Barnhart, Robert K., ed. *Barnhart Concise Dictionary of Etymology*. New York: HarperCollins, 1995.

Bartlett, John. *Familiar Quotations*. Edited by Emily Morison Beck. 15th ed. Boston: Little, Brown, 1980.

Bartley, Bruce. "School Teaches Arctic Skills." Associated Press, 1 February 1989.

Bartram, William. *The Travels of William Bartram*. Edited by Mark Van Doren. New York: Facsimile Library, 1940.

————. *The Travels of William Bartram*. Edited by Francis Harper. New Haven: Yale University Press, 1958.

Bass, Rick. "The Woodland Caribou: They're Still Out There." *Audubon*, May/June 1995, 76–84, 114–15.

Batten, Louis J. *Weather in Your Life*. San Francisco: W. H. Freeman, 1983.

Beardsworth, James D. "State Struts Its Stuffies at 11th Annual Quahog Fest." *Providence Journal Bulletin*, 29 August 1994, 1C.

Bedard, Paul. "Muskrat Season: Time for Serious Skinning & Eating." *Washington Post* (*Maryland Weekly*), 26 March 1981, Md. 8.

Begley, Sharon, with Patricia King and Mary Hager. "Better Red Than Dead." *Newsweek*, 12 December 1994, 79–80.

Bernton, Hal. "In Anchorage, It's Best to Steer Clear." *Washington Post*, 15 February 1995.

Berton, Pierre. *The Invasion of Canada*. 2 vols. Boston: Little, Brown, 1980.

Binder, David. "Tracking Down Michigan Moose No. 9 for a 600-Mile Checkup." *New York Times*, 23 March 1994.

Birket-Smith, Kaj. *The Eskimos*. London: Methuen, 1936.

Boit, John H. "Old Colony Club Marches On." *Quincy (Massachusetts) Patriot Ledger*, 23 December 1996, 1, 9.

Botkin, Daniel B. *Our Natural History*. New York: G. P. Putnam's Sons, 1995.

Boxberger, Daniel L. *To Fish in Common*. Lincoln: University of Nebraska Press, 1989.

Bradbury, L. Joseph. *Old Colony Club, 1769: An Historical Essay*. Plymouth, Mass.: Old Colony Club, 1978.

Bradford, William. *Of Plimoth Plantation*. Boston: Wright & Potter, 1901.

Bragdon, Kathleen J. *Native People of Southern New England, 1500–1650*. Norman: University of Oklahoma Press, 1996.

Braund, Kathryn E. Holland. *Deerskins & Duffels*. Lincoln: University of Nebraska Press, 1993.

Breed, Donald D. "Gay Head's '90s Indian Village Curved Roofs Echo Dwellings of Yesteryear." *Providence Journal-Bulletin*, 13 April 1995, 1F.

Brooke, James. "Battle of What May Be the West's Last Big Dam." *New York Times*, 20 September 1997, A7.

————. "Redwoods Still Inspire Sturdiest of Defenders." *New York Times*, 28 March 1998, A6.

Brooks, Geraldine. "Should the Big Eye Lead to a Greenout, Hey, Have a Homer." *Wall Street Journal*, 1 July 1997, A1, A8.

Brown, Dale, and Editors of Time-Life Books. *American Cooking: The Northwest*. New York: Time-Life Books, 1970.

Brown, Slater. *World of the Wind*. Indianapolis: Bobbs-Merrill, 1961.

Bruchac, Joseph. *Lasting Echoes*. San Diego: Silver Whistle, 1997.

Bruemmer, Fred. "Sentinels of Stone." *Natural History*, January 1995, 56–62.

——— and others. *Arctic World*. New York: Portland House, 1989.

Burch, Ernest S., Jr. "Kotzebue Sound Eskimo." In *Arctic*, edited by David Damas. Vol. 5 of Handbook of North American Indians. Washington, D.C.: Smithsonian Institution, 1984.

Burl, Aubrey. *Great Stone Circles*. New Haven: Yale University Press, 1999.

Burrage, Henry S. *Early English and French Voyages*. 1906. Reprint, New York: Barnes & Noble, 1959.

Burritt, Chris. "Around the South in Praise of Grits." *Atlanta Constitution*, 17 April 1994, A3.

Byrne, Peter. *The Search for Big Foot*. Washington, D.C.: Acropolis, 1975.

Cahill, Tim. "Bigfoot, an Historico-Ecologico-Anthropoidologico-Archetypal Study." *Rolling Stone*, 10 May 1973, 46–48.

Calloway, Colin G. *Indians of the Northeast*. New York: Facts on File, 1991.

———. *North Country Captives*. Hanover, N.H.: University Press of New England, 1992.

Camden-Rockport-Lincolnville Chamber of Commerce. *The Jewel of the Maine Coast*. Camden, Maine: n.p., n.d.

Campbell, Hannah. *Why Did They Name It . . . ?* New York: Ace Books, 1964.

Campbell, Lyle. *American Indian Languages*. New York: Oxford University Press, 1997.

Cannon, Poppy, and Patricia Brooks. *The Presidents' Cookbook*. New York: Funk & Wagnalls, 1968.

Carlson, Barbara. *Food Festivals*. Detroit: Visible Ink, 1997.

Carlton, Michael. "The Fish of 10,000 Casts." *Southern Living*, October 1993, 48.

Carlisle, Tamsin. "A Reporter Finds That Igloo Class Can Be Extremely Difficult to Ace." *Wall Street Journal*, 6 April 1995, B1.

Carmichael, Suzanne. "Around Seattle, an Oversize Clam Shines in Sushi." *New York Times*, 22 November 1992, 6.

Casselman, Bill. *Canadian Food Words*. Toronto: McArthur, 1998.

Catlin, George. *Letters and Notes on the Manners, Customs, and Conditions of the North American Indians*. 2 vols. 1844. Reprint, New York: Dover, 1973.

———. *Life among the Indians*. London: Gall and Inglis, 1867.

C. C. Filson Co. "Might as Well Have the Best." Seattle: C.C. Filson Co., n.d.

Chamberlain, Alexander F. "Algonkian Words in American English." *Journal of American Folk-Lore*, vol. 15, no. 3 (October–December 1902).

Chapman, Joseph A., and George A. Feldhamer. *Wild Animals of North America*. Baltimore: Johns Hopkins University Press, 1982.

Cheek, Lawrence W. *A.D. 1250*. Phoenix: Arizona Department of Transportation, 1994.

Church, Benjamin. *The History of King Philip's War*. Boston: John Kimball Wiggin, 1865.

Clampitt, Amy. *The Collected Poems of Amy Clampitt*. New York: Alfred A. Knopf, 1997.

Clark, Morton Gill. *A World of Nut Recipes*. New York: Avenel Books, 1967.

Clayton, Mark. "'Captain Canada' Just Posing in Fish Fight with U.S., Critics Say." *Christian Science Monitor*, 11 August 1995.

Coe, Sophie D. *America's First Cuisines*. Austin: University of Texas Press, 1994.

Cole, Douglas, and Ira Chaikin. *An Iron Hand Upon the People*. Seattle: University of Washington Press, 1990.

Colin, Mary. "Moose on the Loose." *International Wildlife*, March/April 1993, 38–45.

Collison, Melanie. "Office Cairn Marks Change." *Calgary Herald*, 19 January 1995, D2.

Condon, Garret. "Kayaks on the Coast." *Hartford Courant*, 8 August 1995, F1.

Connable, Alfred, and Edward Silberfarb. *Tigers of Tammany*. New York: Holt, Rinehart and Winston, 1967.

Coon, Nelson. *Using Plants for Healing*. Alexandria, Va.: Hearthside Press, 1963.

Crisman, Ruth. *Racing the Iditarod Trail*. New York: Dillon, 1993.

Cunningham, Patricia A., and Susan Voso Lab, eds. *Dress in American Culture*. Bowling Green, Ohio: Bowling Green State University Popular Press, 1993.

Cutler, Charles L. *O Brave New Words! Native American Loanwords in Current English*. Norman: University of Oklahoma Press, 1994.

Dairy Industries International. "Pecan Power." June 1995, 43.

Damas, David, ed. *Arctic*. Handbook of North American Indians, vol. 5. Washington, D.C.: Smithsonian Institution, 1984.

Davidson, Arthur. "Oil, Caribou and Culture." *Defenders*, January/February 1992, 22–27.

Davies, Mary Carolyn. *The Skyline Trail*. Indianapolis: Bobbs-Merrill Co., 1924.

Deloria, Philip J. *Playing Indian*. New Haven: Yale University Press, 1998.

Demos, John. *The Unredeemed Captive*. New York: Alfred A. Knopf, 1994.

Densmore, Frances. *Chippewa Customs*. 1929. Reprint, St. Paul: Minnesota Historical Press, 1979 .

DePalma, Anthony. "Canada to Preserve Vast Pristine Area in West." *New York Times*, 9 October 1997, A7.

———. "In a New Museum, Canoes Glide Into Mythology." *New York Times*, 28 July 1998, A4.

Derr, Mark. "The Making of a Marathon Mutt." *Natural History*, March 1996, 34–41.

Dictionary of Canadianisms on Historical Principles. Toronto: W. J. Gage, 1967.

Dillard, Annie. *Pilgrim at Tinker Creek*. New York: Bantam, 1975.

Ditmars, Raymond L. *The Reptiles of North America*. Garden City, N.Y.: Doubleday, Doran and Co., 1936.

Dockstader, Frederick J. *The Kachina and the White Man*. Albuquerque: University of New Mexico Press, 1985.

Dodge, Richard L. *Thirty Years Among Our Wild Indians*. Hartford: A.D. Worthington, 1882.

Dolan, Ellen M. *Susan Butcher and the Iditarod Trail*. New York: Walker, 1993.

Donahue, Bill. "A Question for: Peter Byrne." *New York Times Magazine*, 18 June 1995, 14.

Dow, George Francis. *Every Day Life in the Massachusetts Bay Colony*. Boston: Society for the Preservation of New England Antiquities, 1935.

Dretzka, Gary. "Mollusk Monarch." *Chicago Tribune*. 9 August 1995, 8.

Driver, Harold E. *Indians of North America*. 2d ed. Chicago: University of Chicago Press, 1969.

Duke, James A. *Handbook of Edible Weeds*. Boca Raton: CRC Press, 1992.

Dupree, Nathalie. *New Southern Cooking*. New York: Alfred A. Knopf, 1986.

Dybas, Cheryl Lyn. "Tough But Tender Abalone Stage a Comeback." *Sea Frontiers*, May/June 1994, 12–13.

Dykeman, Wilma. "Honoring a Cherokee." *New York Times*, 2 August 1987, XX 21.

Earle, Alice Morse. *Home Life in Colonial Days*. 1898. Reprint, New York: Macmillan, 1926.

Egan, Timothy. "Bountiful Salmon Run Has Anglers Beaming," *New York Times*, 11 August 1988.

———. "Strong-Arming, Profit and Fine Food." *New York Times*, 9 September 1997, A16.

Elbert, Virginie, and George A. Elbert. *Fun with Growing Herbs Indoors*. New York: Crown, 1974.

Ellis, Melvin R. "Skunks Want Peace — or Else!" *National Geographic*, August 1955, 279–94.

Eliot, John L. "Tiny Assassin Foils Maine Caribou Comeback." *National Geographic*, April 1994.

Emerson, Ralph Waldo. "Self-Reliance." In *Harvard Classics*. Vol. 64. New York: P. F. Collier, 1900.

Erath, Sally Larkin, ed. *The Plimoth Colony Cook Book*. Plymouth, Mass.: Plymouth Antiquarian Society, 1957.

Evans, Eric, and Jay Evans. *The Kayaking Book*. Lexington, Mass.: Stephen Greene Press, 1988.

Faber, Harold. "New York Returning Wampum Belts to Onondagas." *New York Times*, 13 August 1989, 39.

Farquhar, Francis P. *History of the Sierra Nevada*. Berkeley: University of California Press, 1966.

Feibleman, Peter S., and Editors of Time-Life Books. *American Cooking: Creole and Acadian*. New York: Time-Life Books, 1971.

———. *The Bayous*. New York: Time-Life Books, 1973.

Fenyesi, Charles. "Unsung Trees: Two, Tall, Fragrant Species with Little-Known Talents." *Washington Post*, 10 May 1990, T28.

Field, Eugene. *The Poems of Eugene Field*. New York: Scribner's, 1924.

Fiske, John. *The Beginnings of New England*. Cambridge, Mass.: Houghton Mifflin, 1898.

Flaherty, Thomas H., and Editors of Time-Life Books. *Way of the Warrior*. Alexandria, Va.: Time-Life, 1993.

Fleck, Richard F. *Henry Thoreau and John Muir Among the Indians*. Hamden, Conn.: Archon, 1985.

Foster, Shawn. "Paiutes, Scientists Sharing Digs and Uncovering History." *Salt Lake Tribune*, 31 July 1995, B1.

Fraser, Frances. *The Bear Who Stole the Chinook*. Vancouver: Douglas & McIntyre, 1990.

Freiberg, Edna B. *Bayou St. John in Colonial Louisiana, 1699–1803*. New Orleans: Harvey Press, 1980.

French, Howard F. "Inheritors of an African Kingdom, Come and Gone." *New York Times*, 21 October 1997, A4.

Frick, George Frederick, and Raymond Phineas Stearns. *Mark Catesby: The Colonial Audubon*. Urbana: University of Illinois Press, 1961.

Fussell, Betty. *The Story of Corn*. New York: Alfred A. Knopf, 1992.

Garber, Steven W. "The Ups and Downs of the Diamondback Terrapin." *Conservationist* 44, no. 6 (May/June 1990), 44.

German, Obadiah. "Unprepared War with England." *Annals of America*, Vol. 4, 323. Chicago: Encyclopaedia Britannica, 1968.

Gibbons, Euell. *Stalking the Blue-Eyed Scallop*. New York: David McKay, 1964.

———. *Stalking the Wild Asparagus*. Putney, Vt.: Alan C. Hood, 1962.

Gibson, James R. "The Maritime Trade of the North Atlantic Coast." In *History of Indian-White Relations*, edited by Wilcomb E. Washburn. Vol. 4 of Handbook of North American Indians. Washington, D.C.: Smithsonian Institution, 1988.

Gilbert, Bil. "A Groundhog's 'Day' Means More to Us than It Does to Him." *Smithsonian*, February 1985, 60–69.

Gildart, Bert. "Hunting for Their Future." *National Wildlife*, October/November 1997, 20–29.

Gillette, Charles W. "Wampum Beads and Belts." *The Indian Historian*, Fall 1970, 32–7.

Gilmore, Melvin R. *Uses of Plants by the Indians of the Missouri River Region*. Lincoln: University of Nebraska Press, 1977.

Goldberg, Carey. "Powwows Change, but Drummer Is the Same." *New York Times*, 24 August, 1997, E4.

―――. "Turmoil Beneath a Land's Tranquility." *New York Times,* 13 July 1997, 12.

Grimal, Pierre. ed. *Larousse World Mythology.* New York: G.P. Putnam's Sons, 1965.

Grinnell, George Bird. *The Cheyenne Indians.* 2 vols. New Haven: Yale University Press, 1923.

Gruening, Ernest. *The State of Alaska.* New York: Random House, 1954.

Gudde, Erwin G. *California Place Names.* Berkeley: University of California Press, 1949.

Gunsky, Frederic R., ed. *South of Yosemite: Selected Writings of John Muir.* Garden City, N.Y.: Natural History Press, 1968.

Guynup, Sharon. "Wetlands for Wildlife." *Audubon,* May/June 1999, 101.

Haekel, Joseph. "Totemism." *Encyclopaedia Britannica Macropaedia,* 15th ed. Vol. 26 (1988), 579.

Haines, Francis. *Appaloosa: The Spotted Horse in Art and History.* Austin: University of Texas Press, 1963.

―――. *Horses in America.* New York: Thomas Y. Crowell, 1971.

Haldane, David. "The Mystery of the Missing Mollusks." *Los Angeles Times Magazine,* 5 January 1992, 23.

Hall, Robert F. "The Tamarack Belongs to November." *The Conservationist,* November/December 1991.

Hamilton, Stanislaus Murray. *Letters to Washington and Accompanying Papers.* 5 vols. Cambridge, Mass.: Houghton Mifflin, 1898.

Hardeman, Nicholas P. *Shucks, Shocks, and Hominy Blocks.* Baton Rouge: Louisiana State University Press, 1981.

Harrigan, Stephen. "Igloo." *This Old House* 25 (January/February 1999), 94–99.

Harriot, Thomas. *A Briefe and True Report.* In *The Roanoke Voyages, 1584–1590,* edited by David Beers Quinn. London: Hakluyt Society, 1955.

Hartford Courant. "State Protects the Turtles." 18 March 1998, A12.

Hartman, Carl G. *Possums.* Austin: University of Texas Press, 1952.

Hatcher, Harlan. *The Great Lakes.* London: Oxford University Press, 1944.

Hauptman, Laurence M., and James D. Wherry, eds. *The Pequots in Southern New England.* Norman: University of Oklahoma Press, 1990.

Havighurst, Walter. *Flags at the Straits.* Englewood Cliffs,N.J.: Prentice-Hall, 1966.

―――. "Three Flags at Mackinac." *American Heritage,* August/September 1978, 50–59.

Hazen-Hammond, Susan. "A Giant Shrugs off Vandalism, Poaching, Tales of its Demise." *Smithsonian,* January 1996, 76–83, 108.

Heckewelder, John. *History, Manners, and Customs of the Indian Nations.* 1819. Reprint, Philadelphia: Historical Society of Pennsylvania, 1876.

Heiser, Charles B., Jr. *Of Plants and People.* Norman: University of Oklahoma Press, 1985.

Hemingway, Ernest. *The Complete Stories of Ernest Hemingway*. New York: Charles Scribner's Sons, 1987.

Henisch, B. A., and H. K. Henisch. *Chipmunk Portrait*. State College, Pa.: Carnation Press, 1970.

Herring, Hubert B. "Crayola Changes Stripes." *New York Times*, 14 March 1999, sec. 4, p. 2.

Hidore, John J., and John E. Oliver. *Climatology: An Atmospheric Science*. New York: Macmillan, 1993.

Hodge, Frederick Webb. *Handbook of American Indians North of Mexico*. 2 vols. 1905. Reprint, Totowa, N.J.: Rowman and Littlefield, 1975.

Holbrook, Stewart H. *The Columbia*. New York: Rinehart, 1956.

Holden, Benjamin A. "The Folks in Dogpatch Don't Like Their Names to Be Taken in Vain." *Wall Street Journal*, 26 May 1994.

Holmgren, Virginia C. *Raccoons*. Santa Barbara, Calif.: Capra, 1990.

Holmstrom, David. "Powwow." *Christian Science Monitor*, 6 January 1994, 12.

Holusha, John. "Where the Muskrat Is a Delicacy for Lent." *New York Times*, 1 April 1988.

Hooker, Richard J. *Food and Drink in America*. Indianapolis: Bobbs-Merrill, 1981.

Hornblower, Malabar. *The Plimoth Plantation in New England Cookery Book*. Boston: Harvard Common Press, 1990.

Hoxie, Frederick E., ed. *Encyclopedia of North American Indians*. Boston: Houghton Mifflin, 1996.

Huden, John C. *Indian Place Names of New England*. New York: Museum of the American Indian, Heye Foundation, 1962.

Huggler, Tom. "Murder in Their Maw." *Outdoor Living*, July 1922, 42.

Hughes, Arthur, and Morse S. Allen. *Connecticut Place Names*. Hartford: The Connecticut Historical Society, 1976.

Hughes, Ted. *Birthday Letters*. New York: Farrar, Straus & Giroux, 1998.

Hultkrantz, Åke. *Native Religions of North America*. San Francisco: Harper & Row, 1987. Reprint, Prospect Heights, Ill.: Waveland, 1998 .

———. *The Religions of the American Indians*. Berkeley: University of California Press, 1979.

Irving, Washington. *The Works of Washington Irving*. Twentieth Century Edition. 12 vols. n.p., n.d.

James, James Alton. *The First Scientific Expedition of Russian Alaska and the Purchase of Alaska*. Evanston, Ill.: Northwestern University Press, 1943.

James, Sarah. "The Caribou People." *Newsday*, 4 December 1991, 106.

Jenkins, Nicholas. "Inventions of the March Hare." *New York Times Book Review*, 20 April 1997, 14.

Johnson, Charles W. *Bogs of the Northeast*. Hanover, N.H.: University Press of New England, 1985.

Johnson, Richard A. *American Fads*. New York: Beech Tree Books, 1985.

Johnson, Stephen S. "Canadian Bacon?" *Forbes Magazine*, 3 June 1996, 38.

Johnston, David. "Spiritual Seekers Borrow Indians' Ways." *New York Times,* 27 October 1993, A1.

Johnston, Patricia Condon. "Seth Eastman's West." *American History,* September/October 1996, 42–51, 65.

Jonaitis, Aldona. ed. *Chiefly Feasts: The Enduring Kwakiutl Potlatch.* Seattle: University of Washington Press, 1992.

Jones, Pamela. *Just Weeds.* Shelburne, Vt.: Chapters, 1994.

Josephy, Alvin M., Jr. *The Indian Heritage of America.* New York: Alfred A. Knopf, 1968.

Jung, C. G. *Civilization in Transition.* Bollingen Series, no. 20. New York: Pantheon Books, 1953.

Kenworthy, Tom, and Steven Pearlstein. "Canada, U.S. Reach Accord on Salmon." *Hartford Courant,* 4 June 1999, A10.

Ketchum, Richard M. *The Secret Life of the Forest.* New York: American Heritage Press, 1970.

Kewanwytewa, Jim, and Katharine Bartlett. "Hopi Moccasin Making." In Museum of Northern Arizona, *Hopi Indian Arts and Crafts.* Flagstaff: Northern Arizona Society of Science and Art, 1951.

Kidwell, Clara Sue. "Food and Cuisine." In *Encyclopedia of North American Indians,* edited by Frederick E. Hoxie. Boston: Houghton Mifflin, 1996.

Kipling, Rudyard. *Rudyard Kipling's Verse.* London: Hodder and Stoughton, 1919.

———. *The Works of Rudyard Kipling.* 33 vols. New York: Scribner's, 1899–1932.

Kisselgoff, Anna. "Symbols and Bravura by American Indians." *New York Times,* 19 September 1991, C15.

Klein, Laura F., and Lillian A. Ackerman, eds. *Women and Power in Native North America.* Norman: University of Oklahoma Press, 1995.

Klimas, John E. *Wild Flowers of Connecticut.* New York: Walker, 1975.

Kniffen, Fred B, Hiram F. Gregory, and George A. Stokes. *The Historic Tribes of Louisiana.* Baton Rouge: Louisiana State University Press, 1987.

Koch, Ronald. *Dress Clothing of the Plains Indians.* Norman: University of Oklahoma Press, 1977.

Kohl, J. G. *Kitchi Gami.* 1860. Reprint, Minneapolis: Ross and Haines, 1956.

Krajick, Kevin. "The Fugitive." *Audubon,* January/February 1997, 69.

Kramer, Marty. "Beauty of the Bayou." *Austin American-Statesman,* 5 March 1995, F1.

Krantz, Grover S. *Big Footprints.* Boulder, Colo.: Johnson, 1992.

Krech, Shepard, III, ed. *Indians, Animals, and the Fur Trade.* Athens: University of Georgia Press, 1981.

Kron, Joan. "For a Perfect Host, *Everything* Goes." *New York Times,* 18 October 1991, C1, 32.

Kuralt, Charles. "Traveling Across America." *New York Times,* 13 April 1997, Advertising supplement, 21 A.

Lacy, Allen. "Pokeweed Grows Up Hardy, Poisonous." *Chicago Tribune*, 25 December 1988, 14; zone D.

Landes, Ruth. *Ojibwa Religion and the Midéwiwin*. Madison: University of Wisconsin Press, 1968.

———. *Ojibwa Sociology*. 1937. Reprint, New York: AMS Press, 1969.

Lane, Charlotte Balcomb. "Clam Farms: The Wave of the Future in Brevard County." *Orlando Sentinel Tribune*, 28 June 1990.

Langer, Richard W. *The Joy of Camping*. New York: Saturday Review Press, 1973.

Latorre, Felipe, and Dolores L. Latorre. *The Mexican Kickapoo Indians*. Austin: University of Texas Press, 1976.

Laubin, Reginald, and Gladys Laubin. *American Indian Archery*. Norman: University of Oklahoma Press, 1980.

Lawson, John. *A New Voyage to Carolina*. Ann Arbor, Mich.: University Microfilms, 1966.

LeDuff, Charlie. "The Man to See for Raccoon Pie." *New York Times*, 19 February 1999, B1.

Le Kernec, Bill. *Alaskan Malamutes*. Neptune City, N.J.: T. F. H. Publications, 1983.

Leonard, Jonathan Norton, and Editors of Time-Life Books. *American Cooking: New England*. New York: Time-Life Books, 1970.

———. *American Cooking: The Great West*. New York: Time-Life Books, 1971.

Lescarbot, Marc. *Nova Francia, a description of Acadia*. Written in 1606; translated by P. Erondelle in 1609. New York: Harper, 1923.

Levi-Strauss, Claude. *The Way of the Masks*. Seattle: University of Washington Press, 1982.

Lewis, Sinclair. *Babbitt*. New York: Harcourt, Brace, 1922.

Lewis, Thomas H. *The Medicine Men*. Lincoln: University of Nebraska Press, 1990.

Linscott, Robert N. "The Money-Maker." *American Heritage*, February 1960, 112.

Lipsyte, Robert. "How Can Jane Fonda Be a Part of the Chop?" *New York Times*, 18 October 1991.

Little, Elbert L. *The Audubon Society Field Guide to North American Trees*. New York: Alfred A. Knopf, 1980.

L.L.Bean, Inc. *Christmas 1995, 1996* catalogs, Freeport, Maine: L.L.Bean.

———. *1995 Fact Sheet*. Freeport, Maine: L.L.Bean, 1995.

———. *Hunting & Outdoors 1997*. Freeport, Maine: L.L.Bean, 1997.

———. *Spring Thaw 1996*. Freeport, Maine: L.L.Bean, 1996.

Lobo, Susan, and Steve Talbot. *Native American Voices: A Reader*. New York: Longman, 1998.

London, Jack. *The Complete Stories of Jack London*. 3 vols. Stanford: Stanford University Press, 1993.

Longfellow, Henry Wadsworth. *Longfellow's Writings*. 11 vols. Cambridge, Mass.: Houghton Mifflin, 1886.

————. *The Song of Hiawatha*. Boston: Ticknor and Fields, 1863.

Lovell, Charles J. "The Background of Mark Twain's Vocabulary." *American Speech* 22 (April 1947).

Lowie, Robert H. *The Crow Indians*. New York: Rinehart, 1958.

Mackie, Richard Somerset. *Trading Beyond the Mountains*. Vancouver: University of British Columbia Press, 1997.

Mackinac Island Chamber of Commerce. "Discover Mackinac Island." Mackinac Island, Mich.: n.d.

Mallory, Keith, and Arvid Ottar. *The Architecture of War*. New York: Pantheon, 1973.

Malone, Dumas, ed. *Dictionary of American Biography*. Vol. 9. New York: C. Scribner's Sons, 1934.

Manaster, Jane. *The Pecan Tree*. Austin: University of Texas Press, 1994.

Markoff, John. "Lessons from Ancients Who Plied the Waves." *New York Times*, 2 December 1990, F9.

Marriott, Alice, and Carol K. Rachlin. *American Indian Mythology*. New York: Thomas Y. Crowell, 1968.

Martin, Laura C. *Wildflower Folklore*. New York: East Woods Press, 1984.

Mathews, Mitford M. *A Dictionary of Americanisms*. Chicago: University of Chicago Press, 1951.

Matthews, Neal. "Half/Shell Highway." *Travel Holiday*, vol. 181, no. 8 (October 1998), 90–95.

Maxwell, Jessica. "Swimming with Salmon." *Natural History*, September 1995, 26–39.

McGillivray, Wesley. "Oh, Those Bright Lights of Moose Jaw." Editorial. *Calgary Herald*, 4 October 1994.

McKeown, Bill. "Pick of the Packs." *Outdoor Life*, January 1988, 58–59, 75–77.

McLynn, Frank. *Carl Gustav Jung*. New York: St. Martin's, 1997.

McPhee, John. *Coming Into the Country*. New York: Farrar, Straus & Giroux, 1977.

Meacham, A. B. *Wigwam and War-Path*. Boston: John P. Dale, 1875.

Melham, Tom. *John Muir's Wild America*. Washington, D.C.: National Geographic Society, 1976.

Mencken, H. L. *The American Language: Supplement I*. New York: Alfred A. Knopf, 1952.

Merriam-Webster's Collegiate Dictionary. 10th ed. Springfield, Mass.: Merriam-Webster, Inc., 1997.

Messiter, Charles Alston. *Sport and Adventures Among the North American Indians*. 1890. Reprint, New York: Abercrombie & Fitch, 1966.

Milewski, Mary. "Rehabilitating and Releasing Wild Animals." *Middletown (Connecticut) Press*, 18 August 1997.

Mitchell, John G. "Oil on Ice." *National Geographic*, April 1977, 104–31.

Moerman, Daniel E. *Native American Ethnobotany*. Portland, Ore.: Timber Press, 1998.

Mohlenbrock, Robert H. "Cupola Pond, Missouri." *Natural History*, January 1988, 62.

Molloy, Anne. *Wampum*. New York: Hastings House, 1977.

Montgomery, M. R. *In Search of L.L.Bean*. Boston: Little, Brown, 1984.

Moore, Patrick, and Angela Wheelock. *Wolverine Myths and Visions*. Lincoln: University of Nebraska Press, 1990.

Morin, Richard. "Money Talks to Business-School Deans." *Hartford Courant*, 19 September 1998, F2.

Morison, Samuel Eliot. *The Story of the "Old Colony" of New Plymouth*. New York: Knopf, 1956.

Morris, William Gouverneur. *Report Upon the Customs District, Public Service and Resources of Alaska Territory*. Washington, D.C.: Government Printing Office, 1879.

Morrison, David, and Georges-Hébert Germain. *Inuit: Glimpses of an Arctic Past*. Hull, Quebec: Canadian Museum of Civilization, 1995.

Mowat, Farley. *People of the Deer*. Boston: Little, Brown, 1952.

Muir, John. *Travels in Alaska*. Boston: Houghton Mifflin, 1915.

Murie, James. *Ceremonies of the Pawnee*. Edited by Douglas R. Parks. Lincoln: University of Nebraska Press, 1989.

Nabokov, Peter. *Two Leggings*. New York: Crowell, 1967.

Napier, John. *Bigfoot*. New York: Dutton, 1973.

National Fisherman. Vol. 79, no. 9 (January 1999), 15.

Native Seeds/SEARCH. *1996 Seedlisting*. Tucson: Native Seeds/SEARCH, 1996.

Nelson, Edward William. *The Eskimo About Bering Strait*. 1899. Reprint, Washington, D.C.: Smithsonian Institution, 1983.

Nelson, Richard K. *Hunters of the Northern Forest*. Chicago: University of Chicago Press, 1973.

———. *Make Prayers to the Raven*. Chicago: University of Chicago Press, 1983.

New England Historical & Genealogical Register. Vol. 24. "Samuel Sewall to Stephen Sewall." Boston, 1870.

New Yorker. "Notes and Comment," 16 March 1946, 21–22.

New York Times. "Indians in Flint, Mich., Win Street Name Fight." 10 March 1973.

———. "Skunks Show Early Signs of Comeback on L.I." 27 December 1992, Sec. 13LI, p. 12.

———. "Wolverines' Defense Holds Down Gophers." 2 November 1997, Sec. 8, p. 5.

Nichols, Frederick Doveton, and Ralph E. Griswold. *Thomas Jefferson, Landscape Architect*. Charlottesville: University Press of Virginia, 1978.

Niebuhr, Gustav. "Indians Blast Imitators." *Washington Post*, 3 September 1993.

Nieves, Evelyn. "Powwows: Path of New Traditions." *New York Times*, 23 July 1992, B4.

Nomadics Tipi Makers. Catalog. Bend, Ore.: n.p., n.d.

Nowak, Ronald M. *Walker's Mammals of the World*. 2 vols. Baltimore: Johns Hopkins Press, 1991.

Obst, Fritz Jürgen. *Turtles, Tortoises and Terrapins*. New York: St. Martin's Press, 1986.

Okie, Susan. "Cradle of Agriculture Found in N. America." *Washington Post*, 25 December 1989, A3.

Oswalt, Wendell H. *Eskimos and Explorers*. Novato, Calif.: Chandler & Sharp, 1979.

————. *This Land Was Theirs*. New York: Wiley, 1966.

Ottawa (Canada) Citizen. 1 August 1992.

Oxford English Dictionary. 2nd ed. Oxford: Clarendon Press, 1989.

Paper, Jordan. *Offering Smoke*. Moscow: University of Idaho Press, 1988.

Parfit, Michael. "Powwow: A Gathering of the Tribes." *National Geographic*, June 1994, 89–113.

Parker, Arthur C. *The Indian How Book*. 1927. Reprint, New York: Dover, 1975.

Patterson, Rich. "The Can't-Win Catalpa." *American Forests*, January/February 1991, 35, 46.

Payne, Jerry A., Gregory Miller, George P. Johnson, and Samuel D. Senter. "*Castanea pumila* (L.) Mill.: An Underused Native Nut Tree." *HortScience* 29 (February 1994), 62.

Pazniokas, Mark. "Planning Missile Strikes 'Sobering.'" *Hartford Courant*, 7 September 1996, B1.

Peattie, Donald Culross. *A Natural History of Trees of Eastern and Central North America*. 1950. Reprint, New York: Bonanza, 1966.

————. *A Natural History of Western Trees*. New York: Bonanza, 1953.

Petersen, David. "Backyard Bandits." *Mother Earth News*, January/February 1987, 66.

Petersen, Robert. "East Greenland After 1950." In *Arctic*, edited by David Damas. Vol. 5 of Handbook of North American Indians. Washington, D.C.: Smithsonian Institution, 1984.

Peterson, Jacqueline. "Plateau Tribes." In *Encyclopedia of North American Indians*, edited by Frederick E. Hoxie. Boston: Houghton Mifflin Co., 1996.

Peterson, Lorin. *The Day of the Mugwump*. New York: Random House, 1961.

Pilgrim Society. "Plymouth Succotash for 100 People." 1995.

Plimpton, George, ed. *The Writer's Chapbook*. New York: Viking, 1989.

Plog, Stephen. *Ancient Peoples of the American Southwest*. New York: Thames and Hudson, 1997.

Polk, Nancy. "Tooling Up Olympic Bobsled Speed." *New York Times*, 8 February 1998, sec. 14, pp. 1, 8.

Powers, Stephen. *Tribes of California*. 1877. Reprinted with an introduction and notes by Robert F. Heizer, Berkeley: University of California Press, 1976.

Preston, Richard J., Jr. *North American Trees*. Cambridge, Mass.: M.I.T. Press, 1966.

Pringle, Heather. *In Search of Ancient America*. New York: John Wiley, 1996.

Proulx, Lawrence G. "Please Your Palate, Pick the Persimmon." *Washington Post*, 28 November 1995, Health Section, 20.

Pyle, Robert Michael. *Where Bigfoot Walks*. Boston: Houghton Mifflin, 1995.

Rand, Silas Tertius. *Lagends of the Micmacs*. 1894. Reprint, New York: Johnson Reprint Corp., 1971.

Randall, Willard Sterne. *Thomas Jefferson*. New York: Holt, 1993.

Random House Unabridged Dictionary. 2nd ed. New York: Random House, 1993.

Random House Historical Dictionary of American Slang. New York: Random House, 1997.

Raver, Anne. "A Desert Survival Team." *New York Times*, 14 March 1993, Sec. 9, p. 14.

Ray, Arthur J. *Indians in the Fur Trade*. Toronto: University of Toronto Press, 1974.

Rayburn, Alan. *Naming Canada*. Toronto: University of Toronto Press, 1994.

Reader's Digest Editors. *America's Fascinating Indian Heritage*. Pleasantville, N.Y.: Reader's Digest, 1990.

———. *Our National Parks*. Pleasantville, N.Y.: Reader's Digest, 1985.

Reddish, Paul. *Spirits of the Jaguar*. London: BBC Books, 1996.

Redford, Polly. *Raccoons & Eagles*. New York: E. P. Dutton, 1965.

Reich, Lee. "Upstart American Persimmons Add to Fall Colors." *New York Times*, 28 September 1997, 42.

Reiger, Barbara, and George Reiger. *The Zane Grey Cookbook*. Englewood Cliffs, N.J.: Prentice-Hall, 1976.

Remini, Robert V. *Andrew Jackson and the Course of American Freedom, 1822–1832*. New York: Harper & Row, 1981.

Rich, Ben. "Inside the Skunk Works." *Popular Science*, October 1994, 52.

Richardson, Robert D., Jr. *Emerson: The Mind on Fire*. Berkeley: University of California Press, 1995.

Richter, Daniel K. *The Ordeal of the Longhouse*. Chapel Hill: University of North Carolina Press, 1992.

Riviere, Bill, with the staff of L.L.Bean. *The L.L.Bean Guide to the Outdoors*. New York: Random House, 1981.

Robbins, Jim. "As Snow Falls in Tetons, Elk Temperatures Rise." *New York Times*, 22 September 1996, 14.

Robertiello, Jack. "Pecan/Pacana/Nogueira Americana." *Américas*, March/April 1993, 54–55.

Rochman, Hazel. "Walk Two Moons." *New York Times*, 21 May 1995, Book Rev., 24.

Roe, Frank Gilbert. *The Indian and the Horse*. Norman: University of Oklahoma Press, 1955.

Roe, John. "Artist Leaves Mark on Millions of Quarters." *Vancouver Sun*, 8 May 1992, A3.

Rogers, Julia Ellen. *The Tree Book*. New York: Doubleday, Page and Co., 1905.

Roosevelt, Theodore, T. S. Van Dyke, D. G. Elliot, and A. J. Stone. *The Deer Family*. New York: Grosset & Dunlap, 1902.

Rosen, Yereth. "Alaskans See More Close Encounters with Marauding Moose." *Christian Science Monitor*, 24 February 1995.

Rosier, James. Quoted in *Purchas, His Pilgrimage*, by Samuel Purchas. 1613. Reprint, Glasgow: James Maclehose and Sons, 1906 (1613).

Rotstein, Arthur H. "Saguaro Cactus Gets Thumbs Up for National Park Status in Arizona." *Los Angeles Times*, 13 November, B4.

Rountree, Helen C. *The Powhatan Indians of Virginia*. Norman: University of Oklahoma Press, 1989.

Ruby, Robert H., and John A. Brown. *The Cayuse Indians: Imperial Tribesmen of Old Oregon*. Norman: University of Oklahoma Press, 1972.

———. *The Chinook Indians*. Norman: University of Oklahoma Press, 1976.

———. *A Guide to the Indian Tribes of the Pacific Northwest*. Norman: University of Oklahoma Press, 1986.

Rudkin, Margaret. *The Margaret Rudkin Pepperidge Farm Cookbook*. New York: Atheneum, 1963.

Russell, Francis. "Apostle to the Indians." *American Heritage*, December 1957.

Russell, Howard S. *Indian New England Before the Mayflower*. Hanover, N.H.: University Press of New England, 1980.

Rutsch, Edward S. *Smoking Technology of the Aborigines of the Iroquois Area of New York State*. Rutherford, N.J.: Fairleigh Dickinson University Press, 1973.

Safire, William. "Maneuvering with Heimlich." *New York Times Magazine*, 7 January, sec. 6, p. 14.

———. *The New Language of Politics*. New York: Collier, 1972.

Scancarelli, Janine. Review of *O Brave New Words! Native American Loanwords in Current English*, by Charles L. Cutler. *ANQ: A Quarterly Journal of Short Articles, Notes, and Reviews*, vol. 9, no. 2 (Spring 1996), 56–59.

Schlesinger, Arthur, Jr. C-Span, 8:00 EDT, 10 May 1997.

Schlich, Kim, and Victor Schlich. "Talking Leaves." *American History*, December 1995, 38–40.

Schmitt, Eric. "Battle Rages Over a 5-Letter Four-Letter Word." *New York Times*, 4 September 1996, A16.

Schrambling, Regina. "A Texas Town Devoted to the Pecan in All Its Forms." *New York Times*, 14 February 1993, 6.

Schueler, Donald G. "Losing Louisiana." *Audubon*, July 1990, 78–87.

———. "That Sinking Feeling." *Sierra*, March/April 1990, 42–45.

Seidensticker, John, and Susan Lumpkin. "Playing Possum Is Serious Business for Our Only Marsupial." *Smithsonian*, November 1989, 108–19.

Shackley, Myra. *Still Living? Yeti, Sasquatch and the Neanderthal Enigma*. New York: Thames and Hudson, 1983.

Shea, Jim. "Smell of Warm Weather Indicates Active Skunks." *Hartford Courant,* February 28, 1997, B7.

Sheraton, Mimi. "Rough Rider, Easy Living." *New York Times,* 4 September 1998, E35.

Sigourney, Lydia H. *Illustrated Poems.* Philadelphia: Carey and Hart, 1849.

Simcoe, Elizabeth. *Mrs. Simcoe's Diary.* Edited by Mary Quayle Innis. Toronto: Macmillan, 1965.

Simmons, Amelia. *American Cookery.* 1796. Reprint, New York: Dover, 1958.

Simmons, William S. *Spirit of the New England Tribes.* Hanover, N.H.: University Press of New England, 1986.

Skinner, Alanson. *Material Culture of the Menomini.* New York: Museum of the American Indian, Heye Foundation, 1921.

Smith, Becky. "When Alaskans Voted Dry: Prohibition in Alaska." *The Alaska Journal,* vol. 3, no. 3 (Summer 1973), 160.

Smith, John. *The Complete Works of Captain John Smith (1580–1631).* 3 vols. Edited by Philip L. Barbour. Chapel Hill: University of North Carolina Press, 1986.

Smith, Marian W. *The Puyallup-Nisqually.* New York: Columbia University Press, 1940.

Society for the Study of the Indigenous Languages of the Americas. *Newsletter.* XVI: 2.

Sokolov, Raymond. *Fading Feast.* New York: Farrar, Straus & Giroux, 1981.

Speck, Frank Gouldsmith. *The Penn Wampum Belts.* New York: Museum of the American Indian, Heye Foundation, 1925.

Stark, Raymond. *Guide to Indian Herbs.* Blaine, Wash.: Hancock House, 1992.

"State of the Union: Being an American." Springfield, Mass., TV Channel 57, 13 October 1997.

Stefansson, Vilhjalmur. *Not by Bread Alone.* New York: Macmillan, 1946.

Stephen, Alexander M. *Hopi Journal of Alexander M. Stephen.* Edited by Elsie Clews Parsons. New York: AMS Press, 1969.

Stern, Bernhard J. *The Lummi Indians of Northwest Washington.* 1934. Reprint, New York: AMS Press, 1969.

Sterngold, James. "A Spirit Lives On, as Magical Masks Guard Indian Traditions." *New York Times,* 26 August 1998, E1.

Stevens, William K. "Make Way for Moose." *New York Times,* 27 October 1998, F1, F4.

Stewart, George R. *American Place-Names.* New York: Oxford University Press, 1970.

Stuebner, Stephen. "The Wanderer." *National Wildlife,* October/November 1997, 40–45.

Stuhaug, Dennis O. *Kayaking Made Easy.* Old Saybrook, Conn.: Globe Pequot Press, 1995.

Sussman, Vic. "For Wetter or Worse." *Washington Post,* 1 August 1995, E2.

Szkotak, Steve. "Rhode Island Clammers Unite to Weather Stormy Seas." United Press International, 19 March 1983.

Taylor, David. "From the Elders to Hi-Tech." *Américas* 50 (July/August 1998), 4.

Teiwes, Helga. *Kachina, Dolls: The Art of Hopi Carvers.* Tucson: University of Arizona Press, 1991.

Tenney, John B. "The Opossum — North America's Australian Connection." *The Conservationist*, January/February 1991, 22–25.

Terrell, John Upton. *American Indian Almanac.* New York: World Publishing Company, 1971.

Thomas, Edward Harper. "The Chinook Jargon." *American Speech*, June 1927, 377–84.

Thompson, Stith. *Tales of the North American Indians.* Bloomington: Indiana University Press, 1966.

Thoreau, Henry David. *The Maine Woods.* Cambridge, Mass.: Riverside Press, 1894.

———. *Walden.* 1854. Reprint: New York: Bramhall House, 1951.

———. *Walden.* 1854. Reprint: Princeton: Princeton University Press, 1989.

———. "Walking." *The Harvard Classics.* Vol. 28. New York: Collier, 1910.

———. *The Writings.* 14 vols. Boston: Houghton Mifflin, 1906.

Thwaites, Reuben Gold, ed. *Early Western Travels: 1748–1846.* 32 vols. Cleveland: Arthur H. Clark, 1904–7.

Time-Life Books Editors. *Algonquians of the East Coast.* Alexandria, Va.: Time-Life, 1995.

———. *Cycles of Life.* Alexandria, Va.: Time-Life 1994.

———. *Indians of the Western Range.* Alexandria, Va.: Time-Life, 1995.

———. *People of the Lakes.* Alexandria, Va.: Time-Life, 1994.

Tixier, Victor. *Tixier's Travels on the Osage Prairies.* 1844. Reprint, edited by John Francis McDermott. Norman: University of Oklahoma Press, 1940.

Todhunter, Andrew. "Gale-Force Kayaking." *Atlantic Monthly*, August 1995, 94–97.

Tombs, George. "Canada's New Arctic." *World Monitor*, July 1990, 42–48.

Tooker, Elisabeth. *An Ethnography of the Huron Indians, 1615–1649.* Syracuse: Syracuse University Press, 1991.

Trager, James. *The Food Chronology.* New York: Henry Holt, 1995.

Trainer, Melissa A. "In Seattle, the Ingredients Shine." *New York Times*, 5 October 1997, sec. 2, p. 6.

Trigger, Bruce G. *The Huron.* New York: Holt, Rinehart and Winston, 1969.

Tunis, Edwin. *Chipmunks on the Doorstep.* New York: Thomas Y. Crowell, 1971.

Twain, Mark. *A Connecticut Yankee in King Arthur's Court.* 1889. Reprint, New York: Oxford University Press, 1996.

———. *Adventures of Huckleberry Finn.* 1885. Reprint: New York: Random House, 1996.

12,000 Words: A Supplement to Webster's Third New International Dictionary. Springfield, Mass.: Merriam-Webster Inc., 1986.

Twichell, Heath. *Northwest Epic: The Building of the Alaska Highway*. New York: St. Martin's, 1992.

Underhill, Ruth. *Papago Indian Religion*. New York: Columbia University Press, 1946.

———. *Red Man's Religion: Beliefs and Practices of the Indians North of Mexico.* Chicago: University of Chicago Press, 1965.

United Press International. "Town Honors the Quahog." 13 July 1983.

———. "Quahog Tradition Tough to Crack." 26 August 1984.

U.S. Distribution Journal. "GoodMark Beefs Up Pemmican Line." 15 September 1991.

VanDerBeets, Richard, ed. *Held Captive by Indians*. Knoxville: University of Tennessee Press, 1973.

Vansun, Tom Henry. "Revival of a Mongrel Tongue." *Vancouver Sun,* 7 September 1991, D6.

Vaught, Susan. "Creating Custom Designs." *Alaska Business Monthly,* March 1992, Sec. 1, p. 56.

Verdi, Bob. "Chinook Turns Calgary into a Melting Pot." *Chicago Tribune,* 14 February 1988, Sports section, p. 1; Zone C.

Verhovek, Sam Howe. "An Expensive Fish." *New York Times,* 17 March 1999, A14.

Verrill, A. Hyatt. *Shell Collector's Handbook*. New York: G. P. Putnam's Sons, 1950.

Vogel, Virgil. *American Indian Medicine*. Norman: University of Oklahoma Press, 1970.

Walden, Howard T., II. *Familiar Freshwater Fishes of America*. New York: Harper & Row, 1964.

Wallace, Anthony F. C. *The Death and Rebirth of the Seneca*. New York: Alfred A. Knopf, 1970.

Wallace, Paul A. W. *Indians in Pennsylvania*. Harrisburg: Pennsylvania Historical and Museum Commission, 1968.

Wallis, Wilson D., and Ruth Sawtell Wallis. *The Micmac Indians of Eastern Canada*. Minneapolis: University of Minnesota Press, 1955.

Walter, Eugene, and Editors of Time-Life Books. *American Cooking: Southern Style*. New York: Time-Life Books, 1971.

Warburton, Eliot. *Hochelaga*. New York: Wiley & Putnam, 1846.

Warsh, David. "The Road from Taxachusetts." *Boston Globe,* 1 November 1994.

Washington Post. "Abalone." 7 September 1995, H19.

Weatherford, Jack. *Indian Givers*. New York: Fawcett Columbine, 1997.

———. *Native Roots*. New York: Crown, 1991.

Weeden, William B. *Economic and Social History of New England, 1620–1789*. Boston: Houghton Mifflin, 1890.

Weiner, Michael A. *Earth Foods*. London: Collier-Macmillan, 1972.

Wetherell, W. D. "After the Maples, the Golden Tamarack." *New York Times,* 24 September 1989, 15.

Whitaker, Alexander. *Good Newes from Virginia*. 1613. Reprint, New York: n. p., 1936.

Whitaker, John O., Jr. *The Audubon Society Field Guide to North American Mammals*. New York: Alfred A. Knopf, 1987.

Whitman, Walt. *Collected Poems*. Garden City, N.Y.: Blue Ribbon Books, 1926.

Wilcox, Bonnie, and Chris Walkowicz. *Atlas of Dog Breeds of the World*. Neptune City, N.J.: T. F. H. Publications, 1989.

Will, George F., and George E. Hyde. *Corn Among the Indians of the Upper Missouri*. Lincoln: University of Nebraska Press, 1917.

Williams, Marla. "Caribou People Welcome Strangers." *Houston Chronicle*, 15 May 1994, 2.

Williams, Roger. *A Key into the Language of America*. 1643. Reprint edited by John J. Teunissen and Evelyn J. Hinz, Detroit: Wayne State University Press, 1973.

Wilson, José, and Editors of Time-Life Books. *American Cooking: The Eastern Heartland*. New York: Time-Life Books, 1971.

Winkler, Robert. "Inside Black Spruce Bog's Spirit World." *New York Times*, 2 November 1997, Sec. 8, p. 12.

Winship, George Parker, ed. *Sailors' Narratives of Voyages along the New England Coast*. New York: Burt Franklin, 1905.

Winslow, Ola Elizabeth. *John Eliot: "Apostle to the Indians."* Boston: Houghton Mifflin, 1968.

Wissler, Clark. *The American Indian*. London: Oxford University Press, 1922.

———. *North American Indians of the Plains*. 3rd ed. New York: American Museum of Natural History, 1941.

Wood, William. *New England's Prospect*. 1634. Reprint edited by Alden T. Vaughan, Amherst: University of Massachusetts Press, 1977.

Woodhead, Henry, and Editors of Time-Life Books. *The Woman's Way*. Alexandria, Va.: Time-Life, 1995.

World Book Encyclopedia. Chicago: Field Enterprises Educational Corp., 1975.

Zuger, Abigail. "Doctor's White Coat Fits All: Jekyll, Kildare, Medicine Man." *New York Times*, 25 November 1977, F4.

INDEX

PICTURE CREDITS